DEVELOPING RESTORATIVE JUSTICE JURISPRUDENCE

This is a welcome addition to restorative justice literature. Tony Foley joins those who argue that restorative and retributive justice can and should be integrated. He proposes jurisprudential and systemic changes that would move criminal justice closer to such a joint purpose. His 'minimalist approach' deserves careful consideration – and adoption.

Daniel W. Van Ness, Prison Fellowship International, USA

A thoughtful and distinctive approach to transforming criminal law jurisprudence. Tony Foley identifies deficiencies in both restorative and criminal justice and then seeks to forge a provocative new amalgam. This is a book serious criminal law scholars must read.

John Braithwaite, Australian National University, Australia

INTERNATIONAL AND COMPARATIVE CRIMINAL JUSTICE

Series Editors:

Mark Findlay, *Institute of Criminology, University of Sydney, Australia*
Ralph Henham, *Nottingham Law School, Nottingham Trent University, UK*

This series explores the new and rapidly developing field of international and comparative criminal justice and engages with its most important emerging themes and debates. It focuses on three interrelated aspects of scholarship which go to the root of understanding the nature and significance of international criminal justice in the broader context of globalization and global governance. These include: the theoretical and methodological problems posed by the development of international and comparative criminal justice; comparative contextual analysis; the reciprocal relationship between comparative and international criminal justice and contributions which endeavor to build understandings of global justice on foundations of comparative contextual analysis.

Other titles in the series:

International Criminal Law
Using or Abusing Legality?
Edwin Bikundo
ISBN 978 1 4094 3867 0

The Dual State
Edited by Eric Wilson
ISBN 978 1 4094 31077

Policing in Hong Kong
Kam C. Wong
ISBN 978 1 4094 1060 7

Criminal Law Reform and Transitional Justice
Human Rights Perspectives for Sudan
Edited by Lutz Oette
ISBN 978 1 4094 3100 8

Codification, Macaulay and the Indian Penal Code
The Legacies and Modern Challenges of Criminal Law Reform
Edited by Wing-Cheong Chan, Barry Wright and Stanley Yeo
ISBN 978 1 4094 2442 0

Developing Restorative Justice Jurisprudence

Rethinking Responses to Criminal Wrongdoing

TONY FOLEY
Australian National University, Australia

Routledge
Taylor & Francis Group
LONDON AND NEW YORK

First published 2014 by Ashgate Publishing

Published 2016 by Routledge
2 Park Square, Milton Park, Abingdon, Oxfordshire OX14 4RN
711 Third Avenue, New York, NY 10017, USA

First issued in paperback 2016

Routledge is an imprint of the Taylor & Francis Group, an informa business

British Library Cataloguing in Publication Data
A catalogue record for this book is available from the British Library

The Library of Congress has cataloged the printed edition as follows:
Foley, Tony (Lawyer), author.
Developing Restorative Justice Jurisprudence : Rethinking Responses to Criminal Wrongdoing / by Tony Foley.
pages cm.—(International and Comparative Criminal Justice)
Includes bibliographical references and index.
ISBN 978-1-4094-6533-1 (hardback: alk. paper)—ISBN 978-1-4094-6534-8 (ebook)—ISBN 978-1-4094-6535-5 (epub)
1. Restorative justice. 2. Criminal justice, Administration of. I. Title.
K970.F65 2014
345'.001—dc23

2014003373

ISBN 13: 978-1-138-25042-0 (pbk)
ISBN 13: 978-1-4094-6533-1 (hbk)

Contents

List of Tables and Figures

Tables

Figures

Preface

This book poses a normative question. It asks how institutional responses to criminal wrongdoing should be reframed so as to better achieve justice. The question is asked in the context of the potential for a wider role for restorative justice, and from the perspective that justice is primarily about distribution. Conventional responses to wrongdoing accept that offenders must be given their just deserts and treated equally, and that all persons affected by wrongdoing must have their rights promoted and protected. However, what is most often distributed to meet all these needs is punishment. Missing is a focus on removing the harm and damage caused to individuals and relationships. Lacking is a more effective means to trigger crime prevention. This book offers fresh insight into what else should be distributed and how this might be done, arguing that it is only by taking into account restorative questions that institutional responses can be truly said to be just.

The book is about how the criminal law might develop from today to bring the need for restoration directly into the mix tomorrow. The restorative practice of justice has many answers but cannot be the sole solution. Restorative processes can begin the process of repair and seek to deter crime through means other than punishment. But restorative practice's own limitations are highlighted when the seriousness of the wrongdoing calls for a strongly retributive response and there is a rushed return to punishment. Rather than seeing restorative justice as a replacement discourse, this book argues that it should be situated in a close complementary role with conventional legal justice.

There is an accelerating adoption of restorative approaches in some countries, often in quite substantial ways, with both adult and juvenile offenders. The book tries to capture some of the imminence of these developments and traces the shape of the growing restorative justice jurisprudence in their legal systems and their courts. It draws upon judicial shifts most apparent in Canada and New Zealand and innovative practice pursued most keenly in the UK, South Africa and Europe. The 'collective effervescence' (Durkheim 1912) that advocates from these programs impart hold out the promise of revolutionizing the practice of criminal justice.

Preface

Introduction

Just Responses to Criminal Wrongdoing

The major question this book addresses is, 'What are the requirements for a just response to criminal wrongdoing?' What follows argues that such a response is one that (i) fulfills certain essential aims, (ii) distributes certain benefits and burdens and (iii) satisfies certain evaluative criteria in order to be just. The critical discovery is that all of this is only achievable when the response is as much about restoration as it is about retribution. We know (or at least think we know) why we respond to crime in the ways we do. We seem to have a ready response to this 'why' question. But what we say and think are often contradictory – that we should aim primarily to 'punish', to 'deter', to 'rehabilitate', to 'protect' or in rare cases to 'restore'. We want all of this to happen in ways that reduce the risk of future offending or address some of the harm caused by the wrong. Rather than needing to be contradictory, this book argues that these purposes can be complementary. We should aim to deliver on the individual and societal pressing need for retribution against the wrongdoer. We should aim to achieve restoration for the personal and normative harm caused by the wrongdoing. We should aim to achieve consequential goals – to deter, to protect and to rehabilitate. All we need is a just means of doing so.

However, the contradictions become deeper when we try to see how justice is done. As its name implies, the 'criminal justice system' sees justice as its guiding light. Responses to wrongdoing must be just, not revengeful or merciful. What is 'just' is often misunderstood. This book argues that a clearer way to conceptualize criminal justice is to see it like any other form of justice – as a process of distribution, as a means of determining a proper allocation of benefits and burdens. This book explores the particular 'harm-related' benefits and burdens that need to be distributed to create the sense that justice has been done. The reason we shy away from seeing criminal justice as distributive is because we are uncertain as to how to measure such justness. It is not enough to simply say that because a response is legal it is just. There needs to be some 'measure' of its justness. This book suggests a response is just if it gives people their deserts (both in a positive sense as much as a negative sense), treats them equally, protects their rights and promotes harmonious social relationships between them. A traditional criminal justice response has regard for desert, equality and rights protection but little or no regard for social harmony. Other forms of response, particularly restorative justice seem to do the opposite. How is the restorative form of response so different? This book explores the behaviours and practices each form gives priority to in promoting justice – legal practice gives prominence to punishment, restorative practice more often to vindication and remorse. Which are the better generators of justice? Is there a missed role for apology and forgiveness in a truly just response which is overlooked?

Much of the early part of the book is speculative. The parts that then follow move beyond speculation to an empirical examination of justice practice. Criminal practice is examined afresh to gauge the justness of its responses. Restorative practice is investigated anew to gain a sense of how its distinctive form of justice is generated. Though restorative justice is not a theory or practice from the discipline of law, it has nonetheless had a profound impact on that practice in some jurisdictions. It has been incorporated into traditional forms of response so that it is now possible to talk of a growing 'restorative justice jurisprudence'. This book explores that jurisprudence to see what restorative justice can add to the responsive mix and how what it adds can have wider exposure.

Synopsis

Part I develops a set of analytical tools by which to investigate justice practice. Chapter 1 applies the concept of distributive justice to the particular context of institutional responses to criminal wrongdoing. While it has long been argued that the distributive conceptualization does not apply to 'corrective forms' of justice because its criterion for determining division is not 'due' but 'moral worth', this proposition is tested. We find that if such distributions are not viewed in terms of 'restoring balance' but rather simply as the means to address certain 'essential aims', a distributive pattern does emerge. It is theorized that three broad aims must be addressed – the need to deliver retribution, the need to achieve restoration and the need to achieve particular consequential outcomes. Consistent with the conceptualization of distribution, these aims are best achieved through distributing 'harm-related' benefits and burdens. The specifics of these benefits and burdens are developed in Chapter 2 through reworking and combining existing retributive and restorative concepts. The distribution of these benefits and burdens achieve just outcomes because they facilitate the essential aims. Some of the benefits are broad and intangible, others narrow and more easily grasped. Burdens range from censure and punishment which need to be imposed to loss and regret which need to be removed. Chapter 3 turns to the question of how such distributions might be justice-promoting. The chapter identifies a set of criteria to determine whether these distributions are just. It draws the criteria from various theoretical suggestions about how 'justness' can be appraised. Beginning with ancient scholars and tracing developing thought from Aristotle's notion of 'justice as entitlement' through to Rawls's theory of 'justice as fairness' and beyond, it settles on four distinct measures of any criminal justice distribution – does it give people their deserts, does it treat them equally, does it protect their rights and does it promote harmonious social relationships between them? If a distribution measures well against these criteria, it promotes justice. Chapter 4 suggests a means to explain how this sense of justice can be generated. Behaving in particular ways and adhering to certain principles is seen as justice-creating. Engendering expressions of accountability and responsibility in offenders and attuning others who are affected by the wrong to deliver censure and vindication are seen as key to justice generation.

Part II turns attention to the world of justice practice. In chapters 5 and 6 the evaluative criteria developed are applied to 'measure' the justness of two forms of practice – restorative and criminal. The analysis highlights deficiencies in both forms of practice. Chapter 5 finds restorative justice's strongest justice claim is its ability to treat people equally and regenerate harmonious social relationships between them, although it clearly has less capacity to satisfy the rights or desert criteria. Chapter 6 finds almost the reverse for criminal practice. It has sound ability to meet the desert and rights measures, but its focus is more on formal than substantive equality, and it has poor capacity to reestablish harmonious social relationships. There is an enticing complementarity to their successes and failures. Experience in New Zealand and Canadian jurisdictions suggests there is scope for embracing restorative practices within mainstream criminal practice. Chapter 7 reviews the developing restorative justice jurisprudence. New Zealand, which began with small-scale conferencing in its criminal courts, is seen to have taken licence from the *Clotworthy* decision of its Court of Appeal to develop real judicial regard for restorative approaches. Canada similarly used its Supreme Court decision in *Gladue* as a catalyst to mandate consideration of restorative requirements in sentencing. Advances and reversals in these and other jurisdictions provide both encouragement and caution.

Part III looks for a way forward. It seeks to remove some of the perceived mystique and mistrust surrounding restorative practice to dispel mainstream doubt about the role it can play in responding to criminal wrongdoing. Chapter 8 provides a comprehensive assessment of existing restorative practice in diverse sites of practice across New Zealand, Canada, Australia, the United Kingdom and Europe. Chapter 9 provides a snapshot of how this practice makes justice restoratively.

Finally, the Conclusion suggests a way to more fully accommodate recognition of the potential of restorative justice within mainstream institutional practice. The growth of a restorative sentencing jurisprudence suggests that criminal practice can be open to accommodating restorative approaches. Nonetheless, 20 years after inroads began there remains limited regard of what these approaches can achieve. Restorative justice is seen as able to address restorative aims and some consequential aims but never any part of retribution. This needs to change if its use is to expand. Without this the practice will remain on the periphery of responses to criminal wrongdoing. But without substantial 'restorative absorption' into criminal practice, many justice needs will remain unmet. A minimalist solution is suggested here, namely mandating a requirement that criminal courts consider 'the restorative question' in its full breadth and capacity each time an offender is to be sentenced. A deceptively simple step, yet one which can provide the key to fuller integration.

This book takes two underlying controversial positions. First of all, it asserts that criminal wrongdoing necessarily has a moral content that must be addressed and resolved. It is not enough to simply focus on the offending behaviour and ignore its moral wrongness or dismiss its social context. Secondly, it asserts that restorative justice is the only way forward from many of the inadequacies of criminal justice. Restorative justice as a distinct theory and approach to justice must necessarily have a place in responding to criminal wrongdoing.

As such, this is a book about changing attitudes. Moving justice practice from where it is now in responding to wrongdoing to where it should better be. Johnstone and Van Ness (2011) delineate a sequence of conceptions of restorative justice's place in the criminal justice system. Some writers have advanced an 'encounter conception' which sees the benefit of bringing together those affected by wrongdoing to agree on how to respond to crime as a positive, and wish to see this develop further. Others have accepted a 'reparative conception' which sees a restorative response to wrongdoing as essential to the effective repair of the personal and normative harm caused by wrongdoing. A smaller group have embraced a 'transformative conception' which accepts that all responses to conflict should be about peacebuilding. The late Canadian criminologist Ruth Morris's writings mark such a move from restoration to transformation, discarding the offence-bound focus that restorative justice still retains.[1] As Van Ness and Strong (2010: 174) have long recognized, 'a hallmark of restorative justice … should be [such a] transformation'. This book allows readers to begin this leap. Its focus is on the transformation of the 'structures' of criminal justice practice which mete out punishment in the flawed belief that this is all that a response to wrongdoing requires. This book accelerates the move from retribution, in the process offering a model for 'transform[ing] a small part of existing criminal justice' (Van Ness and Strong 2010: 178).

1 There is a rich literature on transformative justice. Its beginnings can be traced from the strands of conflict resolution theories of John Burton (*Conflict: Human Needs Theory*, New York, St Martin's Press, 1990; *Conflict Resolution as a Political System*, Fairfax, George Mason University, 1988) and Robert A. Baruch Bush and Joseph P. Folger's writings on transformative mediation (*The Promise of Mediation: The Transformative Approach to Conflict* (rev. ed.), San Francisco, Jossey-Bass, 2005) and from the penal reform lifetime work of Ruth Morris (*A Practical Path to Transformative Justice*, Toronto, Rittenhouse, 1994). It has been swept up and further developed in the restorative justice literature through the pioneering work of Howard Zehr (*Changing Lenses: A New Focus for Crime and Justice*, Scottsdale, Herald Press, 1990) and Daniel Van Ness and colleagues (G. Johnstone and D. W. Van Ness, (eds), *Handbook of Restorative Justice*, Cullompton, Willan Publishing, 2007, 2011; D. W. Van Ness and K. H. Strong, *Restoring Justice*, New Providence, Matthew Bender & Co, 2006, 2010).

PART I

Chapter 1
Responsiveness: The Aims of Institutional Responses to Wrongdoing

Introduction

The conceptual framework of justice employed in this book sees the distribution of benefits and burdens as the core concern of justice, even in situations not traditionally perceived as 'distributive'. This chapter explores the idea of distributive justice in this particular context of 'institutional responses to criminal wrongdoing'. From this analysis it develops a set of 'essential aims' of such responses as a means of seeking to explain the purposes behind any distributive pattern. The aims developed consider the nature of institutional responses and its influence on the priorities set when dealing with 'wrongdoing'. It is theorized that there are three general needs that must be addressed in any such response – the need to deliver retribution, the need to achieve restoration and the need to facilitate a set of consequential outcomes. Consistent with the conceptualization of justice as distribution in this guise, it is surmised that these outcomes are best achieved through a process of distribution. The specifics of these 'harm-related benefits and burdens' will later be developed from retributive and restorative concepts. A rider to understanding the functioning of these distributions is that they must always strive to be justice-promoting. A means of assessing whether justice is promoted in their distribution will come from the conceptual tool termed the 'evaluative criteria of justice' which will allow us to interrogate the distributions developed in this chapter to ask: does this give people their deserts, does it treat them equally, does it protect their rights and does it promote harmonious social relationships between those affected? But first the aims.

The Aims of Responses to Wrongdoing

Influencing Factors

Any response to wrongdoing must address certain discrete objectives, the content of which is influenced both by the institutional means in place to provide them and by the nature of wrongdoing which they address. This section explores the influence that the means of response (referred to loosely as 'justice system responses') and the object of the response (namely 'wrongdoing') have on determining the essential aims.

Justice system responses

The notion of an 'institutional response' is of course a social construct, describing a collection of practices, roles, norms and conventions which structure appropriate behaviour within a particular sphere of activity. 'Institutions' provide a collection of rules, formal or informal, that actors generally follow, for normative, cognitive, material or other reasons (North 1990: 3). So, for instance, in the case of institutional responses to wrongdoing, these rules are influenced by what is understood to be an overriding obligation to promote just outcomes. Obligations to deliver just outcomes similarly arise in 'welfare' institutions organized to ensure fair patterns of distribution of social or economic goods.[1] But in the case of institutions organized to respond to disputes or perceived injustices, the focus is more explicitly on responding to the 'wrongness' of the behaviour and correcting that behaviour (Pettit 1997). Regardless of the particular form of these institutions, these 'confluences of institutional rules and interactive routines [at work in the correction process] … as well as [their] physical structures' are seen as designed to influence the reaching of a just response (Young 2006: 111). It is through such 'structure-constituting behaviour' that these institutions provide a means by which 'members of a society effectively force their fellows to limit their actions to a range of acceptable alternatives', by exercising control and influence over them with a view to preventing or constraining harmful behaviour (Reiman 1990: 213). The institution we know as the 'criminal justice system' forms the core institutional response to wrongdoing. This institutional form emphasizes those practices, norms and rules seen as best able to achieve the required goals by applying the values and norms of the criminal law. The result is that even when exercising broader functions, such as preventing crime, maintaining public safety or expressing normative standards, the criminal justice system still retains an explicit focus on delivering justice through the law.

For Rawls (1985: 233), this 'correctional institution' succeeds in facilitating this 'capacity for [delivering] a sense of justice' because it gives people drawn into its institutional reach the moral power 'to understand, to apply, and to act from [and in a manner consistent with certain] standards of justice'. These standards themselves are seen as explicitly stated in the criminal law in the case of responding to wrongdoing. It is by giving people the moral certainty that the criminal justice system promotes lawful behaviour and keeps breaches of that behaviour grounded in justice concerns that the institution retains its legitimacy.

1 'Welfare' in this sense can be seen as referring essentially to the totality of the happiness and well-being of all persons and particularly to the alleviation of the sufferings of the poor and disadvantaged (Young 2006). The 'welfare system' provides one institutional means of delivering this alleviation.

The familiar concept of 'legal justice' which is at the heart of this system facilitates the path of using law as its means to do justice and provides for a particular form of response. There are of course other 'forms' or 'means' of response, often termed 'non-adversarial justice,' (King, Freiberg et al. 2009: xi) which move away from the mainstream legal justice response. For instance, a growing alternative form of response is 'restorative justice' which in many jurisdictions examined in this book is increasingly co-located within the criminal justice system. In a few of the instances highlighted here, restorative practices fill the wider role as the 'dominant informal justice movement' as regards responses to juvenile wrongdoing (Roche 2003: 25).[2] These different forms of response nonetheless operate under and within overriding criminal justice provisions. Nonetheless, the restorative form of response takes a radically different approach to delivering just outcomes, emphasizing in particular the need to respond to harm in a way that places less emphasis on a strict adherence to legal rules and processes. Both forms of response – mainstream criminal justice practice and emerging restorative justice practice – have clearly distinctive institutional features, but share the same overriding agenda of being 'concerned with justice'. Criminal justice forms the core of institutional responses to wrongdoing, with restorative justice now gaining a growing institutional foothold. Both institutional forms pursue the aim of responding to wrongdoing in different ways. Each lays claim to keeping its responses grounded in justice concerns and not in concerns with promoting expediency, efficiency or in fulfilling particular moral or political desires, be they meting out revenge or favouring powerful influences. It is this avowed commonality of purpose that provides the first influence on the essential aims – that institutional forms (of whatever kind) which respond to 'wrongdoing' profess an overriding emphasis on promoting and championing justice. It is important at the outset to be clear about what is meant by an institutional response to wrongdoing 'doing justice'. 'Doing justice' is used in two distinct but related senses in this book. The first takes it to mean 'creat[ing] a *sensibility* that the wrongdoing has been responded to in a just manner', through morally appropriate behaviour (Shearing and Johnson 2005: 29). The second takes 'doing justice' to mean providing those affected by the wrongdoing (its victims, offenders and the wider community) with *outcomes* seen by them as producing just and proper consequences.[3]

---

2 While restorative practice is new in the context of Western institutional responses to wrongdoing, it has much older historical roots (Braithwaite 2002b). Alternative Dispute Resolution (ADR) can equally claim to have a dominant informal justice role, particularly in civil matters (Sourdin 2004). Therapeutic jurisprudence which informs the practice of many 'problem-solving courts' also has a dominant informal justice role, as a non-traditional judicial response to wrongdoing rather than as a separate informal justice movement (Wexler, Winick et al. 2000).

3 There is some parallel here with the distinction Rawls draws between 'justifying a particular practice' and 'justifying a particular outcome falling under it'. In his famous discussion of punishment, Rawls distinguishes between the justification of morally fitting

Wrongdoing

As well as the explicit 'justice' focus of institutional forms of response to wrongdoing, the very nature of 'wrongfulness' will influence what is required in a response. 'Wrongdoing' is seen as conduct that is both prohibited, and (at least to some degree) invasive of personal liberty. Feinberg (1984: 31–36) captures this essence nicely when he defines 'wrongdoing' as the 'unjustifiable and inexcusable setback or invasion of the legitimate interests or rights of another'. Such 'setback to interests' has as its most distinctive feature the harming of others in ways that are both wrong and rights-violating. In the rare case where there is consent to doing the harm (such as in body contact sports or warfare), this may 'strip it of its wrongfulness', but in most cases conduct that is harmful (because of its invasive nature) is also rights-violating. It is this quality of 'rights violation' that gives such conduct its particular element of 'wrongfulness'.[4] Feinberg's conception of wrongfulness has been critiqued for underplaying the rights-violation aspect when applied in practice. Stewart, for instance, argues that Feinberg's conception centres on unjustified intrusions to interests at the expense of the right-violating aspect of these intrusions, when 'it is supposed to be their combination that produces the distinctive form of harm that is the appropriate target of criminal sanction' (Stewart 2001: 52). Nonetheless, for our purposes this combination of unjustified intrusions and rights-violation is crucial to an understanding of the 'wrongdoing' that gives rise to criminal liability. The requirement for 'rights-violation' is a necessary element for criminalization. In simple terms, where certain types of wrongful harm are caused (essentially harm extending beyond conduct which causes merely social hurt, such as most cases of lying) that conduct has been criminalized. Such criminalized behaviour can be distinguished as *mala in se* – 'things wrong in themselves' – or in moral terms things 'seen as evil' because of their implicit 'wickedness' (Whitman 2003: 34).[5]

Mill's 'harm principle' provides a useful perspective on this conceptualization of wrongdoing. In *On Liberty*, Mill claims that each individual has the right to act

response behaviour and the justification of morally or socially fitting outcomes, that is to say outcomes with a certain utilitarian value (1955: 4–5). A somewhat similar distinction is made here between the just way people are dealt with in institutional responses and the justness of the outcomes imposed on them and others.

4 One obvious example of harmful conduct which is not 'wrongdoing' is the harm done to opponents in contact sports, which is not 'wrongful' provided it remains within permissible limits. Conversely, in other situations the wrongdoing may be such an overriding invasion of personal liberty (slavery, for example) that the rights violation remains even in the presence of 'consent' (Kleinig 2009).

5 This behavior is distinguished from a wide range of essentially regulatory offences which are criminalized not because they are 'wrong' in themselves but simply because they are forbidden for social or regulatory purposes. These *mala prohibita* – 'things wrong only in so far as they are prohibited by the state' (Lacey 2008: 102) – stand outside any explicit notion of wrongfulness but are seen as needing to attract criminal rather than civil penalties to be effective.

as he or she wishes, with the proviso that their actions do not harm others. In this view, an action which directly harms only the actor himself will not be one in which society should intervene since the requirement of 'harm to others' is missing. But as Feinberg points out, the breadth of 'harm' to which the harm principle applies is far wider than the purely 'wrongful harm' or wrongdoing on which the criminal law focuses (1984: 36). Husak explains the distinction Feinberg makes by distinguishing between what he calls 'normative' and 'non-normative' harm:

> In the 'normative' sense of harm, A harms B 'by wronging B, or by treating him unjustly.' In the 'non-normative' sense of harm, A harms B 'by [merely] invading, and thereby setting back, his interest.' (Feinberg 1984: 34; Husak 2008: 91)

It is the normative sense of harm which is the concern of the criminal law. Otherwise, conceivably any result that anyone has ever wanted to prevent and which they felt had set back their interests (for example, being overlooked for promotion) could be construed as 'harmful' to that individual and so forbidden (Fletcher 1978: 402). The concern of the criminal law is much narrower than this. It rests with the particular subset of 'wrongful harm' which is (often morally and normatively) wrong and which will be labeled for discussion purposes here simply as 'wrongdoing'. The immediate question is whether the nature of the behaviour reduced in this way – behaviour which is harmful and wrong – has any influence over what should take place when the wrongdoing comes to light. It does. This can be clearly seen when we consider that the effect of the harm extends well beyond purely material, physical or psychological harm to include damage to normative or social relationships (of friends, neighbours, fellow citizens or communities at large). The effect of this more extensive understanding of harm is that any response must of necessity address both actual and normative harm in ways that are sufficient to 'make it appropriate to desist from anger, to renew trust, and to restore [a sense of] community' (Duff 2002: 86–87). The imposition of punishment is routinely used as a means to address this harm while at the same time communicating the necessary normative condemnation. Therefore, any 'essential aim' in response to wrongdoing must be fashioned in such a way that it can accommodate this twin need to condemn and restore (though the methods of doing so need not be reduced solely to punishment).

There are two final elements to consider about the nature of 'wrongdoing' that may also influence responses. Firstly, 'wrongdoing' as we have described it is often a contestable term for those involved. Offenders may objectively 'do' wrong, but not admit to that wrong, and where they do, they may assert (sometimes correctly) that there was 'wrong on both sides' in regard to their and others' behaviour. When these circumstances arise it makes it much more difficult to fully respond to wrongdoing because the presumed sharp dichotomy between 'offender' and 'victim' is absent. In these instances offenders may admit to committing some particular incident of offending and yet deny that their actions were in fact 'wrong' in the sense used here, believing that their actions were 'responsive' to the willful behaviour of others. They may see themselves as responding to earlier inflicted harm, to a perceived 'need' to address the wrongdoing of others or, more broadly, to the 'wrongness' of their own adverse socioeconomic conditions as compared with others (Alder 2000: 113; Daly 2008: 109). Such missing dimensions of wrongfulness need to be added to the mix in some way when determining what is 'necessary' in responding to criminalized wrongdoing. Secondly, a further dimension of wrongdoing is that it can extend in some situations to harm caused other than by purely individual acts. Young argues strongly that 'some harms come to people as a result of structural social injustice', and that these harms act as 'a kind of moral wrong, distinct from the wrongful act of an individual agent or the willfully repressive policies of a state' (2006: 114). She asserts that 'wrongdoing' of this kind gives rise to special response obligations, suggesting that instead of a focus which is confined to individual responsibility, these responses should embrace a 'social connection model' of responsibility. In this construction all persons who have derived a benefit from particular circumstances of social disadvantage bear some responsibility for addressing incidents of wrongdoing in those situations because they have contributed to its processes, either directly or indirectly (2006: 105).[6] This is a difficult dimension to fit within any conventional notion of wrongfulness, but nonetheless one that cannot be ignored. In summary, institutional pressures to deliver outcomes that are justice-focused will affect any selected formulation of the 'essential aims of a response to wrongdoing'. Similarly, certain aspects of wrongdoing (its rights-violating nature, its concern with personal and normative harm, its potential for contestability and its scope for responsibility wider than mere individual acts) exert strong influence on what should be aimed for in responses to wrongdoing.

Identifying Three Essential Aims

With this background in mind, responses to wrongdoing are seen as needing to address both the consequences of the wrongdoing, as well as the 'morally false message ... of disrespect' implicit in that wrong. In so doing they provide a form of public blaming which transforms the response from one that is purely personal to a form of public normative reinforcement (Garvey 1999: 1821). To do this properly, responses to wrongdoing must also address two other aspects. They must emphasize offending as a breach of community standards (implicit in the criminal law where the breach is proscribed) and so deal with the offender as a violator of those standards. At the same time, they must emphasize the violation of the

6 Young (2006: 107) gives 'the global apparel industry ... [as] a perspicuous example through which I will explain the logic of the social connection model'. In this example, anti-sweatshop activists may press claims on bulk purchasers of goods and their consumers that they have an obligation to take (social connection) responsibility for the poor conditions under which these garments are produced so as to respond to the 'wrongfulness' of that exploitation.

moral rights which the wrongdoing constitutes, and so deal with the harm caused by that violation (Bottoms 2003: 103). These two different points of emphasis often prioritize either 'instruments of censure' or 'measures of remediation' (Ashworth 1993: 283). If the stronger emphasis is on breach of a collective norm, the goal will be more explicitly on censuring that breach so as to ensure 'the maintenance or revitalization of values and norms which lie behind criminal law' (Boutellier 2002: 26). If the stronger emphasis is on the personal harm caused, the goal will be more explicitly focused on remedying that harm and restoring those hurt to something like their former state.[7]

These different points of emphasis provide the source of the first two discernible goals of responses to wrongdoing. Firstly, there must be a concern with 'retribution', so as to address the violation of the moral standard implicit in the wrongdoing. Secondly, there must be a concern with 'restoration', so as to address normative and personal damage caused by the wrongdoing. In addition to these two explicit goals, there must a concern with achieving certain 'consequential outcomes' that can work to 'correct' the wrong. These consequential outcomes look to future rather that past behaviour and have a focus on reducing the potential for further harm by addressing the causes and aftermath of wrongdoing. Any form of justice practice needs to address each of these three overlapping, yet distinct aims.[8]

Retribution

Retributive aims explicitly address the moral aspects of offending. A response to wrongdoing strongly grounded in retribution will emphasize mechanisms such as punishment and be based on principles such as proportionality, to 'determine its standards of justice' (Sadurski 1985: 241). According to one view, justice in this sense is interpreted to mean that 'the primary state response to crime should be to punish offenders in accordance with their deserts' (Duff 2003: 43). In this view, it is assumed that the moral guilt of wrongdoing 'deserves punishment for the sake of justice'. What is made to appear as a necessary and essential connection is the need for retribution and the infliction of punishment. In this conception, punishment is calibrated both in terms of comparative proportionality (relative punishment between crimes), and in terms of its commensurability (that is, punishment relative to the crime itself) (Sadurski 1985: 233). But it is a narrow view which sees punishment as the sole or essential vehicle by which to deliver retribution. It is

7 In pathological circumstances, such as repeated family violence assault, a more pressing aim will be immediate safety, and within the constraints of maintaining that safety the possible transformation or cessation of the relationship, to ensure ongoing safety and restore dignity and equality.

8 That there is a need to address each of these aims is not a view that many restorative justice thinkers, for instance, would share. Braithwaite (2002b) would dismiss the view that retribution is a necessary normative part of a justice response to wrongdoing. He argues that normative retribution is neither necessary nor desirable in such a response.

arguable here that the assumed 'connection between guilt and punishment is not a logical necessity but [more] a moral postulate' accepted by many moral philosophers but not by all (Sadurski 1985: 237). Where it is not accepted, a retributive response can nonetheless say 'the guilty deserve to suffer', without necessarily assuming that it is punishment alone which must constitute such suffering. In this alternative conception 'desert' can remain as the core of retribution and yet mean other things. These can include 'deserving to suffer remorse ... which is necessarily a painful process; [or deserving] to suffer censure from others ... [which] if taken seriously, must [also] be painful'; or it can mean deserving to suffer the denunciation by one's peers of one's wrongful conduct (Duff 2003: 48–49). An approach which addresses retributive aims and delivers desert in this wider sense can still impose the 'deserved suffering' without necessarily extending that 'suffering' to punishment or 'hard treatment'.[9] This broader notion of retribution is better understood when distinguished from a revengeful response. In the case of revenge, the primary aim *is* to use punishment to 'degrade or destroy' the offender's person through that punishment.[10] By contrast, retribution emphasizes that 'offenders be treated with dignity insofar as the point of retribution is ... to vindicate the equality of victim and offender' (Hampton 1998: 41). So, while an approach which emphasizes retribution will extend to punishment in many instances, this punishment is imposed 'with the offender's negative moral deserts in mind', not to mete out some form of revengeful harm (Barton 2000: 56–57). A retributive response in its proper sense is designed to offset and to address ill deserts, and so 'restore a balance [using such] means at our disposal' through deserved deserts (Sadurski 1985: 237). Retribution in this sense should be the first aim of a response to criminal wrongdoing. The censure and sanction implicit in retribution will address the crucial need for public blaming and the need to respond to breaches of community standards by giving the violator his or her just deserts.

Restoration

Restorative aims have a different focus that explicitly seeks 'the retrieval of an original favorable condition' following wrongdoing (Duff 2002: 84). Given that criminal wrongs are 'public' wrongs concerning the community as a whole, the primary restorative focus must be wider than purely personal harm (Duff 2002: 92). Similar to retribution, this necessitates a broader conception of restoration that can extend to restoring the 'offender's normative relationship with his victim as a fellow citizen, and with his fellow citizens more generally' (Duff 2002: 93). There are of course also limitations as to what can be done to address normative and personal harms, such that 'restoration' will need to be narrowed so that there is

9 As to 'hard treatment' see von Hirsch (1993), who describes it as 'visiting a deprivation' on the offender that is burdensome or painful independently of its communicative content.

10 Barton (2003) takes a different view of the purpose of revenge, seeing it instead as a form of the 'true' sense of retribution of 'getting even'. This is not the view taken here.

not a requirement 'to restore the *status quo* … [since] what has been done, often cannot be undone' (Sadurski 1985: 227). Achieving restoration requires some 'process of moral communication' through which the normative repair can be effected (Duff 2002: 97). Punishment is often seen as this communicator, with the assumption that actual and normative damage can be 'repaired' as a consequence of punitive sanctions being imposed on the offender. Punishment in this guise is seen as able to provide the necessary expressive and prudential means to reshape or 'restore' damaged relationships. For the wrongdoer, punishment provides the necessary 'gateway' for reintegration into the community (Kiss 2005: 13). For the victim, punishment signals that their harm 'counts', and that the community acknowledges that their interests and well-being have been violated. The necessary 'restoration' will then be achieved with punishment communicating the effect of the breach on the shared moral environment and reaffirming the importance of the breach of that normative standard (Reiman 1990: 196–197). But punishment is limited in its actual reparative qualities. The necessary moral communication required for restoration can be more effectively provided through the condemnation of the wrongdoing by those directly or indirectly affected by it, and by the provision of some tangible form of repair. The process of restoration is seen as better achieved by communicating normative censure directly rather than by relying on the more remote communicative power of punishment to do so. The restoration of personal harm can be addressed (to the extent possible) by reparation, either in the form of symbolic recognition (through apology or other gestures of remorse) or by more tangible forms of material reparation. Restoration in this sense is the second aim of a response to criminal wrongdoing. Such restoration has the capacity to bring into effect the necessary normative and personal repair by means other than simply through the imposition of punishment, and in doing so can address the need for public blaming and the violation of community standards.

Consequential Aims

As well as seeking to achieve retributive and restorative aims, responses to wrongdoing must also address the consequences and causes of that wrongdoing. These 'consequentialist' aims have a different focus given they seek to achieve instrumental goals rather than simply teach 'morally correct' lessons or restore breaches of community standards. Consequential aims have an explicit forward-looking focus because they endeavor to reduce the occurrence of criminal wrongdoing by removing the desire, opportunity or need for offending in the future. The assumption is that as a result of exposure to some form of institutional response, the likelihood of reoffending can be reduced in a significant way. The consequentialist theory of utilitarianism, for instance, asserts that the utility of 'imposing criminal penalties … [can] outweigh their costs' because the reduced offending that should follow will be socially beneficial (Luna 2003: 208). A core consequential aim is the imposition of rehabilitative measures tailored to match an individual's criminal behaviour and his or her own receptiveness to 'treatment' designed to reduce reoffending (Sherman, Gottfredson et al. 1997). The rationale for such 'treatment' is that it will counteract the causes of the initial wrongdoing and lead to desistence. Enthusiasm for responses which emphasize rehabilitation have waxed and waned over recent decades, with 'treatment [for a time seen as] no longer plausible as the chief aim' in responding to wrongdoing (von Hirsch 1993: 71). More recently, the value of rehabilitative measures has undergone some revival and recaptured some ground as a valid response as better evidence has emerged that particular programs can be effective deterrents (see Cullen and Gilbert 2009). The initial loss of enthusiasm was due in part to concerns that 'imposing' treatment rather than 'inflicting' retributive measures, had meant less stringent regard was given to proper normative procedures and constraints. There were concerns that this had resulted in a 'fail[ure] to provide adequate safeguards to protect offenders from being treated unjustly', but subsequent programs have largely addressed these inadequacies (Dignan 2002: 170). Similarly, deterrence from future offending is a core consequential desired outcome. Criminal justice practice draws a distinction between deterrence that is specific (deterring the particular current offender from future offending) and that which is general (deterring all others who might consider similar offending behaviour in future) (Ross 2009: 19.1720). Though largely dismissed as ineffective in criminology literature, general deterrence continues to be a standard consideration in sentencing principles and practice. As Ross makes clear, general deterrence can only be effective if the criminally minded or the public in general become aware of what penalty is imposed on a particular offender. A not uncommon view is that 'the notion that offenders generally, any more than the rest of the community, are well informed about the prevailing level of sentences is fanciful' (Davies and Raymond 2000: 239). A far more effective deterrent is seen as the certainty or at least likelihood of detection. Recent discussions have focused on the effectiveness of deterrence practice, with some advocates calling for a 'dynamic concentration of deterrence' on the assumption that such concentrated sanctions (or the perception of a heightened probability of their imposition) can reduce the risk of future offending and thereby reduce the levels of overall sanction levels needed (Kennedy 2009; Kleiman 2009). Whatever the merits of this argument, it makes clear that institutional responses to wrongdoing have a role that is wider than simply responding to the individual behaviour of the offenders who commit breaches of the criminal law. Achieving broad consequential aims such as those of rehabilitation, deterrence and protection remain an important part of any response to criminal wrongdoing. Most importantly, they directly address the need to give communities a 'credible guarantee of future right-doing' which remain at the heart of any institutional response (Shearing and Johnson 2005: 35).[11] Meeting such consequential goals is the third aim of a response to criminal wrongdoing where

11 Braithwaite (2002b: 122–123) points out that incapacitation need not refer simply to imprisonment but can include other formal constraints on behaviour such as 'conditional sentences' ('served' in the community) or restraints on practising a profession or filling certain managerial positions. These can also extend to informal restraints on behaviour

the breach of community standards is seen as best addressed by seeking to prevent recurrent breaches. The specifics of each of these aims are summarized as follows:

Table 1.1 The aims of justice responses to wrongdoing

Retribution	Restoration	Consequential
The offender needs to experience	*Those affected need to experience*	*The community needs to experience*
– denunciation of their wrongdoing	– personal and relational restoration through reparation	– deterrence through censure, and penalty
– self-censure of remorse and censure of others	– repair of normative harm through censure	– rehabilitation, through education or treatment
– the pain of sanction, extending to punishment	– repair of relational harm, personal or normative	– protection, through constraints on behaviour, including exclusion

These specifics provide a simple means to assess how well a particular justice practice responds to wrongdoing. Grouped together they provide a measure of 'responsiveness', that is to say a means of assessing programs by the extent to which they exhibit a broad-based response to criminal wrongdoing. Programs can be assessed as 'responsive' by examining how well they address and meet each of the three aims of retribution, restoration and consequential outcomes. In such responses, these aims are best achieved through the distribution of certain 'harm-related benefits and burdens'.

Conclusion

This chapter has provided a set of justice aims for responses to wrongdoing, arguing that the best way to meet these aims is through a distributive process. The next step in the argument about how best to respond to wrongdoing is the assertion that it is only through generating a flow of 'harm-related benefits and burdens' that the core retributive, restorative and consequential purposes be met. Any justice system response to wrongdoing must therefore work to generate the distribution of these 'harm-related benefits and burdens' in order to achieve the essential aims. The content of these benefits and burdens are developed in the next chapter.

---

monitored by family members (such as routine reporting of behavioural compliances or being required to reside with, or be accompanied by, particular individuals).

Chapter 2
Justice as Distribution in Response to Wrongdoing

Introduction

I have argued that the distribution of benefits and burdens is the core concern of justice, even in situations not usually seen as 'distributive'. Justice in all its forms is concerned with questions of such distribution. Understanding notions of justice in these terms is much more familiar when analyzing those social justice practices where the distributive allocation of the benefits of social cooperation is more commonplace. But the same distributive concern can hold just as true for the imposition of benefits and burdens in response to wrongdoing, as it does for the allocation of welfare benefits in response to social need. The distribution of benefits and burdens is necessary to achieve just outcomes in the context of wrongdoing because it provides the best means to deliver the essential aims of retribution, restoration and consequential outcomes detailed in Chapter 1. This chapter answers the question about what flow of 'goods' needs to be generated in the form of 'benefits' and 'burdens' to address these aims. Some of the benefits are broad and intangible, including the restored sense of dignity or relief from emotional distress in victims. They also include a regained sense of security, as well as a sense of private and public catharsis that the moral wrong perpetrated has been confronted and condemned. Other benefits will be narrower and more easily grasped. The repair of damage or injury caused by the wrongdoing can require physical as well as emotional repair, and the replacement of loss caused may call for symbolic as well as material reparation. Similarly, the range of burdens may be wide so as to include the censure and punishment imposed on the offender, or the loss and regret experienced by them as a consequence of their exclusion from society through physical or social separation. It is these social 'goods' which require distribution in response to wrongdoing. Distribution is a well-worked conceptual notion for describing this process of justice. Rawls (1971) conceptualized justice as a set of principles for 'assigning rights and duties in the basic institutions of society' and for defining 'the appropriate distribution of the benefits and burdens of social co-operation' which must flow as a consequence (1971: 4, 10). Rawls's focus was on the distribution of 'primary goods' such as liberties, opportunities, rights and wealth. Yet his emphasis on the foundational idea of 'just distributions' has much broader application including as a means to conceptualize distributions that should take place in response to wrongdoing. Nonetheless, it has been argued that the distributive conceptualization should only apply to 'social' forms of justice, not to its 'corrective forms' (see Barnes 1984). The core of this argument is that corrective justice cannot be governed purely by distributive principles because in responses to wrongdoing the criterion for determining the share or division must of necessity move from 'due' to 'moral worth' when wrong is involved. But much of this criticism can be allayed if the purpose of such distributions is not categorized as 'restor[ing] an overall balance of benefits and burdens', but instead as creating 'flows' of benefits and burdens designed to nullify the illegitimate benefits gained by an offender (Morris 1968: 478; Finnis 1980). If this reconceptualization is accepted then it is possible to envisage a distribution of benefits and burdens following (criminal) wrongdoing, designed not to achieve equilibrium but rather to activate 'flows' of benefits and burdens with a view to meeting retributive, restorative and consequential aims.

Finding the Benefits and Burdens

Distribution not Balancing

Many scholars reject this conceptual extension of distribution to include responses to wrongdoing, arguing that even if such responses do constitute 'redistribution', any such reallocation cannot be governed or understood purely by distributive principles. The principal criticism is that the criterion for determining any 'share' of a division must necessarily move from 'due' to 'moral worth' where wrongdoing is concerned, and that assessing moral worth is not a 'distribution question'. Rawls (1971) takes this view. His argument is that what is at play in responses to wrongdoing is not simply questions of justice alone but much wider moral questions of blame and responsibility which are not and should not be reduced to obligations to be shared among offenders, victims and the community. But there are others who see this critique as an unnecessary and artificial narrowing of the distributive concept. Sadurski's (1985) analysis of justice, for instance, lends some support to the argument being made here that a response to wrongdoing can in fact be conceptualized as distributive (1985: 221–258). There is an important qualification to this assertion. The purpose of such distributions in the case of responding to wrongdoing is not to 'restor[e] an overall *balance* of benefits and burdens' as it might be in social justice terms (Morris 1968; Finnis 1980).[1] If responses to wrongdoing are concerned with 'disturbed' benefits and burdens, their aim should not be to 'rebalance' the disturbance caused to these by the wrongdoing so as to recreate some real or imagined equilibrium. This should be obvious, since finding equilibrium in these circumstances will often simply not be possible given the absence of any preexisting parity or equality to reestablish.

1 A number of legal philosophers, most notably von Hirsch (1976, 1985), came to reject the 'balancing of benefits and burdens' as the aim of responses to wrongdoing.

Distributions made in the context of wrongdoing are much better conceptualized as processes of creating 'flows' of benefits and burdens, with these flows seen as instrumental in some way to meeting the essential aims described above and in establishing just outcomes in the terms discussed in the next chapter.

The unworkability of notions of rebalance can easily be illustrated by examining a classic case of wrongdoing. First, assume that a narrow set of benefits (those concerned with 'rights' to life, liberty, security, property, and so on) is fundamental to all human beings and that this entitlement is 'guaranteed by the rules of the criminal law' (Sadurski 1985: 225). Also, assume that there is an opposing burden of self-restraint on all persons which prevents them from interfering with these benefits in others. When criminal wrongdoing such as assault occurs, this benefit/restraint balance is disturbed. The restraint burden is cast away by the wrongdoer's actions, which have the effect of 'limit[ing] the victim's liberty', security and the like in very tangible ways (Sadurski 1985: 226–227). In the process, the wrongdoer acquires both some of the victim's benefits (a share of their liberty if you like, in the control they exercise for a time over them) and a new benefit for themselves (a new feeling of non-self-restraint). Any subsequent response to the wrong must react to this cumulative unbalancing and redistribute some burden to the wrongdoer as a means to nullify his or her illegitimate benefits. Taking the rebalancing notion to its logical conclusion, the bundle of undeserved benefits obtained by the wrongdoer and the bundle of unfair and undeserved burdens placed on the victim will both need to be rebalanced so as to renew the pre-offence equilibrium. The unworkability that Braithwaite and Pettit (1990) and others see with this conceptualization is that the core burden which guarantees the right (the self-restraint that comes from being law-abiding in the first place) is not really a burden at all for most people. Upholding the guarantee of restraint offers 'no actual inconvenience in its adherence for the bulk of the population' (Braithwaite and Pettit 1990: 158). In the same way, the benefit acquired by the offender (what is his added freedom or new, wider, unrestricted liberty) is not something truly seen as advantageous to most people. It is not a freedom that most would regard as a benefit worth offending in order to gain because it is at best temporary, and necessarily fleeting and insecure (Braithwaite and Pettit 1990: 159). Additionally, the assumption that there was a finely balanced 'equilibrium … there to restore' in the first place is questionable (Braithwaite and Pettit 1990: 159).

Young (1990) makes something of a parallel argument in her work on restrictive social structures which she sees as creating preexisting mal-distributions of benefits and burdens. In Young's view, an unjust social structure entails a 'transfer of energies, whereby the servers enhance the status of the served' by being robbed of a substantial part of their social benefit (once again principally a share of their liberty) (Young 1990: 52). Conversely, the same result is repeated with the privileged beneficiaries acquiring some of the exploited person's benefits (part of their capacity to acquire power, energy and opportunities). The exploiters are thus able to lessen some of their own burdens (for instance, reduce impositions on their own energies or opportunities). But if the assumed response to remedy this social wrong is to again attempt to restore a preexisting equilibrium, this will do no more than restore preexisting imbalances (returning the disadvantaged to their disadvantage, the privileged to their privilege). It will not act to recreate any sort of renewed just balance without some form of fundamental social structure rebalancing. In the light of the infeasibility of rebalancing, the less ambitious alternative is for the redistribution of benefits and burdens following (criminal) wrongdoing to focus not on recreating equilibrium, but on activating 'flows' of benefits and burdens in order to achieve certain stated aims. These 'flows' have as their purpose the need to provide retribution and restoration and to address certain consequential outcomes. The next section develops what is best seen as a taxonomy of the particular benefits and burdens which should 'flow'. The argument is that in responses to wrongdoing, the focus of distribution must be not with seeking to reestablish equilibrium but with ensuring that sufficient 'flows' occur, either 'towards' or 'away from' those affected by the wrong in order to achieve these essential aims.

Identifying Harm-related Benefits and Burdens

The basic premise is this: The harm caused by wrongdoing 'must be restored through [some form of] social action' and this, in turn, involves a process of distribution (Llewellyn and Howse 1999: 357). All such forms of action need to be powered by an overriding 'moral intuition' which can be remedied in some measure by distributing benefits and burdens from the damage caused by wrongdoing (Llewellyn and Howse 1999: 373). The descriptor 'harm-related' is used to capture the idea that the purpose of such distributions relates directly to obligations and entitlements created as a consequence of wrongdoing, rather than as a consequence of the need to create broader social or economic equality. Such distributions provide the means to address the 'How can …?' questions that Bottoms (2003: 97) posed in his discussion about restorative practice:

> How can victims, having suffered a perhaps traumatic shock, be brought again into something like their prior set of social relationships and activities, regaining their self-esteem and confidence to live their lives without undue anxiety?
>
> How can offenders, having been rightly censured (perhaps severely) for their offence, nevertheless be reintroduced into society so that they – and the society – may 'move on' after the offence?

Harm-related Benefits

In an overriding sense, a justice response in itself can provide its own kind of benefit – (ideally) the benefit of being treated justly when one has been affected by wrongdoing. Weil (1951) sees this benefit as a 'kind of nourishment', which is a notion that Gaita rephrases when he says, if we are treated justly then we receive not merely certain natural benefits or goods, but also just treatment as a distinct and irreducible object of gratitude (1991: 77). As well as this underlying benefit of 'just treatment', more specific benefits should flow. One useful starting point to categorize such benefits is Braithwaite's (2002c, 2002e) set of 'maximizing values', which are the particular benefits he specifically ascribes to restorative justice but which can have broader application. Also useful are the insights of desert scholars, most notably Ashworth (1983) and von Hirsch (1993), as to the benefits which should populate the notion of 'positive deserts'. Drawing on these two sources, it is possible to identify a set of specific harm-related benefits which should be added to extend the underlying benefit of 'just treatment':

Repaired, or restored –

- human dignity
- property loss
- safety/injury/health
- human relationships
- sense of community
- emotional states (release from feelings of fear, hate and shame; providing a feeling of vindication)
- sense of freedom
- feelings of compassion or caring. (extracted from Braithwaite 2002e: 569)

Realized, or released –

- sense of public catharsis
- feelings of satisfaction in the victim
- sense of relief in the offender (from feelings of guilt and remorse). (Ashworth 1983; von Hirsch 1993)[2]

Each and every one of these benefits will not be realizable or appropriate in every response to wrongdoing. The actual mix needed in a particular response will be determined at least in part by the relative importance the particular form of justice response places on the retributive, restorative and consequential aims. In summary form, the benefits that may need to flow in responses to wrongdoing in order to meet the three essential aims include the following:

2 There is some similarity in these lists with Edney and Bagaric's summation of what they see as 'the things that are actually conductive to happiness' disturbed when criminal behavior occurs and which need rectification as a consequence (2007: 105–106). It is also reflective in some ways of von Hirsch and Jareborg's 'living standard analysis' of the effect of different degrees of harmful conduct on victims of wrongdoing (1991).

Table 2.1 Harm-related benefits

Harm-related benefits: Repaired or restored
• Safety, injury, health
• Loss
• Relationships
• Sense of community
• Personal dignity
• Emotional relief from feelings of fear, hatred and shame
• Sense of vindication
• Sense of freedom
• Sense of compassion, caring
• Release of public catharsis
• Victim's sense of satisfaction
• Offender's relief

In shorthand form, these specifics can be summarized simply as the distribution of the benefits of 'repair and restoration' and 'normative vindication'.

Harm-related Burdens

Acts of wrongdoing more clearly impose burdens as a consequence of the injustice rendered. Gaita (1991: 77) captures the essence of the burdens the wrongdoing itself has inflicted when he writes,

> A person who is the victim of injustice suffers not merely a determinate form of natural harm [that is, a burden], but also the injustice of it, which is a separate and irreducible cause of his torment.

A purpose of any response to wrongdoing must be to manage the burdens created by wrongdoing in such a way as to ensure that they 'flow away' from victims in order for the work of repair of harm to begin. But at the same time, the retributivist slogan 'the guilty deserve to suffer' misses the full scope of what the burdens that need to be 'suffered' by the wrongdoer can constitute (Duff 2003: 48). A wrongdoer clearly deserves to 'suffer' something 'burdensome and painful', though this can be the burden 'of being censured, of remorse [or] of making reparation' as much as it can be burdensome punishment (Duff 2002: 97). Indeed, Feeley (1979) recognizes that much of the actual burden suffered by a wrongdoer is simply those practical and mundane consequences that flow from involvement in the legal justice process (lost time, perhaps lost employment, added expense, unwanted publicity and personal attention or simply ongoing inconvenience). Other burdens similarly flow as a consequence of the release of emotions, particularly emotions of shame endured by both offenders and victims (Braithwaite 1989). The distribution of these burdens must in some way be managed and controlled in any response process. Similar to the list of benefits, it is possible to distill a set of harm-related burdens that need to flow (or be dissipated) in order to address the injustice of wrongdoing:

Imposed, or released –

- self-censure of remorse
- censure from others
- symbolic reparation
- material reparation
- sanction or punishment
- emotional burdens (feelings of fear, hate and shame)
- burdensome consequences. (Feeley 1979; Duff 1986; Braithwaite 1989; von Hirsch 1993)

In summary form, the burdens that need to be managed or distributed in order to meet the essential aims of responses include the following:

Table 2.2 Harm-related burdens

Harm-related burdens: Accepted or imposed
• Self-censure
• Censure from others
• Symbolic reparation
• Material reparation
• Punishment
• Emotional burdens of managing fear, hatred and shame
• Practical and personal burdensome consequences

The specific burdens can be described in shorthand form as the burdens of 'censure and sanction' imposed on the offender, and the relief from burdens suffered by the victim through 'vindication and reparation'.

These two sets of elements constitute the 'harm-related benefits and burdens' seen as needing to flow in responses to wrongdoing. Any justice response to wrongdoing must distribute some combination of the elements in order to achieve the essential aims identified. The purpose of any such distribution is not to attempt to reach equilibrium, nor to determine a particular 'amount' of a benefit or burden that should be allocated. The task instead is simply to generate flows that might achieve these essential aims. There is one further piece to the puzzle. These distributions must also be just, not merely instrumental in the way they achieve the aims. The next chapter develops a set of evaluative criteria that can be applied to such distributions to assess their justness. To have the potential to be just, they must adhere to the requirements to give people their deserts, to treat them equally, to protect their rights and to promote harmonious social relationships among them. These 'evaluative criteria' provide the means by which to regulate appropriate 'flows' of the benefits and burdens described here in ways that guarantee just outcomes.

Conclusion

This chapter has identified a set of 'harm-related benefits and burdens' which outline the specifics of the goods that need to be distributed in responses to wrongdoing. It has argued that it is through generating a flow of these benefits and burdens that the retributive, restorative and consequential aims can be met. Any justice system response to wrongdoing which fails to generate such flows will fail to deliver just outcomes. While rejecting the need to achieve equilibrium in such distributions, there is still a need to determine the proper 'amount' of flow of each benefit or burden. The argument made in the next chapter is that the proper 'amount' of flow is best gauged by creating distributions in response to wrongdoing which give people their deserts, treat them equally, protect their rights and promote harmonious social relationships among them.

Chapter 3
Meeting Justice Standards in Responses to Wrongdoing

Introduction

This chapter turns its attention to the 'justice' question, seeking to identify a set of evaluative criteria to use to determine whether the distributions of benefits and burdens made in institutional responses to wrongdoing are just. In doing so, it is important to make a distinction between the core *concept* or meaning of justice and various theoretical suggestions or *conceptions* about how 'justness' should be apprised or assessed. It is from such conceptions that the 'evaluative criteria' can be drawn. A distinction also needs to be drawn between those distributions which have as their core concern the provision of a sense of justice and those distributions that serve other useful purposes, such as efficiency or utility. The analysis that follows is a purposive rather than an historical or conceptual examination of justice, though like all other such appraisals it begins with Plato and Aristotle. It traces what is essentially a direct line from Aristotle's notion of 'justice as entitlement' to modern formulations of justice such as Rawls's theory of 'justice as fairness' (1971) and then considers broader formulations of justice as 'more than entitlement' together with critiques of these theories, such as Nozick's entitlement rights theory (1974) and Young's structural critique (1990, 2006). We settle on the view that 'entitlement' still provides the best summation of justice's core meaning and that a concern for entitlement remains consistent within all distributive threads. From an examination of the meaning of justice itself, we then turn to examining various conceptions surrounding the features of a distribution that mark it out as 'just'. These conceptions provide various answers to the question 'When do we know whether distributions (in our case, of harm-related benefits and burdens) are just?' Finding satisfactory answers to this question involves the consideration of a number of possible standards or measures of 'justness'. Some of these are quickly rejected as simply inappropriate in this context (those which seek to measure justice in terms of utility, reciprocity and need for instance). Others are preferred because of their clear explanatory power to illuminate the notion of justness in terms of desert, equality, rights and harmony.

Conceptualizing Justice

We begin by accepting the premise that justice is not concerned with all human conduct, or indeed with all distributions of benefits and burdens. Justice has its own distinct and limited moral terrain. Confining the analysis to this particular moral terrain permits a clearer picture of justice's distinctiveness to emerge. Secondly, using the distinction between the 'concept' of justice as representing justice's core meaning and various 'conceptions of justice deployed to determine that certain types of situation are just or unjust' (Campbell 2001: 10) allows a sharper focus to be turned on justice alone. We put aside (for a time) concerns about what makes a particular situation just or what institutional arrangements might best achieve just outcomes, and first examine the nature of justice.

The Concept of Justice as a Core of 'Entitlement'

Posing the rhetorical question 'What is justice about?' Ronald Dworkin found himself confronted with a myriad of answers (1978: 135). We can follow the same path. To begin with, the ancient Greeks had a deceptively simple notion that justice was essentially *about* virtue. Justice was the first of their virtues, the one which stood above all others in rank and importance. But justice was also their 'chilly virtue', since it regulated 'the dealings of those who are strangers to each other, and who look[ed] to each other neither for intimacy nor for unrequited assistance' (Ryan 1993: 16). This separation of justice from the 'warmer virtues' of affection and love was the first step in giving justice its particular moral distinctiveness.

Early classical scholars saw justice very much in these personal terms, and their writing on the precepts of justice – live in a morally upright manner; do harm to nobody; render to each what is due – reflects this focus on the personal.[1] Aristotle (384–332 BCE) first expanded the notion of justice beyond this idea of a purely individual moral attribute. In *Nicomachean Ethics*, Aristotle drew a distinction between justice in this individual sense of 'all the habits and dispositions of a good citizen' and justice in its broader societal sense as the 'one single and discrete virtue' of the state (1984: Bk V ss2). Plato (ca. 427–347 BCE) had earlier anticipated the same distinction, recognizing that the acts of an 'individual agent' could not be fully understood in isolation from 'the nature of justice in the "larger letters" of the state' (1975: Bk IV 443d; see Miller's analysis in 1987: 373). Plato's prescription in the *Republic* (paraphrasing the earlier formulation of Simonides) that 'justice consists in rendering to every man his due' (1975: Bk IV 433) was the first formulation to capture this wider societal aspect.[2] The requirement to give other people their entitlement as distinct from a purely personal requirement to act in a virtuous, moral manner provided the next refinement of justice's moral separateness. An aspect of this developing separateness was to impose an element

---

1 These precepts have maintained a long history, appearing again in Ulpian's (d. 228) writings and included later in Justinian's *Institutes*, published in 533.

2 A slightly different translation – 'the constant and perpetual will to render everyone his due' – cited in Miller (1987) highlights the sense of justice as being a virtue in need of constant and vigilant maintenance.

of entitlement on the concept of justice. Such claims of entitlement bring with them a 'capacity to demand', making justice distinctive from other moral virtues such as 'humanity, benevolence, charity, generosity and hospitality' where such a capacity to demand would be misplaced (Mautner 1996: 289).[3] The entitlement element meant that justice could 'make the most stringent demands of all the moral virtues', demands that simply cannot be made of generosity or benevolence (Ryan 1993: 11). As a consequence, the moral criticism voiced when conduct is seen as 'unjust' is founded on this recognized failure to deliver on a perceived *entitlement*. Demands for justice that assert a perceived entitlement give rise to obligations to have the injustice corrected and to restore the lost moral status quo in some way (Hart 1961: 164). This capacity for demand provides a further refinement to justice's claims to moral separateness. The element of 'entitlement' adds to justice's quality as a societal rather than a purely individual or personal virtue (Lerner 2002). Maslow (1970) recognizes something of the same supremacy in his hierarchy of needs where he ascribes to justice the status of 'a precondition for the satisfaction of basic needs'. Others have pressed these claims further, suggesting that 'justice is so fundamental, that a case could be made for it to be construed as a basic need' such that 'its observance [is] agreed to be basic to social life' (Maslow 1970; Ryan 1993; Taylor 2003, 2007).[4] Either way, the notion of a demandable entitlement to the maintenance of particular 'publicly agreed terms of social co-operation' sets justice apart from other moral precepts and contributes in large measure to its claims to moral separateness (or in some guises to moral 'superiority') (see Rawls 1971: 3–6; Bix 2006: 105). The strength of the entitlement aspect is well illustrated in the way people recognize and respond to the absence of justice (Shklar 1990: 15). Certain forms of conduct evoke a sense that a moral evil of varying gravity has occurred which requires correction (Allen 1999: 335). An individual's sense of justice mandates that such a failure by society to act in the appropriate moral manner gives rise to legitimate demands for a remedial moral response which *must* be met by society. This brief historical contextualization of the concept of justice has identified its key elements – that it is a broader societal value rather than a merely personal virtue and that the core aspirational essence of justice has to do with delivering a perceived sense of entitlement. Questions clearly remain as to what else besides these qualities sets justice apart as a unique moral claim.

3 'Hospitality' is the term Kant uses to refer to the basic 'moral respect' owed to all persons (Bix 2006: 103).

4 Lerner (2002: 21) argues that human beings have two markedly different 'senses' of justice – a 'normative' sense whichparallels reasoned discourse of justice and an 'intuitive' sense which is more reflective of a primitive, emotional urge to judgment. In an interesting approach, Davis (2007b, 2009) has applied Lerner's Just World Delusion principles to examine the imposition of criminal sentences.

The Concept of Justice as More than Entitlement

Imbuing entitlement with the status of the core concern of justice can often obscure rather than reveal its full distinctive moral terrain (Campbell 2001: 10–12). Describing justice only in entitlement terms, for instance, fails to take into account the legitimate role other moral values, such as liberty, efficiency or utility, play in determining entitlement. An adequate concept of justice therefore needs to be more finely focused if we are to 'deepen the furrows of difference' between justice and these other moral concerns. One useful refinement comes from Hart (1961), who described justice as a precept that aims 'to create among individuals a moral and, in a sense, an artificial *'balancing"* so as to offset preexisting or imposed imbalances or disproportions and thereby make people 'morally more alike' (Hart 1961: 165, emphasis in original). Hart's formative idea helps to push the conceptual boundary of justice beyond simply entitlement. He later confessed 'to an itch to go further' than this to explore precisely which justice principles such a 'moral balancing' should entail (1968: 22). But it was principally Rawls (1971) who sharpened the refinement in his particular focus on the underlying process of distribution.

Rawls's distributive justice

Rawls's (1971) theorizing of justice places the notion of 'distribution' as central to the conceptual meaning of justice. In his seminal work *A Theory of Justice*, he conceptualized justice as a set of principles for 'assigning rights and duties in the basic institutions of society' and for defining 'the appropriate distribution of the benefits and burdens of social co-operation' so to meet those rights and duties (1971: 4, 10). While in later refinements, such as *Justice as Fairness* (1985, 2001), he stressed more explicitly that although his theory was intended as a *political* conception of justice 'worked out for a specific kind of subject, namely, for political, social, and economic institutions', it nonetheless in his view established notions of distribution as the central concern of justice more broadly (1985: 224). Rawls's particular focus had been on the distribution of a set of 'primary goods', such as liberties, opportunities, rights and wealth, but his more general reemphasis on the foundational idea of 'just distributions' had the effect of bringing into sharper focus the core meaning of justice itself. Of course, the foundation which Rawls gave to distribution had deep historical roots. In large measure, it was a refinement of Locke's contract theory. For Enlightenment philosophers like Locke and later for Rousseau, the 'social contract' was the source of political legitimacy, regardless of whether the political structure in question was one of representative or monarchial sovereignty (Locke 1970; Rousseau 1990). Rawls revived this notion of 'contractarianism' and used it as a means to 'demonstrat[e] the *morality* of certain principles of justice' (Sadurski 1985: 60, emphasis in original). The core of Rawls's argument developed from his 'reflective equilibrium' notion, in which he asserted that the principles produced in an idealized 'original position' where principles of self-interest do not prevail are just, because that process itself will only be based upon reasoned debate. It is through such a process of 'reflective equilibrium' that principles of justice can be derived from a hypothetical social contract among imaginary persons in a situation where temptations to further one's own specific needs or interests are eliminated (1971: 48–51). As Sadurski notes, 'the justificatory force of the original position consists in the creation of circumstances in which only the power of reason moulds a contract', and as a consequence the principles produced should in themselves be reasonable (Sadurski 1985: 59). By removing other influences so as to create 'an imaginary, more rational and more moral world', a situation is reached in which the force of moral argument will always win the day. Therefore, any principle produced by rational argument generated within this imaginary world is perforce produced by fully rational human beings agreeing on principles acceptable to all. Any principles so produced will by definition be reasonable and just. It is from such a 'thought experiment' that Rawls finds the emergence of two 'justice principles' for determining what constitutes a 'just' distribution in any given situation (1971: 11). His first principle is that any such distribution should always produce a limited set of 'equal basic liberties', which include political liberty, freedom of speech and assembly, freedom of conscience, the right to hold personal property and the right to fair treatment under the law (1971: 53). His first principle of justice asserts that this basic set of 'goods' should be distributed according to an 'equal liberty principle' where each person has an entitlement to a share consistent with their most extensive basic liberty, provided it is compatible with similar liberty for others (1971: 53–55). Rawls's second principle, 'the difference principle', would alter the original distribution in the face of social and economic inequalities so as to rearrange it in a way that is 'to the greatest benefit of the least advantaged' (1971: 54).

The notion that such distributions should 'maximize liberty' warrants some brief discussion. Liberal notions of justice promote a distribution that essentially maximizes *negative* liberty, which is the absence of interference from others. It is possible to trace to early liberal thinkers this obligation to respect the liberty of others as a core of justice (it is traceable at least to Locke 1970; Kant 1981). As an alternative, republican notions of justice reframe the aim of justice distributions to protecting *positive* liberty. In contrast, positive liberty is *not* the absence of interference by others but rather the overt mutual promotion and protection of one another's freedom which implicitly suggests some interference (see Sunstein 1990; Pettit 1997). This distinction can be sharpened by referring to this mutually protected freedom as 'dominion' or non-domination, rather than using the more familiar term of liberty (Braithwaite and Pettit 1990). In either its negative or positive guise, justice distributions need to follow the Rawlsian prescription to promote a core set of rights which are especially protective of liberty or personal freedom. The core idea that emerges from this Rawlsian analysis is that distributions should be focused on apportioning a set of 'primary goods' so as to provide people with entitlements consistent with their most extensive basic liberty. Maximizing 'liberty' (or 'dominion') then becomes an overriding criterion for determining just entitlements, not utility or efficiency or some other 'moral' virtue (Rawls 1971: 12–13).[5] Any human 'situation' or transaction can be gauged as just or unjust depending upon the extent to which distributions which occur there maximize liberty. Though Rawls's precise formulation of the 'goods' requiring distribution so as to achieve such an outcome has long been debated, there is nevertheless a critical consensus that his emphasis on distributions which maximize liberty 'catches something important about our current notions of justice' (Ryan 1993: 13). Rawls's theory adds this element to the conceptualization of justice – that distributing benefits and burdens in a way that maximizes liberty is at the conceptual heart of the societal value which has as its aspirational heart the satisfaction of a sense of entitlement.

Critiques of distribution

There are several strands of criticism of the centrality which Rawls gives to distribution. Sandel (1982), who pioneered the 'communitarian'[6] ideology, takes issue firstly with the concentration on the individual that these distributions necessarily imply. He argues that the way questions were seen to be posed in the 'original position' unnecessarily prioritized the primacy of individual autonomy, while missing entirely the stronger 'ties of culture and particularity which give our lives meaning and content at their core' (Sandel 1982: 17; see also Campbell 2001: 111). Giving such primacy to individual interests, Sandel asserts, displaces the centrality of community and the obligations and involvements individuals should have in that community. His critique is more a critique of the 'manner' of distribution, rather than of the centrality assigned to distribution *per se* (though it does reject the primacy given to requiring distributions to necessarily maximize liberty). Communitarians such as Sandel explain that distributions should not aim for individual entitlement, but should instead aim for some form of 'central distribution' where the community rather than individuals are satisfied so that 'what each person gets, he gets from others who give to him in exchange for something' (Sandel 1982). Nonetheless, the centrality of distribution remains undisplaced in this analysis.

A second line of criticism seems more substantial since it asserts that the distributive focus should only apply to 'social' forms of justice and not to its

5 Rawls's theory has long been taken to demarcate a fair distribution of benefits and burdens as one of the core elements of the concept of justice. In his earlier, famous article 'Two Concepts of Rules', he does consider a number of justifications for the distribution of punishment (1955). But his concept of justice remains an essentially 'political' one when politics is understood more broadly as 'public decision-making regarding the distribution of goods' (Weber 1947).

6 'Communitarian' is a convenient label to identify a wider ideology which seeks 'to get away from the stark individualism' of liberal rights and regards all values as embedded in a particular social or community culture (see Kennedy 1993, 2000).

'corrective forms', such as responses to wrongdoing (see Barnes 1984).[7] The distinction made between these 'forms' of justice has long shaped some strands of the philosophical debate about the nature of justice (Spader 1988). There has been a strong line of critique that questions of distribution and rectification should be confined to situations of 'social' justice, thereby excluding 'corrective' forms which are more correctly concerned with responding to wrongs and unacceptable harms (Zipursky 2005: 133). But this division is artificial. Campbell rightly asserts that 'justice in all its manifestations [has] to do with questions of distribution' (2001: 22). It seems to be a given that the effect of distributions of economic, social and power-driven 'goods' will always cloud the operation of corrective justice, and that this will be particularly pronounced in 'corrective' responses to criminal wrongdoing (Bix 2006: 104). But that does not undermine the primacy of distribution itself. Accommodating the criticisms of Sandel that justice distributions should be community focused and of Barnes that distribution has no part in correctional responses is reasonably simple. But a more sustained critique of distribution as the core of justice is that offered by Nozick (1974). Nozick sees Rawls's explanation of justice as primarily about distribution as confining the focus of justice far too narrowly into the 'artificial' redistributions of social benefits and burdens at the expense of maintaining preexisting and 'natural' entitlements which should always retain their existing primacy.[8]

Nozick's 'rights conception of justice'

Nozick's (1974: 160) 'historical entitlement conception of justice' appears fundamentally at odds with the assumption that justice is *about* distributing benefits and burdens. As Campbell states:

> [A] major feature of Nozick's theory [is] that the pursuit of all such patterns of benefits and burdens is a violation of rights since it inevitably involves taking away goods from some and redistributing them to other people in order to establish the pattern. (2001: 63)

Nozick's view is that any ordered or 'patterned' distributions, no matter what it is based upon, will always involve violations of rights. This is because maintaining patterns necessarily means 'continually interfer[ing] to stop people from transferring

---

7 Aristotle explained this distinction in terms of mathematical metaphors. Distributive justice is geometric since it involves proportionality in any distribution or allocation. In comparison, corrective justice is arithmetic because it involves adding back that which has been taken, or subtracted, from someone by wrongdoing (Zipursky 2005: 133).

8 There is also an opposite strand of critique positing that justice's distributive reach spreads much farther than simply welfare and correctional situations and in fact intrudes more deeply into human affairs. Putnam (1995), for instance, argues that there is insufficient regard given to the reach of justice into family life, the workplace and the relationship between these two spheres.

resources as they wish to', or 'interfer[ing] to take from some persons resources that others ... chose to transfer to them' (Nozick 1974: 163). So, neither assessing a distribution on the basis of what Nozick refers to as 'time-slice principles' (that is, what is best at any given single moment) (1974: 153), or assessing a distribution based on 'end-result principles or end-state principles' (that is, what is best in terms of outcome) can be the proper basis for justice (1974: 155). Instead, 'a distribution [can only be] just if it arises by just steps from a just initial position' without any preconceptions of 'what pattern will emerge' as a consequence (Schmidtz 2006: 202, 203). For Nozick, whether a pattern of distribution is just 'depends upon how it came about' and as a result, justice essentially reverts to being 'about' historical entitlement (Nozick 1974: 153). One simple response to this argument is to say that Nozick is not rejecting the notion of justice as distribution but merely arguing that such distributions should always be based on historical entitlement. In this sense, he is returning 'entitlement' to the foreground, albeit a different 'version' of entitlement based on rights rather than due. What he does not acknowledge, however, is that there are other 'proper' evaluative criteria on which to base entitlement than simply respecting rights. Entitlement can equally be evaluated in terms of desert, equality, need 'or some other favoured criterion' (Campbell 2001: 64). But Nozick's critique of distribution is deeper than this, as Schmidtz's (2006: 208) analysis makes clear. According to Schmidtz, Nozick provides a theory of justice which is a theory of entitlement that rejects distribution entirely. For Nozick in this analysis, individuals have 'natural rights' to property, life and liberty which give rise to entitlements of non-interference with those rights, that is to say a right to be left alone and uncoerced (negative liberty) (Campbell 2001: 58–59). Because of this 'natural' or historical determinant, no distribution of any kind is necessary to 'allocate' entitlements (since they already exist), and the state should have no justification in 'redistributing' benefits and burdens so as to reach some other ideal equality. Justice is simply a matter of the non-violation of preexisting entitlements. If any 'redistribution' is required it should merely be to recreate historical rights, not for considerations of general welfare or benefit to others given that would mean 'us[ing] one ... for the benefits of others' (Nozick 1974: 33). Nozick's view is that no pattern, howsoever arrived at, should be imposed; whatever pattern happens to be there in the first place should be left alone, undisturbed (1974: 155).

There are substantial problems with substituting this historical entitlement assumption as a descriptive or normative principle. Foremost is that Nozick's rejection of distribution *per se* lacks any normative power in situations where rectification is clearly needed, such as in the case of gross human rights distress. Nozick concedes this to some extent in recognizing situations requiring 'the rectification of justice in holdings' (1974: 152). These redistributions would be justified on grounds of restoring rights or entitlements. But to effect rectification on truly just terms may likely require redistributions as broad as possible, and certainly more than merely reestablishing historical entitlements. Iris Marion Young (1990) strongly asserts that to confine rectification merely to historical entitlements would in fact act to perpetuate preexisting injustice rather than act as a means to deliver justice.

Young's structural critique

Young rejects the notion of reducing justice simply to questions of distribution. She sees justice as much about how people are treated, as about the share of benefits and burdens they may receive (Young 1990, 2000, 2006). She sees these two notions as fundamentally different – 'the ideal of equal treatment is not the same thing as the idea that we ought to have equal shares' (Schmidtz 2006: 112). Young's argument is that it is by unequal treatment, not by unequal sharing that we signal the lack of mutual respect which is indicative of injustice. Therefore, instead of focusing solely on justice as distribution or redistribution, we should begin first by addressing issues of unequal treatment, especially those borne of hierarchical social structures (Anderson 1999: 313). Accepting such a view would displace the prominence afforded thus far in our analysis to distribution. Young's (1990: 26) core critique is that justice 'must involve evaluating not a distributive outcome but [addressing] the social structures that enable or constrain individuals' in relation to such distributions. She explains that the attempt to 'stretch' the distributive concept of justice to account for institutional inequities is doomed to failure because with some crucial situational factors – such as power, opportunity or decision-making – it is simply not possible to reduce people's capacity to questions of distribution (1990: 9). The constraining effect of social structures and relationships will always stand separate and apart from any question of distribution and these need to be properly accounted for first in any comprehensive concept of justice. In Young's view, a sounder concept than 'distribution' is one that begins instead with addressing the reality of domination and oppression born of class, race and gender (1990: 3). Attending to the 'difference' in treatment inherent in these distinctions is much more critical because these constraints prevent what might otherwise be fair distributions from ever beginning to deliver justice (Young 1990: 4).

Young's focus is primarily on institutional conditions which are limiting, in particular two prominent forms of 'disabling constraints', domination and oppression (1990: 149). 'Domination' refers to the structural exclusion of people from any authentic role in deciding how to conduct their own lives. 'Oppression' denotes those systematic institutional processes which prevent individuals and groups from having or utilizing opportunities 'necessary for the development and exercise of [their] individual capabilities' (1990: 39). Within this framework, 'injustice [occurs] where domination leads to oppression' and results in institutionally constrained opportunities (Campbell 2001: 207). Moreover, these restraining conditions are borne of social assumptions that are not 'the result of a few people's choices or policies', but are simply embedded in 'the normal processes of everyday life' (Young 1990: 41). Structural oppression may not be consciously or intentionally exercised, but rather may be an exercise of power in a wider Foucaultian (1977) sense of simply occurring out of everyday, perhaps even socially 'enlightened' practices. Such oppression can be the 'effect of often liberal and "humane" practices of education, bureaucratic administration', and not borne of deliberate policies of exploitation at all (Young 1990: 41). The improper institutional conditions that produce this oppression flow from the fundamental fact that 'some people exercise their capabilities under the control, according to the purposes, and for the benefit of other people' (Young 1990: 49). This constraint has the effect of systematically transferring 'the powers of some persons to others'. Therefore, what is required of justice cannot simply be redistribution. What is needed instead is the overall elimination of the institutional forms that 'enable and enforce this process of transference' and their replacement with more enabling forms (Young 1990: 49–50).[9] Young gives the example of racially specific exploitation occurring in terms of segmented labour markets where oppressed racial groups are confined to menial work lacking in autonomy and which 'entail a transfer of energies whereby the servers enhance the status of the served' (1990: 52).

Young's view is that removing these underlying constraints – domination which prohibits people from controlling their own life choices, oppression which prevents people from acting upon their life opportunities – should be the real concern of justice. Otherwise, such institutional constraints will always preclude people from making the most of any benefits distributed to them (and prevent them from managing their burdens to the least disadvantage). Unless the structural imbalances are first addressed, a focus on justice as distribution will simply perpetuate unjust outcomes. My response is that Young's critique can be addressed by seeing justice conceptually as 'distribution with modifications'. The minimal prescription for overcoming the narrowness of distribution sufficient to satisfy Young's critique would be to add two discrete requirements – that the institutional conditions under which any distribution is made are fair and that the distributions themselves do not add to inequality. This modification addresses Young's mandate that institutional conditions 'contain and support' the scope of individuals to 'develop and exercise [their] capacities and express [their] experience' and 'participate in determining [their] action[s] and the conditions of [their] action[s]' (1990: 37). What this means for justice distributions is that they must be just when measured against both the distributive criterion and the requirement that they not perpetuate underlying justice-preventing institutional oppression and domination in their operation (Young 1990: 8). What this may also mean in practical terms is that the oppressive effect of the structural constraints which Young identifies are accommodated within the distributive framework so that they are not ignored, but rather recognized as a set of particularly heavy burdens which have to be 'distributed away' to the largest extent possible. Young rejected this type of accommodation in the distributive framework as simply little more than amelioration rather than

9 This economic understanding of exploitation can be widened to embrace sexual and racial oppression. 'Women's oppression consists partly in a systematic and unreciprocated transfer of powers from women to men' where 'their energies and power are expended, often unnoticed and unacknowledged' for the benefit of men (Young 1990: 50–51).

change (citing affirmative action programs and the like as examples of largely ineffectual redistributive responses). But seeing institutional mal-distributions as an explicit burden at least openly acknowledges the question of underlying structural disadvantage (Young 1990: 150). There is no simple answer to Young's critique that forms of domination and oppression in institutional constraints should first be eliminated before justice can pursue its distributive course. But in spite of Young's skepticism, my own view is that structural barrier elimination can be incorporated conceptually within distribution so that these social constraints are seen as burdens of which no one should have a share.[10] Young might well argue that justice should be concerned first with restructuring, but it is asserted that these transformations can begin with 'distributing away' as much of the institutional burden as possible.[11]

The concept of justice

Allowing for the strength of some of these critiques, the core concern of justice as distribution is retained as our conceptual framework. Justice is seen to be concerned with the allocation of social benefits and burdens in both social welfare and correctional terms. For our purposes, justice is understood as a moral value concerned with the distribution of the benefits and burdens of social cooperation in ways that maximize liberty. Defining justice in these terms gives centrality to distribution in responses to wrongdoing. Placing distribution at the core of these responses highlights the need for some means of determining whether distributions are in fact just. We will now turn our attention to a consideration of various 'conceptions of justice' from which some suitable means of 'assessing' distributions as just or unjust can be framed.

Conceptions of Justice: Devising Evaluative Criteria

We now have a clearer understanding of what justice 'means', but we are really no closer to having a method for determining whether a particular distribution is just or unjust. For this, we return to the distinction drawn between the concept of

10 Waldron makes a similar argument in *Dignity and Rank* (2008). He asserts that in modern times *everyone* should have the benefit of dignity and respect (as embodied in the notion of human rights) where once it may have been the preserve only of those of rank or nobility. Following this line of argument in a similar way, *no one* nowadays should have the burdens engendered by domination and oppression which are often the lot of those born without such privileges.

11 Young's contention that institutional injustices are often reinforced by 'just distributions' has an interesting parallel in Kennedy's critique that human rights reforms often work to reinforce rather than remove unjust legal orders (2002: 129). Charlesworth (2002) sharpens this critique by reframing it as a question of 'how international lawyers participate in sustaining an unjust legal order while they also seek the role of effective humanitarian reformer'.

justice (justice as 'concerned with' distribution) and various conceptions of justice (or means of determining 'justness'). Schmidtz's (2006: 168–169) adaptation of Hart's (1961) distinction between primary and secondary rules provides a useful means to clarify this distinction. For Hart (1961), 'primary rules' are rules of conduct which 'we normally think of as *the* law' and which define legal rights and obligations. By contrast, 'secondary rules' (in particular 'rules of recognition') identify or tell us what is lawful in particular circumstances (Schmidtz 2006: 167). So, in determining what is just (seen here as a primary rule) in a particular situation, we need secondary rules that 'do the recognizing' of what is a just outcome. The various conceptions or standards of justice (seen as secondary rules) provide these rules of recognition. No single standard is sufficient, because there is 'more than one map, with none guaranteed to be unerring'. While justice will *always* be about distribution in the conceptual framework we have settled upon, how to measure that justness is never fixed. Determining this will always move from prioritizing one rule to prioritizing another as norms shift or as specific circumstances demand (Schmidtz 2006: 178–180). The objective is to identify a set of rules of recognition which can best 'measure' just distributions in the particular context of responses to wrongdoing. Four particular criteria were chosen for this purpose. The selection may necessarily be a contentious one. These are selected from a wider set of 'values' traditionally recognized as comprising the 'canon of distributive justice' (see Rescher 1966; Deutsch 1969; Perelman 1980).[12] This canon provides potential answers (albeit conflicting ones) to the distributive dilemma of how to allocate to each person his or her 'due' in terms of social goods. The range of values in the canon includes:

- utility
- reciprocity
- need
- desert
- rights
- equality
- the 'common good'.

From these potential measures, four have been selected – desert, rights, equality and the 'common good'. Utility, reciprocity and need have not been used as measures of justness. Utility suggests the core test to apply to a distribution is one that 'work[s] to achieve maximum possible satisfaction of the preferences

12 A generally accepted list of the traditional canon includes: to each according to his need, to each according to his merits, to each according to his productivity, to each according to his abilities, to each according to his efforts, to each according to his needs, to each according to his rank or status, to each according to supply and demand, to each according to his right or legal entitlement and to each according to the greater good of the greater number (Spader 1988: 590).

we find distributed in our community' (Dworkin 1984: 162). But what Campbell describes as the 'generally anti-utilitarian flavour of justice' (2001: 49) means that a distribution that best promotes utility is not likely to be one that necessarily best promotes justice. Likewise, reciprocity asserts that part of the answer to the question of how people should treat each other is that they should return favours (Becker 1986). But using this approach as a means to determine the justness of a distribution would have some disturbing implications. If someone has done me a favour, I 'owe' him for what he has done for me. More pertinently, if I have done someone some harm, I 'owe' him for what I have done to him. Becker (1986: 3) says reciprocity in this negative sense mandates a disposition 'to make reparation ... [in proportion to] the harm we have done'. What this may mean in circumstances of wrongdoing is that justice could only be met where the obligation to make up for the 'disfavour' of the wrong is also met. Similarly, a need-based conception of justice would necessarily measure justice by the extent to which its outcomes satisfy various levels of need. The difficulty with such a conceptualization is that it is likely to be focused on seeking out additional benefits rather than allowing for the need to distribute burdens, so that distributions in response to wrongdoing would be essentially one-sided (Spader 1988: 603). Also, assessing the justness of a distribution according to how well it meets needs may simply induce 'people to do what *manifests* need rather than what *meets* need' and in the process leave genuine need unmet, and justice undone (Schmidtz 2006: 167, emphasis added).[13] Therefore, testing the justness of a distribution by its utility, in terms of reciprocity or by how well it maximizes the satisfaction of need are each discarded as inadequate measures. This leaves for consideration those measures which interpret a distribution based variously on desert, equality, rights or the 'common good' (which will be reframed here as promoting harmonious social relationships) as just. The next sections examine the specific moral connection each of these measures is seen to have with justice.

Justice and Desert

Justice in the ancient Greek sense of 'accomplishing the work of living well' was measured in simple desert terms. This means both 'positive' desert where an individual says, 'I deserve this in virtue of my hard work', and 'negative' desert, where an individual says instead, 'the deprivations I am suffering are undeserved' (MacIntyre 1985: 249). Enlightenment philosophers such as Locke enlarged on the positive sense, suggesting that 'people deserve to have those items produced by their toil and industry' since 'the products (or the value thereof) [are] a fitting reward for their effort' (as cited in Lamont and Favor 2007). Moreover, 'what is seen to count [in the case of positive desert] is conscientious effort which has

13 A better way to actually meet need may be to provide social structures that reward exercises of productive capabilities (for instance, efforts towards social repair following wrongdoing) by virtue of which needs are directly or indirectly met.

socially beneficial effects' (Sadurski 1985: 116). Conversely, what is seen to count in a negative sense is that persons adversely affected by wrongdoing should be able to demand to be relieved of the undeserved burdens placed upon them as a consequence of that wrong. This seems uncontroversial. Whether a person has taken on a burden that 'involves some effort, sacrifice, work, risk, responsibility, inconvenience and so forth ... which has socially beneficial effects' is an obviously relevant criterion in determining his or her distribution of benefits and burdens (Sadurski 1985: 116). In this sense, desert can be seen to provide a measure as to whether 'the balance of benefits and burdens in each person's life [are] equivalent to the balance in the lives of other members (see Campbell 2001: 164). But there are difficulties with justice measured as 'desert-based-on-effort' in the context of responses to wrongdoing (Sadurski 1985: 223). If a person takes on a burden, this may provide a legitimate basis for their positive desert. But that does not accommodate two different situations. The first is where structural injustices in fact prevent people from being able to make the effort to assume the additional voluntary burdens (even in the sense of accepting 'obligations') for which they may then gain more positive desert. Secondly, the same can be true in the case of negative desert, where a person's 'just deserts' for wrongdoing may fail to take into account his or her preexisting disequilibrium which may have precipitated events culminating in the offending. Desert alone simply cannot 'allocate good results to good persons without enquiring how much they can do about their goodness', nor can burdens be imposed without a similar inquiry (Ryan 1993: 9). Distributions which give people their strict positive or negative desert may on the surface connote a clear sense of justice, but such distributions still leave underlying unjust social constraints relatively untouched or unquestioned (Sadurski 1985: 226).

Allowing for these important deficiencies, desert has qualities which nonetheless can make it a robust measure of the justness of distributions in responses to wrongdoing. Defined in the following terms for responses to wrongdoing, 'desert' provides our first evaluative criterion of justice:

> The desert standard measures justice by the extent to which people are treated according to what they deserve, so as to address the wrong done to them (in a sense of positive desert), or by them (in a sense of negative desert).

While measuring 'the maintenance of a pattern of distribution' in desert terms is accepted as having merit as a justice standard (Campbell 2001: 155), desert cannot stand alone as the sole measure since it tells only part of the story of what is required for a just distribution. A second standard, that of 'equality', adds a further necessary perspective.

Justice and Equality

Justice measured in equality terms refers to treatment of people *relative* to each other, rather than in terms of purely mathematical equality. Aristotle provided an early acceptance that distributions which treat people equally, though not necessarily proportionally equal are just (Barker 1959: 337). The Aristotelian conception of equality had the twin elements of 'the equal treatment of equals' and 'the unequal treatment of unequals'.[14] Together, these two aspects recognize that while 'all humans may be equal as moral entities, each is unequal to the other in abilities, efforts, achievements' as well as opportunities (Spader 1988: 592). As a consequence, in order to maximize relative equality it will be necessary to treat 'unequals according to their relevant inequalities' (Benn 1980: 31). This can mean the greater allocation of benefits to individuals or groups to ensure that the outcome is equal in relative terms (Vlastos 1970: 49). The Kantian ethic acknowledges this same distinction, that providing 'similar' justice 'requires not [strict] equality but rather differentiation in distribution or treatment' (Stone 1980: 16). Strict proportional equality needs to be tempered to take into account 'justifiable differences' and the 'structuring of justice-precepts corresponding to these differences' for accurate consideration of these differences (Stone 1980: 16). Hart (1968: 51) similarly recognized that 'the pressures of gross forms of economic necessity' are an obvious factor of 'difference' in terms of equality which need to be accounted for in determining responsibility for wrongdoing.

'Equality' seen in this qualified sense provides a potentially robust evaluative standard for measuring distributions in responses to wrongdoing. Needing to accommodate existing inequality may mean having to overtly address differences in terms of gender, race or class when responding to wrong (Minow 1990: 20).[15] Gilligan (1982) argued that the concept of justice itself needs to be enlarged to encompass a wider range of moral qualities central to women if their treatment was to be seen as equal. While later responses rejected suggestions of incorporating qualities such as 'caring' as merely reinforcing the narrower range of moral qualities which women were 'allowed' to embrace in a patriarchal society (see MacKinnon 1989; Daly 1999), Gilligan's critique still has resonance when the question of the equality of distributions of benefits and burdens to women in the

14 In arguing against rigid sentencing guidelines and mandatory minimum penalties, Tonry (1996: 14–20) implicitly recognizes that the justice as equality standard is only partly met in practice. It can mean that the 'treat like cases alike' component is satisfied by focusing attention on the wrongdoing and on the wrongdoer's criminal history. But the companion component of 'treating unlike cases differently' is often *not* satisfied because real differences among wrongdoers (personal backgrounds, effects of punishment on them and their families and so on) are often disregarded.

15 Allowing for 'difference' in terms of justice refers to those differences existing as a consequence of gender, class, race and culture. Two broad schools of thought – critical theory and discourses of identity – represent the most recent attempts to accommodate difference into justice as equality. The guiding principle of critical theory is to examine an area of social life with a view to attaining an 'enhanced emancipation in the future' (Vlastos 1970: 61). 'Discourses of identity' theorists provide a broad description of social analysis in terms of identity and sexuality.

face of wrongdoing are considered. To treat women the same as men in the context of criminal offending, for instance, may well mean treating them unequally. Treating women (and other marginalized groups) justly in terms of the equality standard should mean 'treating them appropriately, given their circumstances and their offending patterns', with the effect that they are treated objectively unequally (Hudson 2003a: 140). Understood in this light, equality does provide a legitimate standard by which to assess the justness of distributions made in response to wrongdoing. Defined in the following terms for such responses, equality provides the second evaluative criterion of justice:

> The equality standard measures justice by the extent to which people are treated equally, with proportionate equality tempered so that actual treatment is equalized.

In a similar way to desert, the equality standard cannot stand alone as a measure of what is required to produce a just outcome. It needs to be applied both alongside desert and together with other criteria. The third criterion of 'rights' adds one further necessary perspective.

Justice and Rights

The rights standard measures the justness of distributions in terms of whether they treat people according to their rights and give effect to those rights. Conversely, a distribution which invades or denies those rights is seen as unjust (Campbell 2001: 76, 88). When measured against this standard, a distribution is considered 'just if, and only if, it is prescribed exclusively by regard for the rights of all whom it affects substantially' (Vlastos 1970: 60).[16] The origin of the idea that protecting rights yields just outcomes is traceable at least to Locke. The source of rights in Locke's view is 'natural' – that is to say people have rights 'by virtue of [their] humanity' (West 2001: xi). Rights act to protect and enhance the pursuit of individual conceptions of the good life. The foundational set of such rights are the 'Lockean pre-political entitlements, namely the right to life, liberty and property' (Buckle 1991: 168). These 'natural law rights' (most obviously the right to life and liberty) act to protect the dignity and 'humanness' of human life.[17] This conception of rights was given normative expression in early aspirational proclamations such as the 1776 American *Declaration of Independence* (as 'the right to life, liberty and the pursuit of happiness') or

16 Through this test, Aristotle's claim that slavery is just is easily rebutted on the basis that the institution of slavery necessarily denies the right of all human beings to personal and political freedom (Sandel 1982).

17 More obliquely, the right to property acts in a similarly protective way 'to secure us against the physical elements, the aggression of others or the tyranny of the state' (West 2001: xi).

the 1789 French *Declaration of the Rights of Man and of the Citizen* (as the 'right to liberty, property, security and resistance to oppression').[18]

Modern formulations of rights see them more as essentially social constructs or 'normatively protected interests' (Campbell 2001: 52) providing 'background guarantees' that certain entitlements will be adhered to if, and when, the expectations of affective bonds which would normally protect and support entitlements break down or in fact remain unformed or rejected (Waldron 1992). Rights in this sense are notions about the proper conduct of human action designed to give explicit content to the more general principle of 'right conduct' (Almond 1991: 262). Importantly, the effect of granting rights is to give individuals the moral power or capacity to compel and constrain the actions of others based on these rights. As Grotius (1583–1645) explained in his early conceptualization of rights 'a right becomes a moral quality of a person', giving that person moral power and capacity to act in certain ways and to compel certain actions in others (1925: 1.1.iv).[19] Nozick (1974), too, makes a strong argument that rights provide the soundest measure of justness. He sees rights as providing entitlements effectively to be left alone, in the sense of 'uncoerced in any manner which violates these rights' (Campbell 2001: 58). An overarching entitlement to be left alone asserts that there are 'things that we ought not to do to other people, no matter how beneficial the consequences might be [for society or for them]' (Campbell 2001: 58). Preventing such interference with others is seen as one way to produce just outcomes. Applying the rights standard therefore constrains the quality of distributions that can be made when responding to wrongdoing. Nozick pressed the supremacy of rights further by arguing that determining the justness of distributions based on other standards should defer entirely to protecting the fundamental moral interests embodied in rights (Nozick 1974: 206). My view is that no single standard can have this overarching supremacy. However, rights protection provides a standard that can be too individual-based and so allow insufficient scope for the importance of dimensions of community connection. As we considered in discussing the concept of justice, communitarians like

18 In *The Spirit of the Laws*, Montesquieu (1689–1755) famously provided one of the means of guaranteeing these rights institutionally in his key tenets of republicanism. He said that despotism borne either of the tyranny of kings or of the majority can best be constrained by political institutions where there is a 'separation of power' among bodies exercising legislative, executive and judicial powers.

19 One expression of rights (specifically that of 'human rights') lies somewhere between the purely natural conception and the positivist notion (Almond 1991: 261). Feinberg (1973: 85) defines human rights as 'generically moral rights of a fundamentally important kind held equally by all human beings, unconditionally and unalterably'. Human rights appear in both detailed contemporary universal declarations as well as in national bills or codes of rights. Some statements have legal force, for example, the European *Convention for the Protection of Human Rights and Fundamental Freedoms* of 1950. Others, for instance, the United Nations' *Universal Declaration of Human Rights* of 1948, primarily have only aspirational or moral force.

MacIntyre (1985) and Sandel (1984) argue for a measure of justness which is more accommodating of a 'situated self' – the person open to and engaged with the influence of community connections rather than a person who is simply the Kantian 'unencumbered self' separate and apart from community.[20] Communitarians assert that rights remain important as a standard of justice but that a balance needs to be struck between individual rights and community obligations and responsibilities, with individual rights needing to defer to community rights in some instances. MacIntyre's (1985) particular critique of rights is stronger still. He rejects the universal attribute of rights, arguing instead that rights will always remain entirely contextual, so that 'what justice demands *in this context*, what rights are operative *in this context*' will never be fixed but will always be open to discourse with individual rights sometimes paramount and sometimes not (Hudson 2003a: 106, emphasis in original). If rights were to lack this universality, this would seriously undermine their usefulness as a measure of justice. Kennedy (2002: 109, emphasis added) makes a somewhat similar critique when he says that rights tend to 'foreground [issues] of *participation* and *procedure*', sometimes with the effect of interfering with the provision of a substantively just distribution. Allowing for these concerns, the rights standard does provide another sound measure of justness which addresses some of the particular deficits identified with respect to the equality standard. Rights by their nature involve adopting the 'viewpoint of the "others" to whom something (including, inter alia, freedom of choice) is owed or due' (Finnis 1980: 205). This quality of inclusiveness has the potential to compensate for the inherent injustices of strict equality. There is of course the risk that by '*particularizing* the rights standard to a community, a tradition or a particular set of circumstances' in order to accommodate difference, its overriding positive attribute of universality will be lost and this needs to be carefully guarded against (Walzer 1994: 4, emphasis added; see also Bix 2006: 114–115).

Given these limitations, rights constitute an appropriate standard by which to measure the justness of distributions. Defined in the following terms for responses to wrongdoing, rights provide the third evaluative criterion of justice:

> The rights standard measures the justness of a distribution in terms of the extent to which the distribution renews and protects the rights of all affected by wrongdoing.

Once again, the rights standard cannot stand alone as a measure of justness. As well as needing to work alongside desert and equality, rights must also sit beside the final criterion of promoting 'harmonious social relationships'. This measure adds the last necessary, though markedly different perspective.

---

20 Some see Aristotelian republicanism as the original source of the concept of the embedded self, in which to act morally is to act as the 'good citizen' (Rowe 1991: 130).

Justice and Harmonious Social Relationships

Using the promotion of harmonious relationships as a measure of justness has its origins with both Plato and Aristotle, each of whom developed the precept of justice beyond the Socratic ideal of the personal to embrace instead the manner in which all elements of society should be arranged. The purpose of such 'arrangements', in their view, was to create overall social harmony. The extent to which distributions contribute to this social harmony can provide a further necessary measure of justness in the case of responses to wrongdoing.[21] Because this measure has much less theoretical currency, our discussion of it is necessarily needs to be more detailed.

An emphasis on maintaining social harmony has its origins in part of the ancient Greek notion of *arête*, or 'virtue', a term that encompasses all that was seen as necessary for human beings to perform their full social function (Rowe 1991: 123). In the context of ancient Greece, only a privileged few could of course perform this full societal role to lead 'whatever life one judges that one desires' (Reiman 1990: 63).[22] Four conditions or 'moral qualities' were necessary to allow this to happen, three of which were under the control of the individual and the fourth of which was socially controlled (Plato 1975: Bk IV 428e).[23] Overlaying each of the other 'personal' virtues, this fourth quality was inherent in the organization of the *polis* itself as crucial to add a stabilizing political effect (Plato 1975: Bk IV 430d). The more personal aspects of *arête* are instead more focused on 'finding a mean between extremes' potentially at the risk of social harmony (Ryan 1993: 8). This fourth quality (which Plato in fact called *dikē*, or 'justice') consists principally in those social arrangements which facilitate what

21 Compare this with the theory of justice that Reiman (1990) defends – that a system of justice is one that satisfies the social 'requirement' that people protect themselves against the subjugation of others.

22 Of course, only a limited subset of ancient Greeks (those adult, free and male) had the possibility of living in more than one kind of way.

23 Those qualities under the control of individuals were 'wisdom', 'courage' and 'discipline'. 'Wisdom' is the quality 'to be found with those who possess ... good judgment and wisdom' and in the *polis* the elite guardians were seen to embody this specific virtue (Plato 1975: Bk IV 428d). This quality is manifest in the way individuals consider 'all the moments of [their] whole life in judging how to act' when following a particular 'possibility of living' (Reiman 1990: 62). 'Courage' is the 'ability to retain safely in all circumstances a judgment about what is to be feared, which is correct and in accord with law' despite facing adversity in that endeavour (Plato 1975: Bk IV 430b). Courage is the virtue specific to the 'auxiliaries' or warrior elite. 'Discipline' or temperance reflects Plato's insistence on the element of self-control or self-restraint as central to performing the functions of a human being. It is the specific virtue of the plebian producers, one that allows 'the naturally better element [that] controls the worse' (in an individual) or 'the desire of the less respectable majority' to be controlled by 'the desires and the wisdom of the superior minority' (in the state) (Plato: Bk IV 430e, 431d).

is variously described as 'minding one's own business', 'doing the job one is most naturally suited for' or 'doing the things that belong to oneself' (Plato 1975: Bk IV 440b).[24] When properly provided, such arrangements bind 'together all the elements [of society] ... into one, temperate and harmonious' whole (Plato 1975: Bk IV 443e). The Platonic measure of social harmony has resonance in later traditions. Cicero (106–43 BCE) in *De officiis* proposed a set of cardinal virtues which for him constituted 'moral goodness'. Cicero's view was that the particular social virtue of 'justice' was a crucial cardinal virtue because it acted to hold society together and enabled people to pursue 'the common good' (Ryan 1993: 9). The Ciceronian notion of justice was that where there were breaches of the common good, there had to be a means to rectify these breaches so as to restore sound social relationships (Ryan 1993: 10). This means of rectification provided a measure of justice, such that the justness of a response to a breach of the common good was to be determined by the extent to which it sought to restore social harmony.

Of the modern canons of distributive justice, the prescription that comes closest to reflecting this harmonious social relationship standard is that which sees benefits and burdens being distributed 'to each according to the greater good of the greater number, or common good, or public interest' (Spader 1988: 590). This prescription holds at its extreme that the interests of the community in establishing and maintaining relationships of harmony should take precedent over the interests of individuals when they conflict. In a more moderate form, this resonates with Durkheim's view that a response to wrongdoing should always seek to reinforce social cohesion (Durkheim 1933; Freiberg 2001a: 273). Dworkin (1978) makes a similar claim about the 'grounding moral principle' of his theory of rights (Campbell 2001: 70), stating that the very foundation of justice is that every person has a right to be treated with 'equal consideration and respect' in order to maximize social harmony. There is also some resonance with Young's (1990) view that the justness of a distribution should be gauged by the extent to which it creates social relationships devoid of 'arbitrary bias or exclusion'.

Recent theorists of restorative justice provide a further perspective on what it can mean to 'promote social harmony'. Braithwaite (1999: 6) makes the argument that social harmony is based on a sense that justice has been done from a 'republican' perspective. More broadly, other restorative justice thinkers see the core normative concern of justice as 'restoration', which they frame in terms of restoring 'relationships of social equality'. Restoration so framed deemphasizes the usual focus on the repair of harm to 'personal or intimate relationships' in preference to wider social repair such that 'each [affected] party has their rights to *dignity*, equal *concern* and *respect* satisfied' (Llewellyn and Howse 1998: 24, emphasis added). It is the restoration of these three elements of dignity, respect and concern which need to be explored further with a view to proposing them as

24 A more recent translation suggests that the Greek phrase most commonly given the conventional meaning of 'minding your own business' is better captured by the modern catchphrase 'doing your own thing' (Plato 1975, editor's note p. 204).

indicia from which to construct a harmonious social relationships measure of the justness of responses to criminal wrongdoing (Llewellyn 2002: 289).[25]

Dignity

The protection of 'human dignity' is connected with historical notions of justice. Feinberg argues that in the act of claiming rights 'as much as any other thing', human dignity must be asserted and promoted (1970b: 257). In right-claiming activities, the dignity of persons is placed at the core of what it is to treat people justly (Campbell 2001: 49). Kleinig (2009: 10) similarly asserts that society should act 'to secure human dignity both as an individual quality and a social value' and 'should support social structures that foster and acknowledge such dignity'. Davis (2007b) more specifically suggests that dignity performs the core function of delivering justice in the criminal law. The key element in all these formulations is that the force of dignity is that it respects a 'capacity to be directed by *moral* considerations' as well as personal considerations (see Meyer 1987). Kant extends the notion of personal autonomy to encompass a notion of 'moral agency' where people are guided by considerations of morality that go beyond their own motivations of expediency or utility (Kleinig 2010: 11–12). In his 1785 *Groundwork of the Metaphysics of Morals*, Kant argued that while whatever is concerned purely with such human inclinations or needs for expediency or utility has a 'price', 'that which [is concerned with] an end in itself ... has an inner worth, this is, dignity' which transcends the purely personal (Waldron 2008: 30). Dworkin (1984) encapsulates the view that the objective value of a human life is to meet a person's own special responsibility for how that life is lived, qualities, he says, 'together define the basis and conditions of human dignity' (2006: 10). It is this dignity with its 'value beyond price' and its 'special responsibility' that adheres in every human being which I suggest can legitimately be seen as the first marker of a relationship of social equality. There is also a close connection between dignity understood in this sense and the 'language of respect' and of 'concern' which forms the other elements in a construction of the harmonious social relationships standard (Waldron 2008: 18).

Respect and concern

Kant argues that it is because persons are ends in themselves that they deserve to be treated as objects of equal respect (Kant 1981). This idea of 'respecting' conveys (as Waldron expresses it) 'some sense of deferring to her, making room for her, listening to her, [or] allowing her will rather than one's own to prevail'

25 There is little analysis in this literature as to what these terms actually mean. Nowhere in her work does Llewellyn (see variously Llewellyn and Howse 1998, 1999; Llewellyn 2002, 2006, 2006a) consider their actual content. Acorn (2004: 23), who draws on Llewellyn's work as 'the most theoretically sophisticated and persuasive writing there is on [this] topic' (though only as a straw horse with which to demolish the notion of 'right-relationship') does not define the term. Braithwaite (1989, 2002b) also does not give these indicia any sustained attention.

(Waldron 2008: 18). This suggests that a relationship of 'respect' is one which acknowledges that an 'extensive and diffuse deference is due' to a person simply as a consequence of their being human (Waldron 2008: 19). Reiman suggests that this 'moral imperative of respect' is an element of justice since respect binds all rational human beings so as to facilitate their own individual pursuit of sovereign interests (Reiman 1990: 123–124). This is the essence of the nature of respect as it relates to the promotion of harmonious social relationships. 'Respect' in these terms entails a mutual recognition of the inner worth of others, and their common entitlement to deference in pursuit of their sovereign interests. Concern can also be understood in much the same way as being an entitlement to equal attention and regard. This notion of 'concern' suggests a social requirement to 'act in ways that respect, [and] so leave intact, others' capabilities to act' in order to fulfill their individual potential (O'Neill 1991: 178). Bringing together these three threads, distributions that promote harmonious social relationships characterized by qualities of dignity, respect and concern are seen as just. This fourth conception of justice is markedly different from the desert, equality and rights standards, and so necessarily more contentious. Reiman cautions that an Aristotelian emphasis on harmony could easily be dismissed as encouraging merely 'a condition of psychic well-being' which acts as little more than 'a corrective to modern-day ethical relativism' (1990: 101, 102). But measuring justice by the additional yardstick of harmony adds a standard that focuses more directly on 'enabl[ing] each person to realize his sovereign interest to the greatest extent possible compatible with the same [realization] for everyone else' (Reiman 1990: 82; see also Burnside and Baker 1994). This is an aspect of justness that would otherwise be neglected amid the other standards of justice. There is also some contemporary re-expression of the standard in the recognition given to indigenous community-based justice responses, particularly in Canada and New Zealand. In New Zealand, the modern recognition of Maori philosophies of justice has influenced that country's criminal justice practice towards embracing concepts of social harmony. One New Zealand judge specifically notes, '[indigenous] harmony ... requires many things, including an attitude of respect for others, a desire to mend the tear in the fabric of the community caused by crime, and a belief that the law is there for the benefit of all' (McElrea 1998: 62).

Defined in the following terms for responses to wrongdoing, harmonious social relationships provide the final evaluative criterion of justice:

> The harmonious social relationship standard measures justice by the extent to which distributions promote relationships of social equality characterized by dignity, respect and concern.

Like the other standards, the harmonious social relationships measure cannot stand alone as a complete measure of what is a just outcome. Each of the measures selected prioritizes a particular and distinctive aspect of what constitutes a just outcome. My argument is that all four measures need to be met in any institutional response to wrongdoing for a distribution of benefits and burdens to be considered just. These four measures provide the set of 'evaluative criteria' by which to measure the justness of distributions made in response to wrongdoing in particular contexts in Part II.

Conclusion

This chapter has argued that justice in all its guises is concerned with distribution, and that the particular focus of all such distributions is to maximize liberty. Following from this, how well a particular distribution delivers justice in its institutional setting can be measured against the evaluative criteria developed here. These criteria argue that a just distribution is one that gives people what they deserve in both a positive and negative sense. Added to this is the requirement that a distribution treat people equally while accommodating their differences. It was recognized that allowance needs to be made for structural inequalities that affect the paucity of the preexisting 'share' of benefits and burdens that persons affected may bring to wrongdoing. As well, a just distribution is one that treats people in a manner consistent with their rights and gives effect to those rights in its responses. Finally, a just distribution is one that promotes harmonious social relationships between persons affected by the wrongdoing. How well the unique moral claims of justice can be met in institutional responses to wrongdoing will be considered in the context of two markedly different settings discussed in Part II. Before doing so, we first need to develop one final analytical tool, namely a means of determining how a sense of justice can be generated.

Chapter 4
Generating Just Responses to Wrongdoing

Introduction

This chapter develops the final analytical tool to explain the behaviours and practices that generate a sense of justice. It introduces the conceptual notion of 'generative mechanisms' and then uses an iterative process to identify the particular mechanisms seen to be at work in responses to wrongdoing. The mechanisms given particular prominence in criminal and restorative justice are identified using a content analysis of each practice's literature. From this analysis, a set of mechanisms (some common to both practices, some unique to one form or another) is distilled and collectively referred to as 'the generative mechanisms of justice'. This typology of behaviours and practices is then examined in terms of particular justice qualities, the importance placed on each mechanism in either practice and the communicative power each such mechanism can bring to justice generation. This final analytical tool is used to consider 'how distributions of the harm-related benefits and burdens are generated in order to produce just outcomes'. The behaviours described include some that focus on accountability and responsibility (behaviour like truth telling, vindication and expressions of remorse are found to be important) and others more attuned to delivering censure and repair (practices like reparation, apology and punishment are important).

Generative Mechanisms

There are specific social behaviours capable of generating particular outcomes in terms of individual behaviour and response. The development of this theoretical construct owes much to the sociological theories developed by Merton in the 1960s. Merton defined such mechanisms as 'social processes having designated consequences for designated parts of the social structure' (1968: 43). More recently, interest has been revived in the explanatory power of such mechanisms in the work of Hedström and Swedberg (1996, 1998), who argue that the 'understanding [of social processes] is enhanced by making explicit the underlying generative mechanisms that link one state or event to another' (1998: 12). They argue that there is a broad typology of 'mechanisms [that] produce observed associations between events' and that the discrete behaviours or social rituals at play in particular situations are thus both identifiable and distinctive (Hedström and Swedberg 1996: 281). In their simplest form, these 'mechanisms' are 'behaviours' of individuals or institutions that bring about certain outcomes through individual action or forms of institutional treatment. As Elster indicates, these mechanisms are 'causal agents' that act as triggers to generate certain effects or outcomes (1989, 2007).[1] Braithwaite and Drahos (2000) made comprehensive use of the explanatory power of such mechanisms in their analysis of global business regulation. They distinguish between 'higher-order mechanisms' (broad behavioural factors, such as rational choice or social norm behaviour) and 'lower-order mechanisms' (individual actions such as coercion, capacity building and modeling) which act to influence and regulate corporate behaviour. The lower-order mechanisms were seen to operate primarily at an 'actor design' level rather than at the level of broader institutional response (2000: 15–16). These generative mechanisms also bear some similarity to the notion of 'coping mechanisms' which is commonly used in conceptual descriptions of motivational posturing theory by Valerie Braithwaite and others. Motivational postures are simply 'coping behaviours' through which individuals send social signals to one another designed to communicate and maintain their preferred social distance in certain personal or institutional situations (Braithwaite 1995). The important similarity for our purposes is that such postures are not confined simply to 'behaviours' in the sense of observable conduct but also extend to 'conglomerates' of social behaviour in the form of 'beliefs, attitudes, preferences, interests, and feelings' expressed by a number of people that together communicate a preferred social outcome which another individual is possibly being pressed to adopt (Braithwaite, Murphy et al. 2007: 138). Each of these theoretical constructs help to fashion the construct of generative mechanisms used here. The lower-order triggers used by Braithwaite and Drahos which involve 'one or more actors (state and non-state) in a series of actions (or reactions) that are linked to the goals and desires of [those] actors' provide the first strand of a conceptual framework for our purposes (2000: 17). Secondly, the idea of generative mechanisms consisting of 'conglomerates' of 'practices, behaviours, approaches and principles' which consist of both social actions and moral practices is more accurately descriptive of the kind of justice-generating triggers we are tracking. A systematic method is needed to isolate such a set of the justice-generating mechanisms at work in responses to wrongdoing. The method applied is an adaptation of the 'difference discovery method' which Parker (1999: 230) developed from the snowballing techniques of Minichiello and colleagues (1990: 80). An adaptation of this approach provides a useful way to capture the 'practices, behaviours, approaches and principles' which can be identified as having particular justice-generating power. Rather than being applied to a series of interview subjects, however, the method is used in the form of a content analysis to interrogate the literatures of the two particular forms of justice practice (legal and restorative) which are the subject of the empirical inquiry described in Part II.

1 Braithwaite (2002e: 571) describes the same phenomena as the effect of 'explanatory dynamics' (such as reintegrative shaming) which provide conditions under which certain outcomes can flow.

Identifying Potential Generative Mechanisms in Criminal Justice Practice

A content analysis of the core criminal justice literature identified a recurrent set of general 'defining features' of legal justice practice. The search for fresh features to add to the list ceased when no new significantly different features were being uncovered. By using this constraint, the sampling strategy can isolate a set of general defining features of legal justice practice. This method identified a range of factors (for example, social control and regulation) obviously important to the broader role of criminal law but more strictly relevant to its non-justice regulatory functions. The features isolated also contained factors (that is, rights articulation and impartiality) which are plainly justice related but have relevance more to law's broader justice role than simply to its practices in responding to wrongdoing. Some features identified (such as truth seeking and fact finding) are also features that are clearly relevant to both criminal and non-criminal practice. Allowing for these qualifications, it is possible to identify a specific set of features seen as descriptive specifically of responses to wrongdoing which can provide one source from which to build the 'generative mechanisms' we are seeking to isolate. These features of legal justice responses seen as more specific to responses to wrongdoing appear in Table 4.1.

Table 4.1 Features of criminal justice practice

Features commonly identified as being prominent in responses to criminal wrongdoing
Accountability
Responsibility
Truth seeking/fact finding
Censure
Remorse
Punishment
Vindication
Deterrence/prevention
Proportionality
Desert
Rehabilitation
Denunciation
Reparation

Identifying Potential Generative Mechanisms in Restorative Justice Practice

A similar content analysis of the core restorative literature provides a picture of its practice's general defining features. From this analysis, a number of recurring features is also identifiable in the same way. The analysis again ceased when no new significantly different features were being uncovered. Many of the features isolated as relevant to restorative responses to wrongdoing are identical to those given prominence in legal justice practice. The defining features of restorative justice practice are also broader than purely justice promotion. The qualities isolated contain normative prescriptions and lesser supererogatory elements variously described as desirable but non-essential to justice promotion. Distinctively, the qualities isolated also contained features more descriptive of purely restorative, rather than justice-generating functions. However, these 'justice' and 'restorative' features were not distinguished, as this literature was strongly marked by its form of justice being promoted *by and through* restoration itself. The full set of defining features identified in restorative justice practice appears in Table 4.2.

Table 4.2 Features of restorative justice practice

Features of restorative justice responses to wrongdoing	
Accountability	Responsibility
Censure	Remorse
Punishment/consequences	Vindication/validation
Deterrence/prevention	Proportionality
Truth telling	Apology
Forgiveness	Reconciliation
Repairing relationships	Harm reduction
Transformation	Developing social capital
Social connectedness	Reparation
Enabling social justice	Distributive fairness
Empowerment	Problem solving

Identifying a Generic Set of Generative Mechanisms

Both justice practices examined profess to provide justice responses to criminal wrongdoing. Inductively, any commonality in their respective defining features should indicate features potentially relevant to promoting this experience of justice. The results obtained from the above analyses were thus cross-matched to highlight this commonality as one means to isolate justice-generating mechanisms. Through this process of cross-matching, it was possible to divide the criminal legal justice and restorative justice features into those for which there was commonality, and those which appear to only define restorative justice practice. From this further exercise, it was possible to identify features which appear to have the particular 'flavour' or quality seen as 'justice promoting ability'. A set of common features and a few of the distinct restorative practice features were said to have this particular potential. Table 4.3 displays the results of this intuitive process of teasing out a distinctive set of features with specific justice-generating capability. Two particular behaviours, those of 'apology' and 'forgiveness', are added from the 'restorative justice features' list, and this requires some explanation. Bottoms (2003: 94) had identified apology as a crucial social ritual leading to 'the restoration of prior social relationships' in restorative justice practice, which suggests that apology has particular justice-generating capacity in those practices. Forgiveness is dealt with much more ambivalently in the restorative practice literature. The practice of forgiveness is certainly ascribed particular moral power, though there is ambivalence about whether it is justice-generating. Nonetheless, the clear 'forgiveness effects' described in its literature are seen as having potentially powerful results and it may be that forgiveness is more broadly justice conducive.

Table 4.3 Justice-generative mechanisms

Justice-generative mechanisms	
Accountability	Responsibility
Censure	Remorse
Punishment	Vindication
Deterrence/prevention	Proportionality
Truth telling	Reparation
Apology	Forgiveness

It is noteworthy that many of these mechanisms have prominence in both practices. Traditional criminal justice responses to wrongdoing give particular prominence to practices like punishment and to principles like proportionality. But surprisingly these behaviours, while they do not appear 'restorative', are given similar prominence in the restorative justice practice literature. Gramsci's concept of cultural hegemony may provide one explanation for this apparent anomaly. Gramsci (1971) suggested that dominant social ideas are maintained partly through the consent of those in subordinate groups which remain actively complicit in their subordinated status. In the case at hand, the hegemonic values of the dominant criminal legal justice system are still pervading restorative justice practice in the form of what are assumed to be 'common sense values' rather than being viewed more critically as specific legal values (Joseph 2002). But putting aside this important reservation, from this series of analyses a set of social mechanisms has been developed which can be applied to explain how an experience of a sense of justice is generated in institutional responses to wrongdoing. The next section of this chapter provides some brief discussion about how each mechanism might be said to work to generate a sense of justice.

Justice-Generating Mechanisms

A review of the individual mechanisms permits a closer comparison of the different priorities given to each mechanism within criminal and restorative justice practice. Mechanisms can be dealt with largely in pairs, based on a perceived degree of similarity or effect. The mechanisms are seen to help deliver justice by helping to create the sensibility that the wrongdoing has been responded to in a just manner and in providing those affected by the wrongdoing (victims, offenders and the wider community) with outcomes seen by them as producing just consequences.

Accountability and Responsibility

'Accountability' and 'responsibility' sit well together as generative mechanisms because they both address the threshold issue of the offender accepting blameworthiness.

Accountability describes the requirement that the wrongdoer give an account of what has happened in the wrongdoing and have that account subject to contestation if necessary in some fashion 'inside a process of deliberation'. Secondly, and more commonly, accountability is used in the sense of 'holding a wrongdoer to account' by, or on behalf of, those affected by the wrong. The assumption is that by doing so those adversely affected by the wrongdoing can begin to experience some sense of relief. The following definition of accountability attempts to capture these two meanings:[2]

> Accountability means the offender giving a public account of his/her responsibility for the wrongdoing which stakeholders in the injustice accept and which the offender is held to own.

Similarly, responsibility is used both in a passive sense of 'taking responsibility for something done in the past', and in a more active sense of 'taking responsibility for putting something right into the future' (Bovens 1998; Braithwaite 2006: 42). It is assumed that if wrongdoers take responsibility in a more active sense, then persons adversely affected by wrongdoing will be more likely to begin to

2 Each of these definitions was used during interviews with informants in the empirical study reported in Chapter 9.

experience a sense of relief and justice.[3] The following definition of responsibility likewise seeks to capture this twin meaning:

> Responsibility means having the offender actively accept responsibility for their wrongdoing and its consequences through confronting them with those consequences.

Accountability and responsibility are central generative mechanisms in traditional criminal justice responses to wrongdoing. Accepting responsibility is constituted by an admission in which the wrongdoer is publicly held to account (Cane 2002: 32–34). The primary focus in this form of response is upon determining and ascribing 'legal liability-responsibility' for the action based largely on establishing the offender's 'intention' and actions (Hart 1968: 215–222). Responsibility is only accepted for 'an action done intentionally or deliberately in order to bring about a result' (Duff 1990: 99–100; Golding 2005: 228). This emphasis on testing conduct against established criteria of legal culpability (intention, liability, *mens rea*, capacity and the like) has the effect that the evident accountability and responsibility are largely passive. Offenders are held to account in the second 'classic sense of accountability' which gives rise to an essentially passive expression of responsibility wherein a personal account of what has occurred is seldom required of the offender, and where responsibility for 'righting the wrong' in any symbolic or practical sense is not expected (Roche 2003: 42).

In restorative justice practice, there is a more overt focus on generating active responsibility since part of its deliberative process is expressly designed to make offenders answerable 'publicly' (or at least to the public of those 'persons affected') for their wrong (Braithwaite and Roche 2001; Braithwaite 2002d: 156). In its processes, offenders are required to provide an account of their actions and have that account subject to contestation by others present so that an account will be reached that 'has been accepted by [all] the stakeholders in the injustice' (Braithwaite 2006: 34). Roche (2003) suggests that the deliberative nature of this practice makes this development of accountability more effective primarily because of its immediacy. Given this immediacy, the deliberation potentially has 'the virtue of [the] authenticity of emotional communication' seen as crucial to a full acceptance of responsibility (Braithwaite 2006: 38). Nonetheless, there is some empirical evidence to support the view that persons affected also perceive offenders as being 'held accountable' in the more formal sense as a consequence of participation in restorative processes and that this aspect of accountability can reinforce a sense that justice has been rendered (see Maxwell and Morris 1993; Bonta, Wallace-Capretta et al. 1998; Poulson 2003).

---

3 For example, an active acceptance of responsibility for their offending is seen as the core therapeutic gateway for addressing abusive behaviour by violent or sexually abusive men (Jenkins 1990).

Censure and Remorse

Censure and remorse are core generative mechanisms that can help to trigger a sense of justice. Censure refers to behaviour which publicly conveys disapproval and denunciation in order to achieve two discrete purposes. Firstly, it provides vindication to persons affected by the wrongdoing while at the same time acting as a moral prompt to help wrongdoers realize that they have done wrong. In the first instance, censure provides recognition that the victim has not only been harmed but also been wronged through no fault of their own. This recognition has the effect of restating the victim's 'moral standing as a human being who demands our concern and respect' (Gaita 1991; Duff 2002: 88). In the second instance, censure acts as a prompt to the offender's own awakening understanding of the character, seriousness and implications of the wrong committed (Duff 2002: 88). The following definition of censure captures these twin purposes:

> Censure means to publicly denounce harmful behaviour and declare it as wrong with a view to having the wrongdoer recognize their wrong.

In a similar way, remorse refers to behaviour through which wrongdoers can express sorrow for what they have done. This is a response distinct from expressing mere sorrow for the effects the wrongdoing has had on their own life or situation. Gaita (1991) identifies remorse as a moral phenomenon which involves what he calls 'the suffering recognition' of wrongdoing occurring as a result of the acknowledgement of one's guilt. In his view, the conditions which gives rise to feelings of remorse have more to do with a recognition of moral responsibility than with simply the acceptance of the actuality of blameworthiness (1991: 44–45). Gaita says that the wrongdoer feels a need to express remorse as a consequence of their feelings of moral responsibility and that these feelings can be experienced independently of an acceptance of culpability.[4] If this is the case, it is arguably not necessary to feel blameworthy in order to recognize the moral responsibility for one's actions which activates remorse.

Remorse is also an emotion which 'sticks with us in a way that is radically different from other forms of suffering' (Gaita 1991: 47). This is because the focus of remorse is on what kind of person we have become (as a consequence of the wrongdoing) as distinct from what kind of person we think we are more generally. Gaita asks why this realization should be so distressing, and thereby similar to what he calls 'a kind of dying to the world' (1991: 48). He offers two reasons. He says that

4 Kennedy (2008) provides an interesting example of the phenomenon of remorse in regard to US soldiers involved in the Second Gulf War. He cites reports of soldiers feeling 'overcome' by remorse for killing civilians in combat, even though they accepted that the deaths were consistent with existing rules of engagement and so did not hold themselves culpable. Their remorse seems to suggest that the soldiers had retained their sense of moral responsibility even though not feeling morally or legally blameworthy.

unlike other suffering, genuine remorse cannot be *shared*; remorse is 'the discovery of a dimension of ourselves ... [about which we] cannot enter into common and consoling fellowship with others' (1991: 49). We are denied the consolation of saying that what we have done has also been done by others, since our particular offending is all our own. As well, the recognition of what we have become as a consequence of our wrongful acts means that we are (at least temporarily) 'placed elsewhere', separate from our fellow persons and unable to simply excuse ourselves by saying that what we have done is 'only human' because our wrong is distinctive (1991: 50). The effect of this (perhaps) temporary exclusion can be emotionally devastating, though its expression is often misconstrued as mere self-absorption and therefore dismissed as self-serving or regarded suspiciously. Properly expressed by a wrongdoer, remorse has positive potential to instill an awakening and recognition of the individual harm done to victims. The recognition of the need for some form of response to an expression of remorse is seen as crucial to its potential to begin the process of justice. The following definition of remorse seeks to capture these aspects:

> Remorse means the offender feeling sorry for what they had done, wishing that it had not occurred and expressing that they are sorry.

Censure as a generative mechanism was seen as important in criminal justice responses principally because it served the purpose of confirming the offender 'as a responsible person who has committed a wrongful act' and therefore deserving of condemnation (Walgrave 2000a: 177). But censure was not necessarily seen as 'a technique for evoking specified [moral] sentiments' from that offender in criminal justice settings (von Hirsch 1993: 10). The assumption is that the wrongful conduct 'deserves' a response which is expressive of censure or reprobation such that there '*should be* a reprobative response to the core conduct' involved in the wrongdoing (von Hirsch 1993: 9, emphasis in original). The legal conception of censure extends to addressing the victim's needs through acknowledging the harmful conduct as wrong (rather than simply injurious) and singling out a particular offender as the agent responsible for that wrongdoing (Narayan 1993). This message of censure is then seen to be 'embodied in the prescribed sanction', often 'delivered' via punishment (von Hirsch 1993: 11). The use of such a penalty to deliver censure is also seen to allow the degree of censure to be appropriately calibrated to reflect the level of reprehensibility of the conduct and thereby express a particular degree of condemnation for the wrongful acts.

Expressions of remorse also contribute to just outcomes in an instrumental sense in legal justice responses.[5] In all the Australian legal jurisdictions, for

5 Illustrative examples are the *Crimes Act* of 1914 (Cth), Section 16A(2)(f), which statess, 'the degree to which the person has shown contrition for the offence' is a 'relevant' factor, and the *Sentencing Act* (Vic) of 1991, Section 5(2C), which indicates that 'in sentencing an offender a court may have regard to the conduct of the offender on or in connection with the trial as an indication of remorse or lack of remorse on his or her part'.

instance, 'contrition, repentance and remorse after the offence are mitigating factors leading ... to some, perhaps considerable reduction of the normal sentence' providing their genuineness is not in doubt (*Neal v The Queen* 1982: 314). But reservations have often been expressed about the generative power of remorse. 'Fundamental problems [were seen] with remorse as a mitigating factor ... [since] it is often indistinguishable from expedience or self-pity' (Edney and Bagaric 2007: 175). The concern was that such expressions of remorse may not be genuine 'since it requires no tangible exertion or demonstrable behavioural change' in the wrongdoer and so remains largely subjective, with its genuineness at best merely assumed (Edney and Bagaric 2007: 175).

Censure has also been seen as an important generative mechanism in restorative justice practice. Restorative practice takes an essentially instrumentalist view of censure because it 'uses' the practice of blaming a wrongdoer primarily with the intention of seeking to strengthen the offender's inhibitions against reoffending in the future (Braithwaite and Pettit 1990). There is criticism that censure thus becomes more of an appeal to a wrongdoer's desire to avoid further disapprobation rather than being more properly directed at increasing their capacity for moral self-assessment (von Hirsch 1993: 24–25). Nonetheless, the form of dialogue that restorative practice facilitates among offenders, victims and other affected persons is seen to provide a potentially effective form of normative discourse through which to convey moral censure. This is both because the process 'afford[s] an opportunity in which both victims and offenders are able to participate constructively' together in discussions, and because the discourse that is generated from such exchanges is more likely to be 'a moralistic form of discourse that offenders may find harder to reject' (Dignan 2003: 144). Importantly, a core element of the restorative purpose of censure identified is the means it offers to vindicate the experience of victims in a way that can vindicate their personal value without needing to necessarily denigrate the wrongdoer (Hampton 1998: 39). Of course, for such an approach to work there must be 'strong procedural safeguards to ensure that the power relationship of the crime is not recreated', or that a substitute power imperative now directed against the offender is not imposed (Hudson 2003a: 183).

Remorse has also been seen as an important generative mechanism for restorative justice practice. There are reports of empirical studies of restorative processes (in particular the South Australian Juvenile Justice (SAJJ) youth conference program) which indicate that more than half the young offenders could be objectively identified as being either 'fully' or 'mostly' remorseful in their response to their wrong and its effects on others (Daly 2003: 224). These expressions of remorse have been seen as contributing significantly to an experience of a sense of justice by persons affected who had participated in these conferences.

Punishment and Vindication

Punishment and vindication are related generative mechanisms in that the imposition of punishment is often seen as a core means of vindicating the victim and reaffirming their worth as individuals. Garvey argues that it is essential to 'vindicate the victim's worth through punishment' in some tangible way in order to reinforce normative bonds (1999: 1844). Punishment serves two interlocking functions – a censuring function and a preventive function. In doing the work of censuring, punishment expresses or underlines the disapproval or disapprobation the wrongful conduct warrants. In terms of its preventive function, the threat or imposition of punishment provides a prudential reason for desistence for this wrongdoer (in the future) and for other potential wrongdoers contemplating similar offending (now or in the future) (von Hirsch 1993: 13). However, these two functions are seen as so intertwined that penalties 'both constitute the hard treatment and express the reprobation' in a single step (von Hirsch 1993: 14). However, disapprobation can be expressed in ways other than punishment. Walgrave, for instance, argues that sanctions which impose 'an obligation to repair' but are not designed to inflict hardship on the wrongdoer can be equally effective in expressing disapprobation (2002: 199). But in many forms of response, the punishment of a wrongdoer is seen as crucial to giving persons affected by that wrong a sense of justice, with disapprobation expressed by imposing some form of hardship. The following definition of punishment tries to capture these various functions:

> Punishment means a sanction which involves a deprivation imposed with the intention of expressing censure for harm done and preventing or dissuading future offending.

In a related way, some means of vindication of the wrong done to persons affected is central to justifying or reaffirming their individual worth. This is more starkly illustrated in responses to widespread politically sanctioned wrongdoing where 'many victims conceive of justice in terms of revalidating oneself, of affirming the sense that "you are right, you were damaged, and it was wrong"' (Minow 1998: 60). Being vindicated in this way gives victims a sense of justice through personal revalidation (which is often effected through the imposition of sanctions on the wrongdoer). Vindication is also understood in a further sense as separate from personal vindication and focused instead on the 'vindication of the law' and the social standards it protects by confirming or reasserting its normative content. The following definition of the term emphasizes more the core sense of personal vindication:

> Vindication means taking seriously the concerns of persons affected in a way that helps them to feel that it is they who have been wronged.

Punishment (and the calculation of the amount of such punishment) has a core generative role in criminal justice responses. Punishing someone involves 'visiting a deprivation (hard treatment) on him [or her], because he [or she] supposedly has committed a wrong' (von Hirsch 1993: 9).[6] Such punishment (which Lacey characterizes more as 'unpleasant consequences' (1988: 7)) is regarded as essential

6 The phrase 'hard treatment' may be traced back to Feinberg (1970a), if not earlier.

to the expression of censure in order to communicate (to both victim and offender) that a wrong has been done and has now been properly addressed. Punishment is designed to induce in the offender 'the pain of condemnation and of recognized guilt' (Duff 1992: 53–54). This recognition in consequence is seen to act as a means to reshape or correct the normative damage to relationships among victims, offenders and the community. An important feature of punishment's justice function is dependent on the amount of punishment being properly calibrated to the severity of the wrong done and the offender's culpability for that wrong. This calibration assumes that offences can be ranked according to their relative seriousness and that this 'seriousness, in turn, is composed of [determined amounts of] culpability and harmfulness' (Ashworth 1993: 288). The calibration of the 'correct' amount of punishment is then seen to satisfy the 'strict obligation to punish in a particular way', and to a particular degree (Allen 1999: 327).

In a criminal justice response, punishment has additional instrumental purposes. This more 'rehabilitative punishment' imposes a deprivation consequential on wrongdoing with a purpose other than to purely penalize. Its further 'essential purpose' is to achieve 'restoration', primarily in the sense of restoring normatively damaged community standards (Duff 2002: 82), but also geared 'towards the pursuit of broadly restorative outcomes – notably compensation orders and reparation orders' (Dignan 2002: 183). Vindication also acts as a generative mechanism in legal justice responses. What 'happens' to the offender in terms of sanction is seen as providing a sense of vindication of the rights of the victim and other persons affected.[7] The full content of 'what happens' to the offender can extend to both the burden of the pre-trial and court process itself in terms of time, expense and stress as well as any overt sanction actually meted out to the wrongdoer through the process (Feeley 1979).

Punishment has a much less central role in restorative justice practice. In the main, restorative practice eschews punishment as its primary means of responding to wrongdoing. But some restorative justice scholars express the view that restorative-type sanctions are in fact 'alternative punishments' which cannot be properly construed as merely 'alternatives to punishment' (Daly 2000: 34). In this view, 'tasks, restrictions or deprivations imposed on an offender in consequence of a criminal act, are [all] punishment' (Hudson 2003a: 187). Punishment in this sense covers 'anything that is unpleasant, a burden or imposition' (Daly 2000: 39). Therefore, paying compensation, attending a counseling session, paying a fine or having reporting conditions to meet all act as 'punishments' to those who must agree with and adhere to these commitments. Daly argues that the work of punishment in delivering censure remains crucial to restoration (2000). However, the key difference she draws is that while restorative justice practice does not

7 In sentencing an offender for murder in *DPP v Dupas* [2007] VSC 305 (para. 16), the Supreme Court of Victoria said, 'this trial was a vindication' of the rights of the victim and suggested that the *Sentencing Act* (Vic) of 1991 be amended to add 'the vindication of the rights of victims' as a specific purpose of sentencing.

exclude punishment, punishment is *not* its vehicle for generating justice. She draws the distinction by saying, 'I am not arguing … that justice is done when punishment is delivered', merely that punishment is implicit in any sanctions imposed, however that sanction is labeled (2000: 40). According to this view, punishment in terms of retributive censure does form some part of what occurs in a restorative justice process (Daly 2000: 40). Its effect is that 'punishment can be seen to make restorative justice possible' since the censure crucial to restoration and the generation of a sense of justice will not otherwise be seen as effective (Daly 2000: 48). However, the mainstream restorative practice literature disputes the requirement that punishment is necessary to express censure. Walgrave (2000: 178), for instance, argues that not all punishments in fact express blame, since in some cases punishment will be seen by potential offenders more as a rationally balanced risk than as a potential penalty. While accepting that wrongfulness needs to be censured, restorative justice practice refutes that this censure is best expressible through punishment. Their core dispute is that censure which is conveyed through punishment will only deal with the offender externally and will not be capable of eliciting the necessary 'moral sentiments of repentance' (von Hirsch 1993: 7). Shearing and Johnson (2005) suggest instead that providing to victims 'a credible guarantee of future right-doing' which better delivers the message that 'this will not happen again' can meet many of the key requirements of censure sufficiently, without the need to also impose punishment (Shearing and Johnson 2005: 35).

By comparison, vindication is a key element in restorative processes. To be effective from a restorative perspective vindication requires the presence of others from whom persons wronged can 'receive acknowledgement and validation' which forms 'a central element of the healing process' (Minow 1998: 71). It is through censuring the wrongdoer's acts in this way that other participants in the process will begin the process of vindication of the worth of persons harmed, which is a crucial first step to their restoration.

Deterrence and Proportionality

Deterrence and proportionality are generative mechanisms which operate as principles affecting behaviour rather than as behaviours in themselves. Deterrence as a principle seeks to dissuade further offending either as a product of the form of response itself (including the 'pre-trial' steps in the determinative process), as well as through the effect of any sanctions or conditions imposed or agreed upon. Measures designed to deter particular wrongdoers can also affect the future behaviour of other unrelated persons so as to dissuade them from similar offending. The following definition of deterrence captures these various senses:

> Deterrence means an intended effect of a response in reducing the tendency of the offender to reoffend, and an effect of a response in reducing the general tendency of other people to offend in this way.

The principle of proportionality suggests that practices which correctly manage the *degree* of response produce important justice-generating effects. For instance, von Hirsch (1993: 6) contends that the principle that 'sanctions be proportionate in their severity to the gravity of offences' is itself a basic element of justice. In its legally conventional sense, proportionality seeks to maintain consistency by linking censure with the objective seriousness of the criminal event. An alternative conception of proportionality which is evident in the restorative justice literature makes the linkage instead between the severity of the harm caused and the degree of restorative effort required to redress that harm. In either view, ensuring that sanctions or obligations to repair are proportionate in their severity or their onerousness to the gravity of the wrongdoing or the degree of restoration required is seen as potentially justice-generative. The following definition of proportionality captures these dual aspects:

> Proportionality means the principle of sanctions being proportionate in their severity to the culpability of the wrongdoing done, or the degree of restorative effort required to remedy the harm done.

Deterrence and proportionality are generative mechanisms given markedly different weight in criminal justice and restorative justice practices. Criminal justice responses give wide prominence to the principle of deterrence. In the case of responses to wrongdoing, it embraces a rationally deliberative model of deterrence which assumes that the likelihood and severity of punishment will affect decisions to offend (Zimring and Hawkins 1973).[8] Deterrence is used in two senses – 'general deterrence [in the sense of] dissuading like-minded persons from committing such a crime as that for which sentence is being imposed' and specific deterrence in the sense of persuading this prisoner from repeating this crime or crimes in general' (Ross 2009: 19.1720). Legal responses likewise embrace the principle of proportionality, particularly in accepting that if sanctions need to be imposed there must be some objective means of correctly determining and managing the amount of sanction. The amount of punishment is variously set by the degree of the offender's culpability, by the degree of 'treatment' needed to promote desistence or by the degree of actual or normative harm caused by the offender. Overriding these different anchors is the controlling restraint of 'upper limits' of penalty (Tonry 1994; Ashworth 2002: 586). Criminal justice's application of its principle of proportionality is guided primarily by the answers to two separate but related questions (von Hirsch 1993). The first asks, 'How much sanction is justified?' The answer offered is that as wrongdoing becomes increasingly more serious, the amount of sanction needs to be progressively increased to 'signif[y] a greater degree of disappropriation' (von Hirsch 1993: 15).

8 Zimring and Hawkins (1973) highlight this model as relative ineffective, particularly as it relates to the use of incapacitation to reduce levels of offending in the community more generally (cited in Tonry 1996: 107).

The second question asks, 'Is there a particular quantum of sanction that is the "deserved penalty" for this particular offence in these particular circumstances given its degree of seriousness?' (von Hirsch 1993: 18). In a purely objective sense, there can be no such 'right amount' of sanction since 'the amount of disapproval conveyed by penal sanctions is [simply] a convention' and not a mathematically calculable amount (von Hirsch 1993: 19). Instead, the use of some basis of relativity for calculating the quantum of penalty is substituted so as to provide usable comparative gravity graduations, boxed by minimum and maximum penalty prescriptions in legislation (Kleinig 1973). Criminal justice practice seeks to overcome some of the limitations of the principle that 'sanctions be proportionate in their severity to the gravity of offences' (von Hirsch 1993: 6), suggesting that proportionate consistency can be retained by linking censure strictly to the objective seriousness of the criminal event. A just legal response therefore says that an offender deserves some degree of punishment and that the degree is ranked in terms of relative seriousness, with 'seriousness' being judged against a combination of the offender's culpability, blameworthiness or the harmfulness of the conduct (Ashworth 1993: 288).

Restorative justice practice also recognizes deterrence, seeing the 'most important function of deterrence is to channel justice into restoration' so as to support a credible guarantee of future right-doing by the offender (Braithwaite 2002b: 121). The 'dialogic social control' model which characterizes much of restorative processes is seen to have potential power to achieve effective deterrence by involving 'many [people] beyond the criminal who can be deterred [so as] to prevent the crime' (Braithwaite 2002b: 121). Restorative practice emphasizes this active form of deterrence that encourages 'third parties [families, friends and the like] ... because of their sense of social responsibility, their caring for an affected party, or because they have [the] power' to contribute their influence in a way that can reduce the likelihood of reoffending (Braithwaite 2002b: 121). By contrast, restorative practice eschews proportionality as a justice-generating mechanism. There is some call in its literature for the substitution of a standard of 'restorative proportionality', whereby a linkage is made between the severity of the harm caused and the degree of restorative effort required to right that harm (see Van Ness 1999: 274–275). Proportionality in this sense would anchor the degree of response to the degree of harm. But using this link between the 'severity of the material, relational and social harm' and 'the degree of restorative effort required by the offender' presents considerable difficulties unresolved in its implementation (Walgrave and Geudens 1996: 376). One difficulty is the potential for an extreme level of sanction being imposed when the degree of harm caused by wrongdoing is itself extreme, and this may not always be warranted (Braithwaite 2005). If the link drawn between the harm caused and the effort is required in this way, with the degree of sanction to be gauged by 'persons affected', then adequate guidelines would need to be strictly in place to avoid unwarranted or disproportionate severity (Van Ness 1999: 274).[9] Balanced against such difficulties may be some potential benefit, in that the degree of culpability and the extent of harm caused by the offence would more likely be made apparent through a deliberative process (Erez 1999). But risks remain where the anchoring point subordinates culpability to consequences (Feld 1999: 38). Victim involvement may also play a destabilizing role where the views of victims are disparate or contradictory, or where some victims are more forgiving and others more vindictive (Ashworth 2002: 586). There is one alternative suggestion as to how to base restorative proportionality. This approach uses instead a consequentialist anchor coupled with fixed 'upper limits' as an overriding constraint (Braithwaite 2002d: 152–155). In this modification, the proportionate standard used is a measure of the likely consequences of the sanction itself in terms of justice promotion (Braithwaite 2002d: 152). A sanction can then be set in such a way that addresses the issue of what response is best to increase 'community safety', 'social harmony' or an 'improved sense of personal safety' in the aftermath of the offending using these benchmarks as semi-objective measures of just outcomes (Braithwaite 2002d: 153). This alternative linkage could remove the risk of excessive sanctions to 'match' the harm done and has the advantage of substituting a measurable level of sanction more likely to provide for the desired credible guarantee of future protection.

Truth Telling

'Truth finding' or 'truth telling' is seen as an essential justice-generating mechanism. In criminal justice responses, the notion of 'truth' is largely confined to 'accurate accounts by competent people of what they genuinely believe from sensory experience' to have occurred (Frankel 1978; Johnson 2002: 17 n11). Markel's definition usefully expands the meaning of truth outside the law to include 'four faces of truth'. In his construction, meanings of 'truth' include forensic or factual truth, personal or narrative truth, social truth and healing or restorative truth (Markel 1999: 408–411). Factual truth is closest to the legal justice notion given that it describes truth as 'a version of events verifiable by forensic techniques'. By contrast, personal or narrative truth refers more broadly to the opportunity given for persons affected by wrongdoing to tell their story and have that story heard, even though it may not be possible to 'argue that just because a story is told it is [necessarily] a *true* story' in a forensic sense (Markel 1999: 409). 'Social' or 'dialogue truth' similarly refers to a more communal notion of truth being shared 'experience that is established through interaction, discussion and

9 Van Ness (1999) suggests that tort law or a desert-based scale be used to gauge how the offence and any sanction impede the standard of living of the typical person. The latter method has resonance with Braithwaite and Pettit's (1990) use of dominion as the target for measuring the harm of criminal conduct in terms of the diminishment of liberty caused by the offending and likely to be caused by imposing sanctions on the offender.

debate' (Markel 1999: 409). Finally, the concept of 'healing' or 'restorative truth' is broader still. It potentially occurs more often in broad political settings where 'facts and what they mean [are placed] within the context of human relationships – both among citizens and between the state and its citizens' so as to effect a sense of communal healing (see Truth and Reconciliation Commission 1998: 114). Allowing for different interpretations as to the relative priority of these 'faces' of truth, truth telling clearly has wide potential as a justice-generating mechanism.

This complexity of truth and its telling presents definitional difficulties, but an essentially descriptive definition is used as follows:

> Truth telling refers to the practice of providing persons affected with opportunities to find or tell the truth of the wrongdoing and its consequences to the extent necessary.

Modes of 'fact finding' or 'truth telling' are seen as fundamental to justice generation in criminal justice responses. How truth is arrived at is basic to its practice since its form of response is predicated upon the identification of a particular offender who has been held or found to be responsible for some particular wrongdoing. The rationale of the criminal justice response is to establish with sufficient certainty whether behaviour which constitutes the violation of a legal norm has occurred. It relies primarily on a system of factual truth finding to arrive at an accepted version of events which is verifiable by forensic techniques. This forensic inquiry is normally confined to investigating those elements of events relevant to establishing responsibility and to arriving at a 'version of events' against which culpability can be determined.

The need to establish forensically verifiable 'truth telling' is less crucial in restorative justice practice given that the offender has invariably already pleaded guilty or acknowledged responsibility before entering the process.[10] The focus of truth telling thus shifts to providing persons affected by the wrongdoing with the opportunity to hear the offender's 'truth', or have their own heard by 'telling the story they want to tell, and for their storytelling to be effective' (Hudson 2003a: 182). This form of truth telling is more along the lines of Markel's 'narrative truth' with the disclosures allowing a potentially fuller picture of events and circumstances to emerge from participants who have direct interest in making and obtaining that disclosure. It is this understanding of truth as something arrived at by discourse which has potential healing force that is its crucial justice-generating role. The focus in restorative practice is also more on the 'truth of the harm caused' rather than the factual truth of the events leading to that harm (Strang 2009). There is thus less need for disputes as to facts and instead more scope for concentration

10 Pleading guilty is the standard requirement, though in New Zealand young offenders have the benefit of a lower threshold of 'declining to deny' culpability, and in the Australian Capital Territory legislation 'acceptance of responsibility in order to participate in restorative justice' is sufficient and is explicitly understood to fall short of a plea of guilty.

on participants' 'own evaluation of what happened' in terms of the harm done to them or others (Hudson 2003a: 182). In accepting responsibility, wrongdoers may not necessarily depart from their own version of the facts but there can still be disputation as to the truth of the ill effects caused (Hudson 2003a: 184). What is also claimed for truth telling in restorative justice practice is that its processes provide discursive capacity for all persons present to arrive at a shared truth. The victim's account of the ill effects caused is more often heard directly. The process also provides the offender with a direct voice about his or her culpability, which is largely undiluted by professional intervention. It is this process of 'truth-finding through undominated dialogue' (Braithwaite 2002b: 87), with its echoes of Habermas's (1996) fundamental discursive rules for 'ideal speech', that can characterize much of the process of restorative truth telling.

Reparation, Apology and Forgiveness

Reparation is a mechanism identified as common to criminal justice and restorative justice responses to wrongdoing. Apology and forgiveness, by contrast, are given little recognition in criminal justice responses, but have significant prominence in restorative justice literature. Reparation is a broad term which covers the means by which harm resulting from wrongdoing can be 'made good'. Reparation can extend to restitution or compensation made by the offender (or provided by the state) including monetary payment, replacement of property or performance of services. But a reparative sanction can be wider than simply restitution, since it can be both material and symbolic in form. Material reparation typically involves the wrongdoer giving undertakings to compensate the victim financially or serve the community in some way directly or indirectly through community service. In its symbolic form, reparation is largely a product of the social rituals of the process whereby those present 'respond in a tangible or symbolic way to the harm done to victims' (Van Ness and Strong 1997: 91). In doing so, it more directly addresses their sense of having been harmed. The definition of reparation captures both the material and symbolic aspects:

> Reparation is the act of making amends, offering expiation or giving satisfaction for a wrong or injury.

Apology was described by Goffman (1971: 113) as 'a gesture through which an individual splits himself into two parts, the part that is guilty of an offence and a part that dissociates itself from the delict and affirms a belief in the offended rule'. The justice-generating claims made for apology are similarly twofold. A meaningful apology is seen to provide a tangible confirmation of an offender's willingness to take responsibility and to thereby leave behind excuses for the offending. Secondly, apology is seen to more directly acknowledge the harm done and affirm the wrongness of the harm. There is some empirical support for the notion that receiving an apology can contribute to a sense of justice, particularly where the apology is seen as genuine and not self-serving. In the Australian Capital Territory Reintegrative Shaming Experiment (RISE) program wherein pathways of response were randomly assigned between criminal justice and restorative justice responses, more than three-quarters of apologies made in the restorative pathway were perceived as 'sincere' or 'somewhat sincere' by victims and their supporters and were seen to contribute to victims' sense that justice was being done in the process (Strang 2002: 115).[11] The following definition of apology captures this:

> Apology means the wrongdoer expressing sorrow about the effect their offence has had on the victim and other persons affected.

Forgiveness stands out amongst the generative mechanisms as more a moral than a social response. Forgiveness, in one view, is 'a power held by the victimized, not a right to be claimed' (Minow 1998). For Minow, the power of forgiveness comes from its 'ennobling capacity, [as] part of the dignity to be reclaimed by those who survive the wrongdoing' (1998: 17).[12] If an offender is forgiven, the effect is not to provide him or her with a release from the consequences of the wrong but simply to communicate that a readjustment of social relationships has now occurred and that this has been bestowed by the harmed on the offender as the harmer (Augsburger 1996). The power of an apology in this respect is that in leaving an offender vulnerable it can enable the victim to confront their own vulnerability and thereby let go of their own corrosive emotions of hatred and anger. As such, forgiveness provides opportunities for moral learning more so than for justice generation. The following definition of forgiveness captures these aspects:

> Forgiveness means people wronged willfully abandoning resentment and endeavouring to respond with compassion. Forgiveness is a response that the wrongdoer has no right to ask.

Criminal justice responses do have regard to material reparation, primarily as a means of confirming that 'the offender has shown remorse for the offence by making reparation for any injury, loss or damage'.[13] But reparation is not

11 Daly (2000) reported similar findings in conference observations in the SAJJ project, with almost two-thirds of young persons apologizing. As to the effect produced by such apologies, while a majority of young persons (61 per cent) said that the main reason they apologized was because 'they were really sorry', this was not the message received by victims, with 'just 27 per cent of victims believ[ing] that the main reason the [young person] apologised was because s/he really was sorry' (Daly 2003: 224–225).

12 In some religious traditions where a wrongdoer has apologized to those he or she has harmed, the wronged are seen as religiously required to grant forgiveness. For instance in Judaism, the teachings of Maimonides counsel the injured party to be magnanimous and offer forgiveness.

13 New South Wales *Crimes (Sentencing Procedure) Act* 1999, section 21A(3)(i).

recognized as a primary means of sanction. Apology also has relatively little role in criminal justice responses either as a means to generate censure or as a form of sanction. Apology is accepted as a means of demonstrating contrition, as well as tangible evidence of the offender's remorse. It is also a legally recognized mitigating factor capable of reducing the objective culpability of the offender, although its scope is limited (Edney and Bagaric 2007: 161). There is also concern that the genuineness of apology cannot be readily appraised and that specious or false apologies are commonplace.[14] Forgiveness is seen as a discretionary moral practice with 'no place in a system governed by law, where the rules must apply equally to all' (Edney and Bagaric 2007: 177). Nonetheless, courts accept that in some instances forgiveness may affect the severity of sanctions imposed, since it 'may reduce the possibility of re-offending, [and] may reduce the danger of public outrage', both of which are positive instrumental outcomes (Edney and Bagaric 2007: 177).

Restorative justice claims to explicitly facilitate both material and symbolic reparation in its responses. In restorative practice, the communicative and symbolic meanings of reparation are seen as more important than any simple exchange of material detriment for material advantage. The attraction of restorative processes is that they can 'facilitate the negotiation of much more flexible forms of reparation that should, in principle, be capable of responding more appropriately to more of the particular harms that victims have experienced' (Dignan 2003: 144). Apology is also identified as a primary generative mechanism in restorative practice, seen to 'help to transcend breaches of the normative order within a given group or community' (Bottoms 2003: 96). The restorative process provides the opportunity for the disassociation between the wrongdoer and the wrong that Goffman (1971) notes needs to occur for apology to be effective. Apology can be verbal, and accompanied by physical acts (such as a handshake or hugging), or can be more formally delivered in writing, either prepared before or after a restorative encounter. Apology in the restorative sense is directed not so much at society's normative damage but at the victim's own personal harm. This is so even where it may have been society's 'moral imperative' which first compelled the offender to take steps towards apology (Tavuchis 1991). Forgiveness is also identified as a core value of restorative practice. Empirical research suggests that when offenders receive 'perceived forgiveness', their experience of that feeling has a positive effect on their level of reoffending (Ahmed and Braithwaite 2006: 351). In a similar manner, self-forgiveness by the offender allows release from the pervasive feelings of shame and guilt without excusing or minimizing the wrongdoing and without excusing the offender from censure or sanction (Woodyatt and Wenzel 2013: 2013). But expressions of forgiveness have been seen to have less

---

14 The New South Wales Law Reform Commission suggested that 'genuine' remorse may be evidenced by: (i) a plea of guilty, (ii) cooperation with police, (iii) making reparation, (iv) apologizing and (v) self-inflicted injuries or attempted suicide (New South Wales Law Reform Commission 1996: 192).

direct justice-generating power and to operate instead more as expressions of mercy or compassion, which sit adjacent to but not necessarily within the realm of justice.

Conclusion

This chapter has developed a set of generative mechanisms which can be used to more closely investigate justice practice. These mechanisms suggest various ways those who participate in institutional justice responses to wrongdoing can generate and come to experience a sense of justice from the social interactions involved. A unique set of behaviours, approaches and principles are seen to have particular generative force. The importance placed on each mechanism in the respective practices of criminal and restorative justice has been canvassed and compared. Some mechanisms are valued by both forms of justice practice, while others are favoured by only one or the other. There is clearly some suggestion of a paradigmatic unity in the two practices in the mechanisms they use, particularly with respect to accountability and responsibility. There is also clearly a paradigmatic shift. For instance, in the means used to generate censure, criminal justice practice often resorts to punishment while restorative justice disavows punishment and favours instead the censuring power of apology and reparation. What can usefully be made of this unity/disunity in institutional settings is returned to later in the Conclusion. We now have a collection of analytical tools with which to examine justice practice. In Part II, the evaluative criteria are first applied to 'measure' the justness of responses to wrongdoing in the two practices discussed here – the newer (and as yet marginal) practice of restorative justice and the prevailing and much more pervasive practice of criminal justice. The results of this analysis are reported in chapters 5 and 6. The analysis shows worrying deficiencies in each practice in how well justice is realized. Neither practice alone provides a full or indeed adequate 'justice discourse' for responses to wrongdoing (Dignan 2003). Nonetheless, there remains a potentially encouraging symmetry between the two practices in their respective adherences and non-adherences to provide scope for a form of integration which can draw on the justice strengths of each practice.

PART II

Chapter 5
Restorative Practice: Is It Just?

Introduction

In the next two chapters, the justice evaluative criteria are used to compare two forms of practice – restorative practice and criminal justice practice – and to 'measure' the justness of their respective responses to wrongdoing. This chapter applies the criteria to restorative practice in the context of responses to wrongdoing. Chapter 6 does the same with regard to criminal justice practice. It has been asserted that restorative practice is not 'just another version of existing juridical approaches' (Walgrave 2000a: 166), but instead a justice practice that follows a 'fundamentally different path' to create a response to wrongdoing where explicit 'moral learning [can] take place' (Schweigert 1997: 23; Van Ness 1999: 263). Participants are encouraged to take on particular healing roles so as to activate this process of moral development. The process ideally begins with a (relatively) brief personal encounter among 'those affected by the wrongdoing', usually the offender, the victim and their families and supporters. The structure and form of the encounter are guided by a particular set of process and particular standard prescriptions to which programs must adhere (Walgrave 2000a: 167; Braithwaite 2002e). Underlying each of these prescriptions is an overarching assumption that the best response to wrongdoing is 'restoration' in some form. A key assumption of such 'restoration' is that all participants will bring with them unresolved (and potentially undiscovered and unacknowledged) emotional consequences from the wrongdoing. It is seen to be through addressing these consequences that a catalyst for repair of harm is found. For the offender, the emotional consequences of their offending may include anger (at themselves or others) as well as fear, hostility, embarrassment, shame and guilt. For victims affected by the offending, very similar emotional consequences may be manifest and unresolved as a consequence of the harm done to them. Restorative practice's focus is on directly and openly addressing both sets of emotional consequences. Given this deliberate emotionally open nature, encounters are managed by trained facilitators. Applying the evaluative criteria to restorative justice practice suggests that the relationship between restoration and justice is necessarily mediated by particular internal commitments (we will find that criminal justice practice is similarly mediated by its own set of internal constraints). These include commitments to managing shame, anger and guilt in an integrative way, in order to allow opportunities for the communication of emotion, and to seek to generate some form of collective censure. Such commitments heighten adherence to certain of the evaluative criteria, particularly positive desert and harmonious social relationships. Yet these commitments leave open the potential for deficiencies in meeting the rights and desert standards. Before we apply the criteria to its practices, it is useful to review features of the restorative process in terms of form, functions and values to highlight the contrasts with criminal justice practice.

The Difference of Restorative Justice

The factors that make a restorative response to wrongdoing different from a standard criminal justice one can be conveniently divided into three categories – form, function and values. These differences can be considered individually, but can also be conveniently grouped together using Roche's (2003) set of shortform 'restorative value prescriptions' of participation, personalism, reparation and reintegration. Firstly, we examine differences of form.

Differences in Form

The unique form of a restorative response is clear even from the most commonly cited definition of 'restorative justice':

> Restorative justice is a process whereby all the parties with a stake in a particular offence come together to resolve collectively how to deal with the aftermath of the offence and its implications for the future. (Marshall 1996: 37, 1999)

The formulation of 'restorative process' endorsed in United Nations instruments is slightly different but highlights similar distinct commitments:[1]

> 'Restorative process' means any process in which the victim and the offender, and where appropriate, any other individuals or community members affected by a crime participate together actively in the resolution of matters arising from the crime, generally with the help of a facilitator. (United Nations Office on Drugs and Crime 2006a)

These two definitions can be combined and reworked slightly to emphasize the practice's differences in form:

1 This definition has its origins in the Working Party on Restorative Justice created by the United Nations Alliance of Non-Government Organisations on Crime Prevention and Criminal Justice, which formulated a set of fundamental principles of restorative justice. These principles were endorsed by the UN Office on Drugs and Crime in December 2006; http://www.unodc.org/pdf/criminal_justice/06-56290_Ebook.pdf, accessed 16 October 2013.

> Restorative justice is a process that *brings together* all *persons affected by wrongdoing* to consider such wrongdoing and the *harm caused*, and to decide *collectively* on a consensual basis *how to deal with its aftermath.*

Each of the highlighted elements represents a different aspect of the practice seen to contribute in some respect to its distinct form of response. Their significance is briefly considered.

'Brings together'

The 'bringing together' of the parties expresses a commitment to creating a forum that directly involves all affected persons as participants rather than merely as observers.[2] A fundamental part of any restorative process is some form of 'encounter' between persons affected by the wrongdoing. In various practices this encounter will involve either direct face-to-face engagement or variations of indirect engagement. In terms of its immediacy, the level of the encounter can be categorized in terms of its degree of 'restorativeness'. McCold and Wachtel (2003) capture this well in their 'restorative practices typology':[3]

Where all three groups are actively involved (as they are most usually in the peace circles, family group conferencing and community conferencing options which appear in the 'restorative justice' sector of the model), the process is rated as 'fully restorative' in a participatory sense.[4] Other forms are classified as 'mostly restorative' and 'partly restorative', so that while they remain part of restorative practice more broadly they involve potentially less 'bringing together' and as a consequence, potentially less immediacy and restorative potential.

'Persons affected'

The 'persons affected' referred to notionally consist of the victim(s), offender(s) and their 'communities'. 'Victim' and 'offender' are of course not simple 'uncomplicated and homogenous categories of self' (Cunneen 2003: 192). Each apparent 'victim' and 'offender' experiences or occupies these categories in different ways. As well, the categories may well not be mutually exclusive; people can simultaneously have both experiences. Additionally, participants who sit in the 'victims' category' will 'come to conferences with different orientations and expectations' because of their personal factors, because of the harm done to them and

---

2 This element may be better expressed as providing an 'opportunity' for all persons affected to attend if they wish. In the case of some victims (such as victims of large-scale fraudsters, for instance), the number of persons adversely affected may be huge and individual attendance may need to be replaced by representative appointment.

3 Reproduced at http://www.iirp.edu/article_detail.php?article_id=424, accessed 18 October 2013.

4 Bazemore and Schiff (2005: 29, emphasis in original) rightly make the point that the application of this 'three-dimensional focus' excludes informal encounters *outside the context of formal programs* but which may still fully engage all three 'stakeholders'.

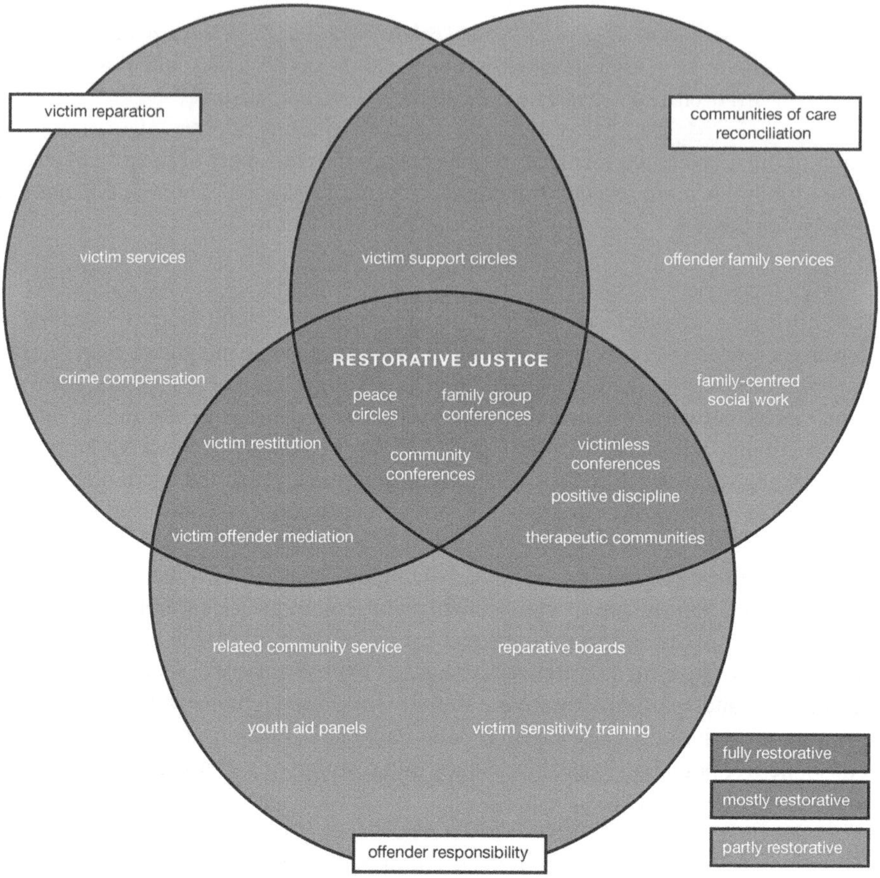

Figure 5.1 McCold and Wachtel's restorative practices typology

because of differences consequential on the form of restorative program in which they are asked to participate (Hayes 2005: 96). Notions of an 'ideal victim' who is 'vulnerable, respectable, not contributing to their own victimisation' (Cretney and Davis 1995: 160) are simply artificial in that setting. Likewise, notions of a typical 'offender' who is 'powerful, bad [and] a stranger to the victim' are equally artificial (Cretney and Davis 1995: 160). The identification of a particular 'community affected' is equally troubling, particularly when attempts are made to draw together a community that can yield 'meaningful standards' against which the particular wrongdoing can be judged (Brown 1994: 1292). Even if such a community can be 'found' for each offender, there will potentially be significant issues of conflict, power, difference and inequality inherent in the existing community relationships of the group that will need to be accommodated. There is also a potentially 'dark side to the quest for community', given that 'a spontaneously shared community often involves images of exclusion' and such perceptions will need to be closely managed (Pavlich 2001: 58). The bitter reality may be that any apparent 'ideal community' is in fact 'marked (and sustained) by social exclusion, forms of coercion, and the differential distribution of power' (Crawford 2000: 290–291). These communities may not be 'the havens of reciprocity and mutuality, nor ... the utopias of egalitarianism' that the notion of 'community affected' may connote, and their negativity will need to be controlled (Crawford 2002: 110).

To accommodate these negatives, restorative practices have put in place protections to prevent encounters intended to be restorative from becoming processes which 'close, limit and exclude individuals, rather than reintegrating them' (Cunneen 2003: 186). One strategy is to acknowledge that the 'ideal' of community may be better seen as a 'collective solidarity' such that deliberate attempts are then made to exclude potentially parochial factors and instead artificially 'create' communities seen as more nurturing (Pavlich 2001: 59). Some restorative practice advocates recognize a need to 'reshape' existing communities to ensure that those who are actually 'brought together' emphasize inclusion over exclusion and aim to open up the potential to activate 'a virtue of care hospitable to the non-member' (Braithwaite and Strang 2001: 8). In pragmatic terms, this may mean convenors 'build[ing] a community' around each single offender (or victim) by drawing widely from any conceivable base of support (Bottoms 2003: 109).[5] However, adding such artificial extensions of community (including 'community representatives') runs the risk of the created group adopting purely external standards of 'wrongness' and thereby losing any discrete or tailored community focus relevant to the participants (Ashworth 2002: 582).[6] Of course, in the absence of such an artificial creation the alternate risk may be that the internal standards which do prevail become 'the norms of a micro-community' where majoritarian opposition to offending is weak or compromised. In such cases, the involvement of support groups to provide the absent normative voice may well be the only way to provide the necessary denunciation of the wrong (Coker 2002: 129; Stubbs 2004: 7).

5 In some circumstances, it would be necessary to relax this limitation to allow structuring of restorative processes to minimize power imbalances by giving a supporting voice to organized advocacy groups. The 'community' description used in the Australian Capital Territory's Restorative Justice Unit (where restorative justice is currently confined to juveniles), which characterizes 'the people most affected by an offence' as 'the victim, their family and friends and the young person who committed the offence and their family and friends', is commonplace.

6 See Ali Wardak's work on integrating local institutions of informal justice (*jirga*) within a postwar justice system in Afghanistan. *Jirga* is an example of a local institution of decision-making and dispute resolution that 'incorporates the prevalent local customary law, institutional rituals, and a body of village elders whose collective decision about the resolution of a dispute (or local problem) is binding' (Wardak 2004: 326). But fitting this process into a restorative-style model may prove difficult where the traditional community does not reflect equality for women and others.

'Wrongdoing'

The prescription of 'wrongdoing' used in this work envisages conduct which offends accepted normative standards in some serious way such that it has been criminalized. Restorative practice's initial focus is on wrongdoing in its 'determination of "what happened" in the process of deliberation' (Hudson 1998b: 251). However, there seems to be an awareness of the risk that conceptualizing wrongdoing as separate 'incidents' may exclude persistent patterns of conduct of which the offending behaviour is but a single manifestation. The limits and risks of an 'incident-based definition of domestic violence', for instance, are all too well known. Restorative processes responding to such forms of wrongdoing attempt to expand their notions of wrong where appropriate, to see it instead as 'part of a pattern of repeated violence or other abuse' (Stubbs 2004: 14, 2012). Additionally, restorative processes recognize that an emphasis on the moral nature of the 'wrong' should not exclude the fact that the wrong is also 'criminal'. As such, there needs to be an explicit emphasis on public censure in addition to emphasizing the need to address the harm caused to individuals (Duff 2003: 47).

'Harm caused'

Restorative practice resets the core criminal relationship of offender and state so as to 'make the relationship between victim and offender central', with the harm caused becoming the key focus rather than the normative breach (Hudson 1998b: 247). Making 'the victim's perspective central to proceedings' (rather than simply a prosecutorial tool or a consideration in sentence) brings the relational aspect of the harm directly into play (Hudson 1998b: 248).[7] Offenders are then confronted not so much 'with the power of the state acting on behalf of (or in the place of) the victim' but with the potentially direct exposure to the harm their wrongdoing has caused to individuals (Hudson 1998b: 247).

'Collectively'

'Collectively' implies the reaching of a mutual decision in which all 'persons affected' have a say in 'how to deal with the aftermath' of offending and arrive at some consensus about what needs to be done. In this collective sense, victims and their supporters are a core part of the decision-making, along with offenders and their supporters. This raises the risk that each *side's* obvious partiality may curtail or interfere with the right to 'a fair hearing' in an 'independent and impartial

7 Pelikan describes this in empirical work she undertook in a pilot project in Austria on the use of victim-offender mediation (VOM) as a diversionary response to domestic violence. She found that in VOM 'the victim is at the centre. It is about her we are talking; it is her suffering, her fears, her apprehensions, her anger, and her reactions' (2000). More traditional forms of response have been used to give victims an independent voice in the form of a subsidiary prosecutor in Germany, Austria, Norway, the former Yugoslavia and Sweden (Joutsen 1987: 114).

tribunal', which the law mandates.[8] This right is seen as expressing a 'fundamental principle of justice' and as such should apply equally to any 'sentencing stage' of proceedings, which clearly includes restorative processes (Ashworth 2002: 586). One means of protecting this right has been to withdraw from the restorative phase any determinative role as regards sanction, so that sanctions imposed (even when recommended by the process) are subject to external and final judicial determination (Roche 2003: 42–46).

'How to deal with the aftermath'

The focus of a criminal justice response is primarily on an 'act' (which may include harm, both actual and normative) and a 'mental element' (such as intention or willful indifference). By contrast, the restorative focus more often highlights the 'aftermath' or consequences of the offending. Such consequences are addressed as part of the process through internal mechanisms such as apology or reparation. There is also an explicit recognition that harm itself will release relational, material and emotional needs in victims, offenders and affected community members and that meeting these needs is also core to any effective restorative response (Pavlich 2005: 40). In summary, these are the measures of the unique form of restorative practice that sets it apart from criminal justice responses to wrongdoing. There are also differences in function and values which warrant similar brief review.

Differences in Function

The range of processes described as 'restorative' is clearly broad, as McCold and Wachtel's (2003) typology indicates. It is therefore useful to categorize such processes in terms of their function as a means to highlight their degree of restorativeness. This can be done by categorizing a process in terms of whether the response deals with criminalized or non-criminalized wrongdoing, whether it is diversionary or supplementary and whether it involves direct or indirect deliberations among persons affected.

Responding to criminalized or non-criminalized wrongdoing

The use of restorative justice extends well beyond responses to incidents defined as criminal. Indeed, as Charlesworth points out, 'restorative justice is not a theory from the discipline of law' and that although its influence is strong there it goes much beyond criminal justice (2002).[9] Restorative responses are widely used in the resolution of non-criminalized disputes in areas such as schools

8 As seen, for example, in the requirements of Article 6.1 of the *European Convention on Human Rights*.

9 Hilary Charlesworth in her nomination of John Braithwaite for the 2012 Future Justice Award; http://regnet.anu.edu.au/news/john-braithwaite-wins-2012-future-justice-award, accessed 16 April 2014.

and workplaces, where law seldom has direct involvement (Morrison 2007). Restorative responses are also utilized in larger 'transgressions *by* the state through truth and reconciliation commissions' in the context of 'large scale historical, social and political [mal]practices' as well as in peace operations (Sherman and Strang 2007: 32).[10] It is in these guises that restorative justice functions both as a response to wrongdoing and as part of a process of societal reconciliation. The focus of this study concentrates attention on wrongdoing defined as criminal, where an identifiable and affected offender and victim are involved, and so where some form of encounter takes place.

Responses which are diversionary or supplementary

When functioning as part of a response to criminal wrongdoing, restorative justice can be diversionary or adjunctive in form. If its form is diversionary, the restorative response usually sits outside the formal legal process as a substitute response and is utilized where a wrongdoer is diverted by police, prosecutors or courts. When its form is ancillary, the process instead acts to supplement the criminal justice response, with an offender participating in a restorative process but still returning to the formal criminal justice system for final disposition and sentence. Additionally, some restorative processes are post-sentence or pre-release and so operate well after any disposition of penalty.[11] The focus of this comparison is once again principally with those restorative practices which act in an ancillary role and to a lesser extent those that are diversionary.

Responses which involve direct or indirect deliberation

Restorative practice which is 'face-to-face' involves direct and personal deliberation among the parties affected in some form of encounter. In most instances, a convenor with primary responsibility to manage the process facilitates these deliberations. In some instances of direct deliberations, such as circle sentencing, a judicial officer and/or tribal elder(s) will be present and play a more interventionist rather than facilitative role.[12] The direct deliberation approach is preferred by many restorative advocates because 'the emotional power generated in this way is [seen as] crucial to the process' being restorative (Sherman and Strang 2007: 33). Additional restorative

10 See Morrison (2007) on its use in schools, Llewellyn (2002) on its use in residential care abuse disputes and Roberts (2003) on its use in transitionary justice contexts.

11 See, for example, the post-sentence program run by Corrective Services New South Wales involving serving prisoners (Milner 2012).

12 Circle sentencing now operates widely including in Canada, such as in the Carcross Circle Program, Yukon Territory, and in Australia with Circle Sentencing in New South Wales, Victoria's Koori Courts, South Australia's Nunga Courts, Queensland's Murri Courts and the ACT's Galambany (formerly Ngambra) Circle Sentencing Court. In New Zealand, there is a Maori Land Court. However, this does not deal with criminal wrongdoing, although its proceedings deal with issues in a traditional and appropriate manner, including being conducted in the Maori language. But many mainstream restorative processes are conducted on the *marae* (Maori traditional meeting place) by indigenous conference providers.

processes such as 'shuttle diplomacy' style mediation and victim-absent or offender-absent conferencing are also used as preparatory steps to face-to-face deliberations. The focus of the comparison made in this volume is principally on those practices that adopt the direct personal deliberative model and seek to involve some form of restorative 'encounter'. As well as these variations in form and function, there are also distinctive 'restorative values' that inform the restorative justice process.

Differences in Values

Processes involving restorative encounters are seen to be informed by a distinctly 'alternative value base' (Bazemore 1996: 37). In his 1996 study of restorative practice, Braithwaite writes that early formulations of these values left the response to the core question 'What is to be restored?' essentially in the hands of the persons participating to determine the dimensions of restoration that mattered to them. What 'mattered' was found to include restoring property loss; injury; a sense of security, dignity and empowerment; and creating the sense that justice had been delivered (Braithwaite 1996). Braithwaite refined and expanded these early formulations into a more comprehensive set of values grouped into three sets, each with differing priorities (2002c, 2002e). The first, 'constraining standards', specifies procedural guidelines and emphasizes rights and limits. The second group is 'maximizing standards' which when adhered to provide the process with its restorative quality. The third set is 'emergent standards' which are seen to sometimes emerge of their own accord in the course of encounters but which cannot be planned or pushed for.[13] While each of these value sets is aspirational, the threshold commitment is to 'honour the constraining standards' (Braithwaite 2002e: 569). The constraining values are those that '*must* be honored and enforced as constraints' since they set standards 'that are so fundamental to justice that they must always be guaranteed' in any response to wrongdoing (Braithwaite 2002c: 253). The constraining values are:

- non-domination of the proceedings by any party
- empowerment of participants to tell their story
- the honouring of legally defined upper limits on sanctions[14]
- respectful listening

13 The emergent standards are those values that *may* emerge in restorative practice but which are not seen as morally appropriate to expect or demand. The presence of these values provides strong evidence that the process is both restorative and justice-enhancing (Braithwaite 2002c). These emergent values include remorse, apology, censure of the act, forgiveness and mercy.

14 New Zealand data especially supports the notion that courts rarely invoke proportionality to reduce restorative justice sanctions but much more frequently do so to increase the level of sanction (Maxwell and Hayes 2006). This empirical data bolsters the general view that the public is more tolerant and less punitive than politicians would have us believe (Roberts, Hough et al. 2002).

- equal concern for all stakeholders
- accountability of the proceedings
- the opportunity for appeal
- respect for basic human rights.[15]

The restorative encounter is seen as 'a space that tries to maximize the possibility of staying close to those values in our behavior' when responding to wrongdoing (Pranis as quoted in Braithwaite 2002e: 573). The other value set of most interest here for the purpose of comparison is that of 'maximizing values' (which have already been used as one source to inform the conceptualization of the harm-related benefits developed in Chapter 2). The maximizing values are those 'values against which the success of restorative processes must be evaluated' since they are concerned with achieving 'restoration' which is fundamental to delivering justice through restoration (Braithwaite 2002c: 250). These value prescriptions once again related to the repair or restoration of:

- human dignity
- property loss
- safety/injury/health
- human relationships
- sense of community
- emotional states (release from feelings of fear, hate and shame; providing a feeling of vindication)
- sense of freedom
- feelings of compassion or caring.

Braithwaite formulates this set of values as 'represent[ing] what restoring justice means for participants' and sees them as the 'values against which the success of restorative processes must be evaluated' (2002b: 250). These value sets provide a useful summation of the principles under which restorative processes operate when they are used to respond to wrongdoing.

---

15 The final value of 'respect for basic human rights' is intended to encompass respect for the fundamental human rights specified in the *Universal Declaration of Human Rights*, the *International Covenant on Economic, Social and Cultural Rights*, the *International Covenant on Civil and Political Rights* and its *Second Optional Protocol*, the United Nations *Declaration on the Elimination of Violence Against Women* and the *Declaration of Basic Principles of Justice for Victims of Crime and Abuse of Power* (Braithwaite 2002e). The recently adopted 2006 UN *Convention on the Rights of Persons with Disabilities* and the 2007 UN *Declaration on the Rights of Indigenous Peoples* should now be added to this list of instruments so as to incorporate additional principles, such as self-determination, that have 'a direct impact on how restorative justice programmes that are respectful of indigenous rights might develop' (Cunneen 2003: 188). Interestingly, three of the four nations which voted against the adoption of the last-named declaration in the General Assembly in September 2007 were Canada, New Zealand and Australia.

Differences in Summary Form

The value prescriptions that make restorative practices distinctive are those that constrain its processes so that they adhere to certain procedural requirements and seek to maximize certain deliberative outcomes. It is convenient to have a shortform summary of these distinctive form, function and value differences, and Roche's (2003) prescriptions are useful for this purpose. Roche (2003) cites four core 'value prescriptions' of restorative practice – participation, personalism, reparation and reintegration.[16]

Participation

'Participation' refers to the encouragement of the persons most affected by the wrongdoing to involve themselves directly in resolving the harm caused. Participation encapsulates much of what has been said about the centrality given to 'restorative deliberation'. This participation is seen to ideally extend involvement to those affected so that they too can contribute to deciding how to deal with the aftermath of the offending (Roche 2003: 30). Restorative practice ideally promotes full participation above other forms of indirect involvement.

Personalism

'Personalism' denotes the perception that wrongdoing is first and foremost a violation of people and their relationships. The emphasis is that the focus of any justice response should be the *impact of that offending* on the victim, the offender, their families and the wider community. This emphasis contrasts with a criminal justice focus where 'the physical and emotional damage [that] crime does [may be] suppressed, if not completely ignored' (Roche 2003: 27). Restorative practice promotes personalism above perceptions of the offence as a public wrong.

Reparation

'Reparation' refers to the emphasis restorative practice places on repair, specifically on repair of the harm caused by wrongdoing. Its focus is on the identification and repair of harm, be it material, physical or emotional (including such harm as 'loss of dignity, happiness, confidence, security, personal power, and sense of self-worth') (Roche 2003: 27). This contrasts with the criminal justice focus on sanctions designed to provide normative repair. Restorative practice promotes reparation above sanctions as its means to express censure.

Reintegration

'Reintegration' refers to the focus in restorative practice of assisting offenders to rebuild ties with their community following wrongdoing (Roche 2003: 29). Restorative processes emphasize 'the responsibility of the wider community

16 Roche drew on Van Ness's (1993: 259) statement of 'the foundational principles of restorative justice' in drafting these prescriptions.

to ensure offenders are accepted and included' in order to promote community harmony and 'with an eye to prevent future offending' (Roche 2003: 29). This contrasts with criminal justice's sharper focus on punishment and rehabilitation. Restorative practice promotes opportunities for reintegration above a focus on punishment or on purely rehabilitative measures.

These four descriptors are used in this comparison as a simple means to highlight the distinctive qualities of restorative justice practice. Programs which manifest all four value prescriptions are those that strongly promote the particular restorative view as to how wrongdoing and the response to it should be conceptualized. It is to these processes that the evaluative criteria can now be applied.

Evaluating the Restorative Practice of Justice

This section considers the potential of restorative justice practice to meet various aspects of the evaluative criteria set in Chapter 3 in order to test the assumption that a sense of justice can be generated through restoration.

The Desert Standard

The desert standard measures justice by the extent to which people are treated according to what they deserve, so as to address the wrong done to them (in a sense of positive desert) or wrong done by them (in a sense of negative desert). In the negative sense, offenders are given what they 'deserve' in restorative processes primarily because they suffer the burden of their emotions being exposed in the presence of others during the encounter. Offenders who acknowledge their wrongdoing (even if only to themselves) leave open a wider range of painful emotions (founded primarily on feelings of self-indignation) than would be the case in mainstream criminal justice responses (Moore 1993: 13). Harris (2001) finds the mix of negative emotions created by this indignation to be a 'shame-guilt' combination and sees it characterized 'by feelings of having done wrong, concern that others had been hurt, feeling ashamed of oneself and one's act, feeling anger at oneself and [feeling a] loss of honor among family and friends' (extracted from Ahmed, Harris et al. 2001). This composite emotional burden can be overt or latent in the offender and can arise as a consequence of the internalized values, normative expectations and social context of the process just described. The activation of a desire to confront this emotional burden is one key to generating justice in a desert sense. Rather than simply allowing these emotional deserts to fester, the restorative process seeks to facilitate their disclosure in a way that may be emotionally painful yet one the wrongdoer is prepared to embrace (Harris 2001: 184; Braithwaite 2002c).

If this outcome is successful, offenders may then experience the benefit of positive desert where the process relieves them of some of their emotional burden through 'the removal or transformation of [their preexisting] shame'

(Zehr 2004: 310). It is the effect of this potential 'redemption ritual' that Maruna identified (2001, 2004) as giving offenders a sense of positive desert as a consequence of their own recognition of the harm they have done. It is by firstly shouldering and revealing their own deserved burden of shame/guilt that they can obtain in return a deserved relief from some of that burden through the integrative process (Braithwaite and Braithwaite 2001: 9–10; Harris 2001: 77).[17] The emotionally latent nature of the restorative encounter also provides a means for the burdens suffered by victims to be similarly addressed. Bringing together persons affected by wrongdoing to discuss its consequences can have an effect of restructuring the shame, anger and outrage which have been imposed on victims by the wrongdoing (Braithwaite 2002b: 74). The 'intentionally emotional' meeting can explore these emotional responses, firstly through looking back to expose the fullest possible truth of the details of the wrongdoing and by looking forward to ways in which to repair the physical, emotional and social harm caused by that wrong (Braithwaite 2002b: 251).

Retzinger and Scheff (1996) suggested that there is a crucial sequence of emotional stages required to activate this flow of deserved benefits to victims (Retzinger and Scheff 1996: 316). They saw a need at the outset to provoke the offender's own expression of shame and remorse so as to elicit positive rather than negative responses from the victim (1996: 316–317). In their view, the offender must be brought to the point of sharing and communicating his or her 'visible expression of shame' to the victim (1996: 321). This display is best provoked through 'refram[ing] displays of moral indignation against the offender' into some other form that will elicit the 'vivid expression of painful emotions' from the offender (1996: 321). Structuring the encounter in a way that gives victims first opportunity for their own 'expression of painful emotions' can provide this trigger. If this works, the victim's expression of emotion (even if it begins with outrage and anger) can provoke the expression of shame/guilt by the offender which, in turn, can act as the trigger for emotional repair to begin for all those affected by the wrongdoing.[18] It is through such a sequence outlined by Retzinger and Scheff that restorative justice practice can begin to release the

17 Reintegrative shaming provides one explanation of how this is done. The premise of reintegrative shaming is that social disapproval which is respectful and healing can prove more effective in harm reduction and restoration than stigmatizing shame (Braithwaite 1989).

18 Reservations have been expressed about shame as the assumed pathway to reintegration, particularly in relation to certain offences and offenders. These concerns have been most persistently expressed in relation to family violence offences and young women offenders (Alder 2000; Strang and Braithwaite 2002). In the case of family violence offending, there are concerns about how the power imperative that underlies such offending can be neutralized in a conference. In the case of young female offenders, a specific critique is that to assume a generic, rather than a gendered population may fail to consider the particular dimensions of acknowledging shame (even in a shaming process focused on reintegration) which confront young women (Alder 2000: 109).

burdens of negative emotions and engender the benefits of emotional repair. The process then can give persons affected by wrongdoing their 'positive desert' through relieving some of the emotional harm caused to them. The restorative encounter provides the forum in which to elicit these expressions of shame/guilt and remorse which the offender deserves to suffer. Their expression acts as the catalyst for the relief of some of the undeserved emotional burdens imposed on victims and so can provide them with a measure of positive desert. It is clear from this analysis that desert does have a part to play in restorative justice practice. As Ashworth (1998: 305) notes, meeting the desert measure is an aspiration restorative practice strives for when the question of 'decid[ing] how much damage has been done to the community and how it needs to be restored' is at issue. Ashworth states that some restorative justice writers (in his view, 'notably Van Ness') 'come close to embracing a desert-scale' by the use of 'degree measures', such as degrees of harm or degrees of culpability, as their 'metric' for determining the level of restoration required to address the harm caused (1998: 305).[19] But there are key differences as to how desert is managed in restorative practice. Unlike the 'authoritative model of deserved punishment' that more often characterizes a criminal justice approach, a restorative response has at its core a 'negotiated process between offender and victim [and others]' to arrive at a sanction (von Hirsch, Ashworth et al. 2003: 26). This negotiated process is seen as a discourse 'closer in certain respects to informal moral discourses in everyday life' (von Hirsch, Ashworth et al. 2003: 26). Its crucial effect is that the response is more reparative in focus and less directed towards delivering authoritative blaming. The affected persons 'brought together' are deliberately not armed with authority to express blame by means of sanctions or punishments and so the focus is not simply on satisfying the desert standard through penalty. The process deliberately excludes any 'right of victim allocution on the appropriate *retributive* sentence' with such determinations specifically left to be made elsewhere (Cavadino and Dignan 1997: 352, emphasis in original). The effect of this is a necessarily less overt focus on punishment and negative desert.[20] As a result, while restorative justice practice does have the potential to meet the desert standard of justice, most notably in terms of providing all persons affected with their positive deserts, its means of rendering justice is not focused on desert. The restorative process deliberately steps aside from a role

19 Interestingly, in Roberts's rewrite of the introductory section on 'restorative justice' in the third edition of the von Hirsch, Ashworth and Roberts (2009) *Principled Sentencing* collection, more common ground with restorative practice is recognized than previously. Restorative programs' potential 'to express some normative censure of culpable conduct' (2009: 166) and the advocacy by some of 'a middle ground, one which might invoke both retributive and restorative elements', is now acknowledged and accepted (2009: 171).

20 Victim allocutions in the form of victim impact statements are now common in a number of jurisdictions, and though these statements do not call for a particular sentencing outcome they attempt to affect sentencing outcomes (Kennard 1989; Booth 2005).

in the imposition of negative burdens in terms of punishment and thereby by definition has limited scope to give offenders their full deserts, in cases where they may be necessary in response to serious criminal wrongdoing.

The Equality Standard

The equality standard measures justice by the extent to which people are treated equally, with proportionate equality tempered so that actual treatment is equalized. Restorative practice has regard for this standard in a significant way. One summation of the intended focus of such practices indicates that their concern is 'with establishing or restoring actual equality and respect between particular persons in a given context following a particular set of actions or events' (Law Commission of Canada 2003: 120). Importantly, within this form of response there are overt attempts to address difference in terms of gender, race or class when seeking to frame just treatment (see Hudson 1998a, 1998b, 2000).

An issue which arises with this overt approach to equality is the degree to which restorative responses depart from considerations of proportionate treatment of offenders. Proportionality anchors the 'equal' treatment of offenders to align with their degree of culpability. By releasing this nexus between offenders and the degree of seriousness of their offending, restorative practice constitutes a significant realignment from the equality standard used in criminal justice. Victims and others affected are treated with 'equal concern and respect', with their 'entitlement to reparation [not] governed by the [relative] seriousness of the offence' (Cavadino and Dignan 1997: 352). This further uncoupling acknowledges that the impact of crime can extend well 'beyond the person formally noted in police records as the victim' but once again involves a substantial departure from traditional equality standards (Zedner 1994: 243). In the case of offenders, restorative practice openly acknowledges 'the social context of structural disadvantage in which many offenders act' and attempts to bring this background to bear in its response (Zedner 1994: 230). Such 'crafting' has given rise to claims of inconsistent treatment, which are critiqued as equality damaging (see Van Ness 1999: 274–277). Traditional proportionate responses have the benefit of matching the degree and form of sanctions to the gravity of the offence and the objective offender's culpability, and restoration departs from this. Attempts to substitute other bases such as 'restorative proportionality' (where the linkage is made with the degree of restorative effort required) or 'consequentialist anchors' (where the coupling is with the likely consequences of the sanction itself) run the risk of being neither generally workable in practice nor necessarily equality protecting in their effect (Braithwaite 2005).

Restorative practice may be better seen as aligned to parsimony than to equality (Braithwaite and Pettit 1990). Its response to 'equality of treatment' is to treat offenders of 'equal culpability given knowledge of [their] circumstances' the same, yet simultaneously avoid imposing 'a simplified sameness' in penalty (Hudson 1998b). In practice, this will likely mean wide departures from strict proportionality (see, for example, Tonry's (1994) suggestion of giving offenders who are severely socially disadvantaged credit for their past restraint from crime) with a focus on lesser penalty.[21] This 'individualized equality' which restorative practice seeks to deliver may in one sense be better off rejecting any notion that it is 'a requirement of [its] justice' to adhere to strict proportionality of treatment and instead find a different anchor for its responses (von Hirsch 1993: 6). The concern with this is that such an avowed departure would mean that sanctions were instead based on 'attitudes' or other 'non-offence' factors, and therefore clearly potentially equality defeating (Warner 1994). The best protection from this risk would be for restorative approaches to deliberately depart from a sanctioning role and focus instead upon providing reparative responses only (Braithwaite 1999a). Yet in other ways, restorative processes do accommodate equal treatment more directly by providing a voice for people who might otherwise have virtually none, particularly, it is said, women's voices. Daly's (1996) observational work on restorative conferences in Adelaide, Port Augusta and Canberra provides vivid evidence that conferences can become highly gendered events, in which female voices for once often predominate. She notes a significant female presence in conferences with the majority of non-offender attendees (victims and their supporters and offender supporters) being women (Daly 1996; see, too, Daly and Stubbs 2006: 15). Researchers in the Canberra RISE program reported similar patterns indicating that 'women's voices in restorative conferences are often extremely influential' (Braithwaite 2002d: 154). The same findings were seen in youth conferences in New Zealand, with Maxwell and Morris (1993: 292) concluding that they were 'places where women's voices are heard'. Alder (2000) was concerned that such voices may reinforce cultural restraints on the 'dissent' voice of a young female offender who has departed from acceptable female stereotypes by her offending. Daly's findings, however, suggests that 'female offenders [are] as self-assured as their male counterparts', and are seldom cowered or stereotyped in their participation (2008: 113). Restorative practices have similarly been seen to accommodate equality-promoting scope for indigenous voices. Sentencing circles in particular help to address 'important social justice aspirations of indigenous peoples searching for empowerment' (Braithwaite 2002d: 151). These aspirations are best addressed through tailored restorative processes, with 'restorative circles' managed and facilitated by indigenous providers. Restorative processes do have potential to meet the equality standard in ways that are different from traditional criminal justice responses, though at times nonetheless substantial. Restorative justice deliberately focuses on addressing individually needed benefits and burdens rather than on meeting strict proportionality requirements. While this is

21 A restorative approach might agree that parsimony is better served by abandoning discounting for guilty pleas, as Tonry (2004) suggests. He says that such discounts unfairly disadvantage black youth in the UK and USA who will not plea because the criminal justice system lacks legitimacy for them and as a consequence receive more severe penalties when convicted.

seen as a beneficial development, critics retain nagging doubts that discarding proportionality can mean that other sources of inequality will necessarily creep in. The internal protections that restorative approaches employ in the value prescriptions (together with an exclusion from the determinative sanctioning function) provide one means of ensuring that determinations of 'equal well-being' are 'created or achieved' by those who are direct participants in encounters rather than externally imposed (Sullivan and Tifft 1998: 40).

The Rights Standard

The rights standard measures the justness of a distribution in terms of the extent to which the distribution renews and protects the rights of all affected by wrongdoing. There are two main issues which arise with respect to the adherence of restorative processes to this standard. The first deals with the broader overriding issue of whether its processes adopt a rights-based approach to justice delivery in an overall sense. The second is concerned with how well restorative justice handles discrete aspects of procedural rights which necessarily must be afforded to offenders and victims in all stages of responses to criminal wrongdoing, including restorative procedures. With respect to the question of a 'rights-centred approach', restorative justice involves a departure from a strict approach in the way in which it determines distributions of benefits and burdens. The restorative focus on individualizing justice can run contrary to giving people their entitlements in a strict rights sense. Restorative practice does not accept the assumption, for instance, that 'differences and imbalances can [necessarily] be addressed by guarantees of sameness in treatment and procedural requirements' which a rights-centred approach implies (Law Commission of Canada 2003: 127). Restorative practice looks instead to outcomes that repair the harm done by wrongdoing and these may or may not be rights-focused. As a comparison, the adherence to a rights-based approach gives criminal justice the capacity to explicitly protect rights in its responses (as well as to give expression and recognition to rights more broadly through the law).[22] Clearly, restorative responses do not have this rights-creation capacity, but the concern expressed is that the protective function itself may also be absent at times. Zedner (1994: 249), for instance, conveys the fear that a combination of 'reparation' with 'retribution' (which he sees as representative of some forms of restorative practice) could act to 'recreate [and] … accentuate social inequality' and so violate rights. But restorative justice's notions of 'reparation' are clearly wider and not tied simply

22 Criminal justice can do this either under the general law or by legislative recognition given to specific social and economic rights in human rights instruments. See the ACT *Human Rights Act* of 2004, which has provision to add such rights, and the Victorian *Charter of Human Rights and Responsibilities Act* of 2006, which includes some provisions. More comprehensively, the South African Constitutional Court has developed a significant socioeconomic rights jurisprudence (Mokgoro 2009).

to the constraints of 'retribution'. Properly managed, its approaches are much more likely to accentuate and renew social rights, rather than curtail or erode them.

The second issue is restorative justice's capacity to protect specific procedural rights accepted as essential to ensure fair treatment in responses to wrongdoing. This concern has two aspects. The first is whether offenders are inadequately rights-protected when they are referred to or dealt with in restorative processes. The second concern is the protection of victims' rights. Braithwaite recognizes the concern that restorative practices 'can trample rights because of improvised articulation of procedural safeguards' (2002b: Chapter 5). He acknowledges this concern as potentially well founded but indicates that it could be addressed by 'a creative interplay between restorative forums and traditional Western courts' (2002b: 166). It is useful to examine the potential for this 'interplay' more closely. The 'constraining values' discussed earlier can bring into effect a range of protective mechanisms through its key 'respect for basic human rights' value. Adherence to internationally accepted standards is essential to provide the overriding 'moral framework through which we can assess and evaluate the behaviour' of all participants involved in restorative processes (Braithwaite 2002c: 253). If the standards are strictly adhered to, the externally prescribed moral framework can add content to fundamental notions of justice and ensure that procedural and substantive values of voluntariness, non-domination, accountability and appeal rights are properly recognized and respected. But there are strong concerns as to the adequacy of the protection this 'interplay' can provide. The argument is that fairness requirements make it essential to protect rights since restorative processes involve a form of 'imposition' on the offender (even if the 'imposition' is agreed or voluntary). As Cunneen suggests, calling for an acknowledgement of fault in itself can involve an 'imposition' (2003). It is obvious that such outcomes can result in 'dispositions that may deprive the offender of important interests' with regard to property or to his or her freedom to act and so are patently rights-invasive (von Hirsch, Ashworth et al. 2003: 27). There must therefore be clear limits in restorative processes 'to prevent violations of rights behind a mask of benevolence' (Ashworth 2002: 592). Van Ness sees these limits as operating in the best restorative processes. In a series of analyses, Van Ness (1996, 1999, 2003) examines the particular procedural rights which require protection and considers the ramifications of their non-adherence. Using a set of 'fundamental rights of persons accused or convicted of criminal offences' which he gleaned from both 'international accepted' and national instruments, Van Ness (1999: 266–269) identifies the rights most at risk of non-adherence in restorative processes:

1. the right to equal protection under the law
2. the right to freedom from degrading treatment or punishment
3. the presumption of innocence
4. the right to a fair trial
5. the right to counsel.

His conclusion is that in 'programs observing good practices' there is 'no reason to conclude that [these programs] will inherently result in due process violations' (1999: 270). Van Ness (2003: 170–171) suggests that abiding by a standard set of 'basic principles on the use of restorative justice', such as Braithwaite's (2002e) constraining values, can ensure that essential procedural rights seen as most at risk in restorative processes can be well protected.

There is also the issue concerning the protection afforded to victims' procedural rights. Claims have been made that victims are promised too much in terms of rights assertions in restorative justice. Ashworth (2002) argues that the protection and promotion of rights for victims in responses to wrongdoing have long been properly limited and that restorative justice guarantees unsafe departures from this constraint. In particular, Ashworth is concerned that giving 'substantive and procedural rights [to] victims at the stage of disposal (sentence)' is in itself justice defeating. Ashworth (1993: 281–282) says that in not adhering to these constraints, restorative practices blur the line between victims' legitimate 'rights to services' (support, assistance, state compensation and the like) and their illegitimate rights to participate in and influence 'the appropriate retributive sentence' (Cavadino and Dignan 1997: 352). The extension of rights to victims to be consulted on decisions to prosecute, on bail determinations, on acceptance of a plea, on submissions on sentence and the like, concerns Ashworth the most. He writes that the 'determination of what procedural rights (if any) victims should have' is never a matter solely related to victims' needs and desires, as restorative justice seems to imply (Ashworth 1993: 282). Instead, these determinative decisions should be calibrated against the rationale of the criminal process which of necessity will diminish the relevance of individual personal desires against community needs (von Hirsch, Ashworth et al. 2009). Ashworth's concern is that if restorative practice overemphasizes the deliberative priority of victims over society, justice will be ill served. The usual safeguard is to remove any unmediated determinative function from victims and put in place systems of accountability in the form of legal checks (the presence or availability of advocates during conferences, for instance) or judicial oversights (the requirement that restorative outcome agreement provisions be reviewed). These measures seem to be an effective constraint on the scope of the role given to victims, a constraint which Roche, for one, sees as essential in accountability terms (2003). Restorative justice does adhere to the rights standard in that its dealings with people involved in its processes are consistent with their rights entitlements. Provided its practices adhere to best practice protocols, there is a balanced articulation of procedural safeguards among offenders, victims and the affected community. Restorative justice does not assert a broader capacity to give expression and recognition to rights more generally in the way that legal justice clearly does, although it can use its commitment to individualizing just outcomes in ways that can positively reinforce rather than diminish rights.

The Relationships Standard

The relationship standard measures justice by the extent to which distributions promote relationships of social equality characterized by dignity, respect and concern. Measuring the justness of a response to wrongdoing in terms of its potential to contribute to harmonious social relationships is a standard with explicit restorative content. Restorative responses place direct emphasis on the effect of harmful behaviour on social and normative relationships (Llewellyn and Howse 1998). Such practices also recognize that individuals form social relationships of some kind with those they come into contact with, even when this arises from wrongdoing.[23] As such, its justice responses are concerned with repairing damage done to those relationships as much as possible (Luna 2003). This obligation to repair can usefully be conceptualized as a requirement to make 'atonement' for wrongdoing so as to reestablish preexisting 'relational harmony' (Garvey 1999). This does not mean that restorative processes themselves are 'harmonious' or without tension and distress, since the processes aim to explore aspects of necessarily unpleasant events and to give expression to negative emotions suffered as a result of that harm (Braithwaite 2002b: 251). Nonetheless, the focus of these processes is the collective censure that can begin the work of repair. It is through this catalyst that harmonious social relationships can begin to be reestablished. There remain difficulties with this approach, in that any apparent 'harmony' may be mistaken for unvoiced opposition or dispute. Ashworth (1998: 305) argues that giving prominence to notions of 'reassurance' as a feature of the restorative response overlooks the wider aspects of societal harmony which should be considered important in a response to wrongdoing. The 'reassurance' of a restorative perspective may be specific and contextual in providing places of safety for individual victims, but his concern is that this might mean that broader societal concerns such as restraints (through separation) on offenders' behaviour necessary to protect the broader community are potentially ignored. Ashworth (1998) argues that prioritizing narrowly conceived views of what 'harmonious social relationships' means runs the risk of dangerously downplaying the more pressing concerns of societal harmony (such as overall 'public safety'). There is also criticism that the assumption that 'having crimes dealt with through interaction between victim and offender' would by definition be more likely to produce personal or societal harmony, remains an essentially unexamined and untested assertion (von Hirsch, Ashworth et al. 2003: 24). Effective measures need to be in place to address these limitations. Some illustrations of these in a number of existing programs are reviewed in Chapter 8. An analysis of the checks and balances at work in these programs suggests that attempts to ensure 'harmony' can create outcomes which are both individually and socially beneficial.

---

23 Derksen (2009: 163) refers to the victim-offender 'trauma bond' which, until there is some resolution, can bind them 'together in an unfinished justice agenda'. See the effect the use of conferencing with imprisoned offenders can have in releasing these bonds for victims (Milner 2012).

Restorative justice has a high potential to meet the harmonious relationships standard as a direct consequence of its focus on repair. Its restorative encounters provide forums where movements towards such harmony can begin to develop out of the collective response.

Conclusion

This chapter firstly examined the restorative practice of justice in terms of its form, functions and values. It then investigated its justice potential assessed against the evaluative criteria, finding its strongest claims to justice in its potential to satisfy the harmonious social relationship criterion and, to a lesser degree, its ability to meet the equality standard in ways that more fully accommodate difference. It found that restorative practice has lesser potential to satisfy the rights standard and much poorer potential to meet the negative aspects of the desert criterion. Given these findings, it is not feasible to see restorative justice as a complete form of response in itself that has the capacity to provide ‘an overarching standard’ of justice in place of a criminal justice response (Schmidtz 2006: 17). The next chapter applies the same evaluative criteria to delve into the legal practice of justice. What it finds is largely the reverse – good potential to meet the desert and rights measures and to meet the equality standard in its emphasis on notions of formal equality. It also finds little commitment or capacity to meet the harmonious social relationships, although there is evidence in some jurisdictions of a developing therapeutic jurisprudence that embraces restorative principles prioritizing social harmony.

Chapter 6
Criminal Justice Practice: Is It Just?

Introduction

This chapter applies the justice evaluative criteria to criminal justice practice and considers whether its responses to wrongdoing are just when assessed against these measures.[1] Wrongful behaviour which has been criminalized constitutes a breach of the normative system of law. The criminal justice response is to use the coercive powers of the law to respond to the breach. At issue here is whether this response is just. The evaluative criteria provide one means to assess this. This chapter firstly examines the extent to which criminal justice compliance with the four justice standards is mediated by law's own internal commitments to the rule of law, to formal equality and to rights protection. On the face of it, these commitments should heighten adherence to the evaluative criteria, most obviously as regards the rights and equality standards. However, when critically explored the effect of these commitments is seen to have a number of deficiencies. While criminal justice is found to have sound potential to meet the desert and rights standards, it provides considerably less potential to meet the equality and harmonious social relationships standards. Criminal justice's strong emphasis on retribution means that it should deliver well on the need for negative desert. But its weak emphasis on restoration gives it less chance to distribute positive desert and more of a bias to imposing negative deserts. The strict formalization that the law brings to notions of equality and rights protection may mean that while these particular standards are explicitly addressed, the very formality of entrenched commitments can result in a closer adherence to the form than the substance of equality. Criminal justice has no intuitive concern with promoting harmonious social relationships, yet it is apparent from developments in sentencing jurisprudence in a small number of jurisdictions that an exposure to restorative forms of justice are starting to become influential.

---

1 The 'criminal justice process' referred to here is that which operates in modern Western legal systems. It fits best into Weber's 'formal-rational' category of systems of law. Weber's four-cell scheme differentiates systems of law as combinations of 'formal' or 'substantive' and 'rational' or 'irrational' (1947). In the formal-rational 'ideal-type' category, a legal system is based on courts making formal decisions according to laid-down rules which are both general in application and case-specific (see discussion in Hudson 2003a: 176).

The Normative Function of Law

Law has the capacity to conceptualize normative principles of approved or proscribed conduct into rule-like form and to then maintain and enforce adherence to these forms. It is in this way that law makes determinate the relatively unformed 'principles' which social or political processes may have proposed for what is hoped will be more effective reform or regulation (Murphy 2005: 18). In the case of responses to wrongdoing, the practice of law has the crucial capacity to coerce compliance with normative prescriptions by providing a means to determine culpability where non-compliance occurs and to impose sanctions where necessary to affirm rights and responsibilities (Fiss 1984: 19). It is in this context that the claim can be made that 'law is not *any* set of norms; [but] a system which [also] provides a method of settling disputes authoritatively' (Finnis 1980: 59, emphasis added). Law is often referred to as 'the law', with the definite article 'reflecting a sense of law looming large over society' and claiming normative supremacy over other forms of regulation (Laster 2001: 1). The suggestion implicit in this assertion is that while law may only be something 'made and remade by human beings in practices and traditions' (Sypnowich 1994: 77), once it is in place it can transcend its simpler origins and becomes 'higher and distinct' from other normative expressions (Davies 1999: 120). Alongside this coercive and normative role, law also has the broader role of setting 'the tone or background noise for private exchanges' (Tuebner 1998), even while it 'rarely intrude(s) into everyday conduct' in an overt sense (Campbell 1996: 255). Through its background presence, law shapes conduct by providing a source of stable expectations and by 'constitut[ing] forms of thinking' which then becomes commonplace currency for behaviour (Zipursky 2005: 135). In affecting conduct in this way, law may still sit alongside other means of social control (such as adverse social opinion, economic influences or external moral pressures) while always having the advantage of its own coercive force. Consequently, criminal justice responses to wrongdoing will always see wrongdoing first and foremost as a breach of its own normative constraints and will focus fundamentally on that breach of constraint in its response. The question here is whether this particular focus influences its capacity to deliver what are truly just outcomes.

What is claimed on behalf of law and justice is an interrelationship that principally delivers just outcomes. In its role as 'a device for ordering society' (Fuller 1964), law has broader functions to control human behaviour, resolve conflict, aid economic and social efficiency and ensure social and personal predictability. But even when carrying out these functions, law is seen to have the capacity to deliver justice whether by mediating state power or by protecting individuals against private exploitation. This provides an important reminder that to 'de-emphasise law may mean taking away the only resource the powerless have for achieving justice' (Parker 1999: 56). Whatever its failings, law retains an inbuilt capacity to promote justice precisely because it can 'explicate and give force to values … crystallised into legal doctrine'

(Fiss 1984: 1085).[2] But simply because the practice of law is referred to as 'legal *justice*' is an insufficient basis on which to say that justice 'simply exist[s] as [a consequence of the application of] law' (Davies 1999: 126). Certainly, there is an 'institutional edifice' that provides 'a critically important method of justice in certain situations ... [primarily] because it can coerce compliance' (Parker 1999: 49). However, merely saying that law delivers justice by enforcing 'formal and universal principles that define a context in which each person can pursue her or his personal ends' is not a sufficient basis on which to assert that law automatically 'does' justice (Young 1990: 121).[3] This highlights the need for a more accurate measure of the relationship between law and justice than merely an assumed presence. The evaluative criteria of justice provide one such alternative. To set the context, we first need to consider briefly the quality of the relationship between law and wrongdoing.

Law and Wrongdoing

In the specific context of responses to wrongdoing, law's coercive approach is most starkly evident. Law's primary focus when wrongdoing occurs is neither to address the wider harm done to victims and the community nor to consider the underlying causes of the wrongdoing. Instead, law principally addresses the normative breaches constituted by the wrongdoing and may inflict its own harm upon a wrongdoer in response to those breaches. Its 'just outcomes' may in fact serve to restore or reinforce preexisting disequilibria 'imposed on those already unfairly low on the scale of benefits and burdens' in socioeconomic terms (Goldman 1982: 61). The procedure of criminal justice is necessarily based around the need to establish criminal responsibility for normative breaches so that those breaches can be justifiably dealt with in a coercive way. The allegation of such a breach in practice gives rise to a 'charge', usually laid by police. As a consequence of this charge, the alleged offender appears before a court to have their criminal

2 At the same time, law's contribution to the promotion of justice by adapting society to social change seems sorely limited. Rosenberg found that the effect of US appellate decisions was of very limited use in achieving broad social change (1991). However, there are some more positive indications about the effect of legal intervention in producing behavioural change in discrete areas, such as with family violence offenders (see Lewis, Dobash et al. 2001). Particularly apposite here is Rudin's despair over the failure of restorative measures in Canadian legislation to address extreme levels of Aboriginal incarceration, 'If Aboriginal overrepresentation was a crisis in 1999, what terms can be applied to the situation today?' (Rudin 2008: 452).

3 A persisting question is whether the incorporation of alternative practices of justice (such as restorative justice) can add to both the quality and quantity of justice delivered in the criminal justice system. A well-established example of incorporating such ideas outside the criminal justice sphere is the use of 'cooperative compliance' strategies in the enforcement activities of the Australian Competition and Consumer Commission (ACCC) (see Yeung 2001; Parker 2004).

responsibility determined. Two distinct pathways then emerge. If criminal responsibility is accepted, a plea of guilty is usually entered and the offender is subject to a sentencing process which determines the form of response. Conversely, if criminal responsibility is denied (and for a large body of strict liability offences, such denial may not be feasible), culpability is determined through an adversarial process, sometimes in the form of a jury trial but more often in the form of a hearing before a single judicial officer. If culpability is established via this process, the offender is subject to the same sentencing procedure as for a plea of guilty. If culpability is not established, the offender is discharged or 'otherwise dealt with'.[4] It is therefore primarily within the sentencing part of this process that our focus on justice responses lies.[5]

Evaluating the Legal Practice of Justice

Its avowed 'justice performance' as a consequence of law's adherence to the 'ideological tripod' of the rule of law, 'formal equality' and 'rights protection' (West 2003: 8) is testable more objectively against the evaluative criteria.[6]

The Desert Standard

As we have argued, the desert standard measures justice by the extent to which people are treated according to what they deserve, both in a negative and positive sense. Applying this measure to distributions made in response to wrongdoing assumes that treating people in accordance with their deserts is the first requirement of justice (see MacIntyre 1985: 249). Recall that the desert standard measures justice by the extent to which people are treated according to what they deserve, so as to address the wrong done to them (in a sense of positive desert) or by them (in a sense of negative desert). 'Desert' provides the foundation of law's response to the offender. The wrongdoing proscribed by the criminal law does not necessarily equate to moral wrongdoing. Criminal law in many instances 'de-moralises' behaviour, so that what is right and wrong in legal terms is not necessarily equivalent to moral wrongness (Norrie 2005: 85). The result can be that the desert that is imposed in a criminal justice response

4 For instance, confinement for treatment if mental health issues are seen as the cause of the offending.

5 Certainly, there are strong justice considerations in the culpability-determining phase, but these are not strictly responses to (established) wrongdoing in the sense used here.

6 The division into three separate commitments is artificial since all three are aspects of the one core legal justice commitment to the 'rule of law'. It is clear that the 'rule of law' principle encompasses both 'the similar treatment of similar cases' (Raz 1975) and the 'protection of a regime of liberal individual rights' (Hutchinson and Monahan 1987).

may equate at times to being 'just deserts from one side, [and] social injustice from another', given the particular circumstances and background of the offender (Norrie 2005: 90). But desert is a measure which has clear resonance with criminal justice practice and is a standard which it has the potential to meet substantially, particularly in its negative sense. The criminal justice response may presume that desert necessarily equates to 'deserved punishment for the sake of justice' and so fail to embrace the need for positive desert as well to address the harm done (Sadurski 1985: 233). Nevertheless, recognizing this strong emphasis on negative desert (while acknowledging its scant attention to positive desert), criminal justice responses to wrongdoing have significant potential to meet the desert standard.

The Equality Standard

Recall that the equality standard measures justice by the extent to which treating people equally can provide them with a sense of justice. This standard says that in the case of responses to wrongdoing the harm-related benefits and burdens should be distributed in a way that satisfies this requirement. Actual proportionate equality may need to be tempered to take account of 'justifiable differences', in order to equalize the distribution of benefits and burdens (Stone 1980: 16). Equality is a measure which has clear resonance for criminal justice responses. The premise is that when responding to harmful conduct, treating offenders equally in a legal sense will mean 'treating [them] ... appropriately, given their circumstances and their offending patterns' such that justifiable differences in their background and offending behaviour are accommodated in the sanctions imposed (Hudson 2003a: 140). Similarly, in the case of those harmed by wrongdoing (either directly or normatively), treating people equally will mean acknowledging the harm done to them and allowing for the need to address differing levels of impact from that harm. Criminal justice's internal commitment to the 'rule of law' (in its simplest sense, meaning fidelity by the judiciary and the executive to existing 'rules' of law) is seen as the first basis for this implicit suggestion that the law treats everyone equally.[7] Waldron's (2000: 1) more comprehensive list of the principles and ideals referred to collectively as 'the rule of law', such as 'the subjection of government and state to law', the importance of 'legal predictability', the requirements of 'due process', the idea of 'one law for all' and the ascendancy of law over 'controversial ideologies' all suggest a single overriding purpose of maintaining law's predictability, consistency and independence so that all people

7 The literature speaks of 'thin' or 'thick' versions of the rule of law. In its 'thin' version, the rule of law represents the minimum adherence required to avoid the tyranny of the sovereign or of the majority satisfied by regular compliance with clear, general and validly enacted rules. If the content of those rules is morally sound so much the better, but this is not essential (Dyzenhaus 2003). By comparison, the 'thick' version of the rule imposes more detailed obligations of deeper pervasiveness and particularity such that there is a stronger element of moral soundness.

are treated the same.[8] This internal principle of 'one law for all' does suggest a strong resonance with the equality standard. Even reading the rule narrowly to simply mean 'judicial fidelity to law' imposes obligations of consistency and predictability which on the face of it aid equal treatment.

Nonetheless, there are persistent critiques that legal justice processes are not equality-enhancing after all. Critical legal scholars have long argued that the rule of law imposes obligations of fidelity that are simply unworkable and thereby defeating of law's equality-treating assertions. Both Unger and Singer agree that the very indeterminacy of legal rules makes it impossible to fulfill the obligation of judicial fidelity in the sense of excluding all other reasons for decision-making (Unger 1975; Singer 1984). They argue that what judges actually do is 'some admixture of will and reason, of passion and disinterest, of discrimination and discernment, and of judgment and deduction', none of which equates to strict rule fidelity or gives the promise of equal treatment before the law (West 2003: 23). Posner (1990: 73) is more disparaging still, describing legal reasoning as 'a grab bag that includes anecdote, introspection, imagination, common sense, empathy, imputation of motives, speaker's authority, metaphor, analogy, precedent, custom, memory, "experience" intuition, and induction'. If the notion that it is not possible to 'carve out a pristine space for the law to operate' free from other influences on decision-making gains currency (West 2003: 24), this leaves serious doubts as to whether the rule of law can really work to promote equal treatment. If all that the best legal rules do is 'under-determine the decision' (Leiter 2001: 295), what claims does law have other than fidelity to legal rules for claiming that its outcomes necessarily treat people equally?

The other potential equality-protecting feature of legal justice response is its focus on checking the excesses of private power (Hobbes 1996; West 2003: 34–43). Hobbes saw law as 'the positive edicts of a sovereign authority' designed more to protect citizens from a state of 'no law', in which the violent propensities of individuals would hold sway (1996: Chapter 17). Law in this sense does constrain the consequences of private lawlessness which would otherwise lead to violence, forceful subordination and unequal treatment (West 2003: 38). In Rawls's view, the Hobbesian thesis is feasible because, 'although men know that they share a common sense of justice and that each wants to adhere to the existing arrangements, they may nevertheless lack full confidence in one another's compliance'; therefore, law provides some compliance certainty (Rawls 1971: 240). Law provides a surer footing by securing from private domination certain entitlements to non-interference (West 2003: 41). The 'value' of law in these terms is that it can ensure that private

8 The law is often seen as a 'fragile body of principles and ideals' (Waldron 2000: 4), but with such fragility tempered by the development of principles to explicitly support the ideal of law in particular, distinct circumstances. In the case of the criminal law, for instance, the rule of law is supported by principles of the presumption of innocence, the privilege against self-incrimination, the requirement of proof beyond reasonable doubt and trial by an impartial and open tribunal according to fair procedures (Cowdery 2006).

interactions will not be the product of force or undue influence. In his American Revolution pamphlet *Common Sense* (1995), Thomas Paine expressed the value of law in this fashion in his famous dictum that 'In America, the Law is the King'. If a criminal justice response to wrongdoing can act to protect people from private vengeance by subjecting offenders to rules of restraint, then this provides a sounder basis for asserting its potential to meet the equality standard. Law's own notion of equality expressly makes a commitment to such a 'like treatment of like cases'. Rawls suggests that 'this precept that similar cases be treated similarly [alone] ... does not take us very far', unless 'the criteria of similarity are given by the legal rules themselves and the principles used to interpret them' (1971: 237–238). But arming people with the certainty of like treatment has the potential to allow them 'to establish for themselves [their own] greatest equal liberty' (Rawls 1971: 240). The basis on which 'treating like cases alike' is said to be justice-promoting in this sense is because of the certainty it provides (Posner 1990). In Posner's view, this capacity to benefit from certainty of treatment should be universal, unrelated to gender, race or class (although initial opportunity to make meaningful choices is clearly influenced by such factors). The formal equality of law will reinforce this certainty, so that any bargain entered into should be enforced and protected within existing law. Rawls argues that by minimizing the threat of uncertainty in this way, law does maximize the risk people are prepared to take in exercising their capacity for choice which can be equality-enhancing (Rawls 1971: 237). But this assumption rests on the shaky premise that it is in fact possible to 'treat like cases alike'. Assuming that a process of reasoning by analogy will assign any seemingly novel 'case' so that it is 'subsumed within yesterday's settled practice' can be fraught (West 2003: 119). There are strongly divided views about the usefulness of analogical reasoning itself. Sunstein (1992) argues that analogical reasoning has distinctive properties that aid principled consistency, but Posner dismisses it as being at best part of 'an unstable class of desperate reasoning methods' (1990: 86).[9] More importantly, the core difficulty with the 'like treatment of like cases' approach is, as Holmes (1918) argued, that it is simply not logically possible to reason purely by analogy. Any 'novel' case does not in fact 'fall' into a predetermined legal category, but needs to be first 'placed' there based on some means. Any such means of legal placement is necessarily based on a preference for one point of comparison above another. This preferment can never be neutral but will always be the product of commitments, values or prejudices that are 'political, cultural or moral but decidedly non-legal' (West 2003: 124).[10] The result is that the selection method of preferment in fact treats people differently rather than equally, solidifying all the while the perceived 'normalcy' of the particular worldview on which the selection was based. People may have been treated the same from the perspective

9 Farrar provides a critical review of this literature in his article 'Reasoning by Analogy in the Law' (1997) and his more recent presentation of the same title (2009).

10 For a recent strong defence of the process of analogical reasoning, see Weinreb (2005).

of that worldview, but the preferment is based upon a narrow criterion and will of necessity produce a very limited form of equality (Littleton 1987). 'Treating like cases alike' in this way therefore does not have an acceptable basis on which 'likeness' can be expanded to include 'otherness'. At its extreme, law's formal equality of 'treating like cases alike' offers no necessary moral gain over simply *ad hoc* decision-making. This is a somewhat circuitous way to arrive at a view about whether criminal justice practice's internal commitment to formal equality does equate to equal treatment in the sense of meeting the equality standard. The law seeks to ensure that the principles embodied in its legal rules are enforced equally by adherence to certain commitments. But its potential to actually meet the equality standard is significantly diminished by the distance between the artificiality of its notions of equal treatment and the substantive equality called for by justice.

The Rights Standard

The rights standard measures the justness of a distribution by the extent to which it has 'regard for the rights of all it affects substantially' (Vlastos 1970: 60). 'Rights' in this sense are 'normatively protected interests' which give the holder the capacity to compel or constrain somebody or some action because they 'would be wronged if denied that something' (Finnis 1980: 205). The rights standard measures the justness of a distribution in terms of the extent to which the distribution renews and protects the rights of all affected by wrongdoing. Criminal justice responses appear to measure well against this standard because the law gives primacy to a set of rights designed to preserve and protect individual freedoms. It does so by providing a formal enforcement structure, enabling reliance on the power of normal social pressures or 'ties of affection' to be supplemented when necessary (Waldron 1992). The conception of rights that legal justice supports assumes a need to 'preserve and protect' individual freedoms and restrict encroachments on aspects of those freedoms. The institutionalizing in law of specific positive rights (to free speech, to the exercise of religion, to privacy and to property) provides one means to protect and guarantee this individual autonomy from public and private interference. When there is interference with these rights, the assumption is that the law is there to provide its remedy to address that interference (West 2003: 72).

In his consideration of Bentham's (1824) famous dismissal of rights as 'nonsense on stilts', Waldron traces a shift in the source of legal rights from one based purely on 'natural rights' to views that move beyond 'mere truths' about human nature (1987: 163). Waldron suggests that the firmer foundation for rights justifying 'these irksome requirements' is now widely recognized as being because rights are explicitly justice-enhancing (1987: 163). Rights seen in such terms do not arise purely from the *fact* of being human, but are articulated because human beings deserve to be treated justly and that treating them in a manner consistent with their rights achieves justice. This is a view that Rawls shares when he argues, 'each person possesses an inviolability founded on justice' rather than on their humanness (1971: 3–4). If this foundation is accepted, then there are certain 'rights secured by justice' which need to be upheld and it is law that provides the means. This formulation strongly suggests that the rights protection powers of the law are justice-enhancing. The question remains, how effective is legal justice in providing this protection? Tushnet (1984) argues that giving rights 'legal' form is not automatically an effective means of their protection since personal rights encapsulated in legal form can have the counterintuitive effect of limiting the state's authority to protect freedoms. This may mean that at times the state cannot do what is required to secure the necessary preconditions for justice. Tushnet's argument is that in order to secure the minimal preconditions of the good society for all, the state will need to violate the equal application of rights in some instances. Providing legal protection for rights may result in the state being robbed of its capacity for the positive (but unpopular) action necessary to promote just distributions.[11] Additionally, by curtailing state intervention, legally enforced rights may act to entrench private inequalities and provide 'in effect, a privilege to exploit others' (West 2003: 77). In this way, the negative operation of legal rights may disguise or give scope to private abuses which become sites of injustice (Glendon 1992: 520–523). Kennedy (2002: 110) argues that 'the legal formulization of rights and the establishment of legal machinery for their implementation makes the achievement of these forms an end in itself' and leaves the actuality of rights and justice unmet or constrained. There is, of course, no logical reason why legal rights could not be fashioned to avoid this outcome. For instance, in West's view, giving rights positive legal form (such as welfare rights, education rights, environmental rights,'relational rights' or civil and political rights[12]) has the potential to both protect existing freedoms and at the same time 'goad the state, in the name of justice, to govern toward the end of creating the good society' (2003: 89). The law can provide the institutional means of legitimizing, protecting and enforcing such positive rights. Legal rights do constitute an effective coercive mechanism to support claims of rights in situations where communal attachments have been breached or are not yet established. If legal justice can realize its potential for rights enforcement so that rights 'can be relied on to survive as a basis for action no matter what happens to [communal] attachments' (Waldron 1992: 379), justice interests are well met. The protection of rights by their legal enforcement in criminal justice proceedings

11 The constraints that a strict rights adherence focus could place on certain forms of 'positive discrimination' such as equal opportunity employment schemes are an obvious example.

12 'Civil and political' rights are those most often protected in legislation. See, for instance, the Canadian *Charter of Rights and Freedoms* of 1982, the ACT *Human Rights Act* of 2004 and the Victorian *Charter of Human Rights and Responsibilities Act* of 2006. But pressure exists to extend the range of rights protected legislatively in some jurisdictions to include economic, social, cultural and environmental rights (as is the case in Chapter 2 ('Bill of Rights') of *the Constitution of the Republic of South Africa* of 1996, the United Kingdom *Human Rights Act* of 1998, and Part 3A of the ACT *Human Rights Act* of 2004).

means that there is a high potential for the rights standard of justice to be delivered. This is qualified by the need to ensure that the legal enforcement of rights protects their substance and not just their form.

The Relationships Standard

The relationships standard of justice measures the performance of justice by the extent to which distributions in response to wrongdoing promote restoration of 'relationships of social equality characterized by equal dignity, respect and concern'. Measuring the justness of a distribution by this standard is consistent in some respects with law's emphasis on ensuring that 'each person [realizes his or her] sovereign interest to the greatest extent possible' within the constraint of what the law permits (Reiman 1990: 82). But historically there has been very little to suggest that actively seeking to maintain or restore social relationships in response to wrongdoing has been of any real concern of criminal justice. There is, however, some evidence of change in this regard in those jurisdictions which have had more sustained exposure to the principles of restorative approaches (most notably New Zealand and Canada, and to a lesser extent South Africa[13]) and which have attempted to accommodate a concern for promoting social harmony as a consequence.

Broadly speaking, elements of the form of retributivism favoured in criminal justice embrace the idea that paying the penalty for wrongdoing leads the wrongdoer to 'restoration' in the sense of readmittance into society in a way that could arguably be seen as promoting social harmony. For example, some justifications for inflicting punishment in proportion to desert are that it treats morally responsible wrongdoers with dignity and respect and leaves open to them (at least in the abstract) their potential for a full return to society. Separate from this direct influence on individual wrongdoers, legal decisions can send a self-regulatory message to a broader audience so that these decisions are capable of maintaining general harmonious social relationships on a much wider scale. Dworkin suggests that simply by carrying its 'familiar moral judgments and principles into ... practice' (2000: 4), legal justice acts to 'quell controversies' caused by wrongdoing through 'the application of the law', and that this in itself gives law a wider, harmonizing effect.[14] But save for these relatively scant indications, the law's primary focus has not been with 'harmonization'. It has not concerned itself with reestablishing individual social relationships following wrongdoing (indeed, if we accept Foucault, 'law is not [in fact about] pacification ... for beneath the law, war continues to rage in all the mechanisms of power' (2003: 51)). It is all the

13 See Skelton (2013).

14 'Quelling controversies' was the High Court of Australia's view of the purpose of law in *D'Orta-Ekenaike v Victoria Legal Aid* [2005] 223 CLR 1 (para. 43). In a dissenting voice, Kirby J reminded the court that 'controversies must nonetheless be "quelled" justly' (para. 225).

more interesting to see inroads of principles which prioritize restoration of social relationships into the criminal sentencing jurisprudence.

Conclusion

A primary focus of criminal justice responses to wrongdoing is on repairing 'the tear in the normative fabric' brought about by wrongdoing. This is a different focus entirely from the restorative justice focus of repairing personal or individual harm. That difference has directly impacted criminal justice's potential to promote justice in terms of each of the evaluative criteria. Criminal justice favours distributions of deserved benefits and burdens which impose negative desert on the wrongdoer. It favours treatment which deals with people equally in a formal way but one which may negate substantive equality. It favours treatment that respects people's rights in a way that has much stronger potential to promote just outcomes. Overall, its strongest potential to deliver justice is its adherence to the desert and rights measures, and to a lesser extent its commitment to notions of formal equality. Although traditionally there has been little commitment to shift its focus away from only promoting normative harmony to more explicitly promoting harmonious social relationships, there is evidence of a developing sentencing jurisprudence in some jurisdictions which suggest a new preparedness to consider principles and practices that address relational aspects of offending. If it is accepted from the reviews in Chapter 5 and this chapter that neither legal nor restorative conceptions of justice has the capacity to provide 'an overarching standard to which the others [must] reduce' when responding to wrongdoing, something further seems called for (Schmidtz 2006: 17). Each form of response may have a clear aspirational reach towards different standards, but there is something of an enticing complementarity that suggests they could work together. If criminal justice is the 'semi-autonomous institution' (Moore 1978) it is said to be with an avowed capacity to enlarge its justice capability through 'borrowings' (Norrie 2005: 81), might not restorative justice be one such potential borrowing with much more to offer than merely being 'borrowed'? There are two common law jurisdictions where there is real and sustained evidence of this occurring. Chapter 7 examines the developing restorative jurisprudence in these two countries – New Zealand and Canada.

Chapter 7
Developing Restorative Justice Jurisprudence

Introduction

This chapter considers developments in criminal sentencing jurisprudence in a number of jurisdictions (predominantly New Zealand and Canada) to gauge the influence of an exposure to restorative justice principles and practices on the criminal law's response to wrongdoing. Jurisprudence (generally, but more specifically here in response to criminal wrongdoing) develops essentially from a combination of legislative provisions as to sentencing, and the general law developed in judicial sentencing decisions dealing with offenders which consider those provisions and general principles in practice. The expression, development and critique of this combination constitutes the 'jurisprudence' of sentencing, which produce a set of principles that perform both the practical and 'symbolic function[s] of pronouncing on the wrongness of the behaviour with which [courts] deal' and facilitating a coherent form of response to that behaviour (Hudson 2002: 628). Traditionally, criminal justice jurisprudence had prioritized retributive elements designed to provide an 'authoritative condemnation of the class of behaviours' proscribed by the criminal law (Hudson 2002: 629) and as such were more likely to 'disgorge [primarily] retributive responses' (Bowen and Boyack 2003: 6). This focus expanded to include addressing desired consequential outcomes, particularly rehabilitation and prevention. But there has been little focus on meeting restorative aims or contributing to providing justice in any relational sense. A small number of jurisdictions have responded to this deficiency and begun to give scope to both the restorative aims and the relational aspects of justice. In the process, its courts have pointed the way to how these distinctive justice aspects might be accommodated within existing jurisprudence.

Towards a Restorative Jurisprudence

Restorative jurisprudential developments can be traced in any significant way to only two jurisdictions – New Zealand and Canada. In New Zealand, the then small-scale use of restorative responses to wrongdoing in its criminal courts was judicially approved by the New Zealand Court of Appeal in 1998 in the decision of *R v Clotworthy* [1998] 15 CRNZ 651 (CA). The '*Clotworthy* principle' which developed from this decision gained some judicial currency and came to be applied in ways that marked a clear departure from existing judicial approaches. Similar in many respects is the Canadian experience, where the 1999 Supreme

Court decision in *R v Gladue* [1999] 1 SCR 688 saw certain parts of otherwise apparently 'neutral' national sentencing legislation being interpreted to mandate consideration of restorative requirements. In a like manner, the '*Gladue* principle' promised the adoption of restorative principles and a much wider departure from traditional sentencing jurisprudence. Judicial reluctance to adopt the principles as fully as anticipated saw the *Gladue* principle revisited in a 2012 'sequel' in *R v Ipeelee* [2012] 1 SCR 433.

In the case of other jurisdictions, there is both an absence of mandatory requirements to give consideration to restorative approaches and the absence of a single guiding jurisprudential response to restorative practice similar to *Clotworthy* or *Gladue*. In Australia, this can partly be explained by the absence of national sentencing legislation, and partly because most restorative practices operating in the Australian jurisdictions deal only with juvenile offenders and so produce fewer appellate decisions. Two pathways of response are discernible in individual Australian state or territory legislative reforms. The first is a minimalist approach where 'restorative aims' are added to sentencing principles and implicitly allow for the possibility of wider sentencing aims being delivered by ways other than through punitive means. The second, more substantive approach explicitly permits the use of 'restorative processes' as a means to address some of the 'relational requirements of justice'. In early pilots of restorative conferencing in the United Kingdom, a number of appeal court decisions, notably *R v Collins* [2003] EWCA Crim 1867 made reference to the offender's attendance at a conference, saying that this was 'a factor properly to be taken into account' on sentencing (para. 7). This principle was noted with approval in two subsequent cases, *R v Barci* [2003] ECWA Crim 2816 and *R v O'Brien* [2004] EWCA Crim 2572. However, following the cessation of the pilot programs any principle that participation in a restorative encounter 'before sentencing can provide evidence of mitigation that should normally reduce the length of imprisonment' (Sherman and Strang 2007: 13) was not revisited. There is no evidence that this has developed further in any substantial jurisprudential way, with only minor references in caselaw to 'restorative principles' or 'restorative remedies'.[1]

Each of the Australian states and territories has sentencing legislation potentially capable of accommodating restorative responses to varying degrees. However, other than relatively incidental remarks in sentencing decisions there is in no sense a developing restorative jurisprudence. This in large measure is due to the absence of mandatory requirements in any of the jurisdictions requiring courts to take account of such approaches. The NSW Court of Criminal Appeal in *R v Qutami* [2001] NSWCCA 353 gave some initial promise in a Crown appeal against the adequacy of a sentence for solicitation to murder (where the planned arrangements did not eventuate). In reviewing the original sentence, the Court of Appeal recognized that:

1 A *Westlaw International* database search of 'restorative justice' in UK caselaw discloses 36 references, all relatively minor.

> Over recent decades the issue of restorative justice has been of considerable and growing significance in discussions about the operations of the criminal justice system … The role of victims has also been given more weight in matters of sentencing. This has included questions of empowering the victims in a restorative context such as conferencing. Attention has also been given to the significance of reintegrating offenders into their communities, including smaller communities such as extended families. (para. 74)

A similar anticipation was given in *R v Seet* [2001] 2 DCLR (NSW) 192 in an assault sentencing matter where the court noted 'practices and facilities growing for restorative justice', saying, 'Hopefully, there will be opportunities in this jurisdiction in appropriate cases for such a path to be followed in appropriate cases' (para. 24). Sadly, this hope has not been borne out. The only jurisdiction in which there has been any development is in a series of cases involving environmental damage. In *Environment Protection Authority v Waste Recycling and Processing Corporation* [2006] NSWLEC 419, the NSW Land and Environment Court considered this in a case of toxic pollution from a waste disposal landfill which had killed most of the aquatic life in a creek area. In a passage that in many respects reflects the need to address retributive, restorative and consequential aims, the judge stated:

> In sentencing for environmental crime, the court ought take into account such [polluter pay] considerations in selecting the types and the severity of sentencing orders. In so doing, the court better achieves, first, retributive aims by ensuring the sentence is proportionate to the objective gravity of the offence, the offender is adequately punished and the conduct of the offender is denounced; secondly, deterrence aims by deterring the offender and other persons from committing similar offences which cause or are likely to cause environmental harm; and thirdly, restorative aims by achieving restoration of the environmental harm and reparation for the environmental harm caused. (para. 23)

In a further decision, that of *Garrett v Williams* [2007] NSWLEC 96 involving damage and disturbance to a large number of Aboriginal artefacts through mining operations, the court recommended the defendant participate in a restorative conference with representatives of affected Aboriginal communities. The outcome report detailed steps to foster indigenous employment opportunities in the affected remote community (para. 63). In considering whether 'the fact and the results of the restorative justice intervention can be taken into account in this sentencing process' (para. 64), the court held that contrition and remorse were retributive aims that could be met by restorative outcomes of apology and reparation. However, that court's sentencing jurisprudence has not developed further in this direction.[2]

2 A *Westlaw International* search of Australian jurisdiction for 'restorative justice' produces approximately 80 responses, but all of these are relatively incidental and provide no indication of a developing restorative jurisprudence.

Skelton (2013: 123) derives the origins of fledgling but more significant developments of restorative jurisprudence in South African courts to the connection its Constitutional Court has drawn between traditional African customary notions of *ubuntu* (formally acknowledged in the epilogue to its post-apartheid 1993 Interim Constitution), with its emphasis on 'the virtues of … dignity in social relationships and practice' (citing Mokgoro 1998: 17) and the need for both wider societal and individual reconciliation. She traces this in civil proceedings with the court's development and expansion of the common law concept of 'meaningful engagement', firstly in housing and eviction law in a series of cases including *Port Elizabeth Municipality v Various Occupiers* [2005] (1) SA 217 (CC), *Occupiers of 51 Olivia Road, & 197 Main Street v City of Johannesburg* [2008] (3) SA 208 (CC), *Residents of Joe Slovo Community, Western Cape v Thebelisha Homes* [2010] (3) SA 454 (CC) and *Abahladi Basemjondolo Movement SA & Sibusiso Zikode v The Premier of the Province of Kwazulu-Natal* [2010] BCLR 99 (CC) (Skelton 2010, 2013). The effect of these judicial developments is that meaningful engagement in the sense of a new procedural requirement for pre-litigation mediation before eviction proceedings 'has become central to the application of eviction law in South Africa' (Skelton 2013: 132). In defamation proceedings, the Constitutional Court similarly introduced procedural requirements for mandated apology initially through the influence of two minority decisions of Mokgoro J and Sachs J in *Dikoko v Mokhatla* [2006] SA 235 (CC) (*Dikoko*), wherein Sachs J specifically promoted apology in terms of *ubuntu* 'as a concept highly consonant with the rapidly evolving international notions of restorative justice' (Skelton 2013: 134). The majority of the Constitutional Court subsequently endorsed this view in *Le Roux and Ors v Dey* [2011] (3) SA 274 (CC), with the court saying, 'it is time for our Roman Dutch common law to recognise the value of this kind of restorative justice' (para. 197). However, concerns have been expressed that the procedural ordering of apology (an order made in subsequent defamation proceedings of *The Citizen 1978 (Pty) Ltd and Ors v McBride* [2011] (4) SA 191 (CC)) in fact robs the apologetic behaviour of its restorative flavor, given that 'the moral power of an apology will be destroyed if an offender is placed under any form of coercion to apologise' (Doak 2011: 444). Nevertheless, these are significant steps towards restorative principles in South African civil law. Restorative justice developments in the criminal law have been comparatively more modest and still somewhat short of 'infus[ing its] sentencing with restorative justice thinking' (Skelton 2013: 142). Restorative justice has been raised in sentencing offenders most particularly in fraud matters. In *S v Saayman* [2008] 1 SACR 393 (E), a requirement (redolent of an Australian conferencing proposal for a young man to wear an 'I am a thief' t-shirt) that the accused stand on the court steps holding a placard bearing an apology and seeking forgiveness was rejected by the High Court which specifically referred to the minority decision of Sachs J in *Dikoko* when stating, 'if restorative justice is indeed to make a significant contribution to sentencing options then it must be applied only in appropriate circumstances and must be developed in a constitutionally acceptable manner' (per Pickering J at p. 13). In a further fraud matter of *S v M* [2007] 2 SACR 539 (CC), a term of imprisonment which had been set aside in a High Court appeal and substituted with by a period of correctional supervision (which nonetheless required some eight months' initial jail time) was replaced by the Constitutional Court with a restitution order, community service and counseling requirements. In the majority decision Sachs J was not critical of the substitution of correctional supervision in lieu of the full time jail, saying it showed 'a multifaceted approach to sentencing comprising elements of rehabilitation, reparation and restorative justice' (para. 59) but he took the view that the statutory prerequisite for jail time was inappropriate. The application of restorative principles in these cases is, as Skelton (2013: 143) says, heartening, giving signs of 'a uniquely South African brand of restorative justice'. However, its 'brand' does not as yet equate to encounters in the 'fully restorative' sense of the McCold and Wachtel (2003) typology.

New Zealand Jurisprudence

The Clotworthy Principle

The decision in *Clotworthy* provided a strong guiding principle on restorative justice in New Zealand.[3] The case involved an unprovoked attack during which a drunken offender slashed the victim's face with a knife and stabbed him six or more times in the chest and stomach. The attack caused life-threatening injuries and permanent facial scarring. The offender pleaded guilty and the court delayed sentencing in order to allow the defendant's request to participate in a restorative justice conference facilitated by a community-based group. A report of that conference was considered by the judge (before sentencing). The sentencing decision referred to this:

> The main emphasis of submissions today have been for me to consider the implications of the restorative justice conference. In a rare and almost

3 *R v Clotworthy* includes a first instance sentencing decision in the District Court at Auckland (Thorburn J 1998) and a Crown appeal (Court of Appeal of New Zealand 1998). Prior to *Clotworthy*, a series of lower court sentencing decisions had begun to introduce restorative approaches into sentencing practice beginning in about 1995. These included *R v Symon* [1995] Unreported High Court Auckland S64/95 (Tompkins J) which involved a street robbery where a referral was suggested by the judge for a conference 'generally described as restorative justice' (Thorburn 2005: 5); *R v Taparau & Ors* [1996] NZDCR 774 (a serious assault on police); *Police v Currie* [1996] NZDCR LEXIS 8 (a shaken baby syndrome assault); *R v Murphy* [1996] Unreported District Court Auckland S151/96 (Hansen J) (a kidnapping at knife point); *R v Miskea* [1996] Unreported District Court Auckland, CR No. 5204003944-45 (McElrea J) (an assault with a knife) and *R v Akurangi* [1997] Unreported District Court Otahuhu CRN 60040709-2-7 (Mather J) which involved an assault. An illustration of how these developments were judge-driven is evident in *R v Akurangi* where the judge said to defence counsel, 'I would like to see the possibility of some restorative justice initiative being undertaken in this matter' (Bowen and Consedine 1998: 143).

> unbelievable communication from the victim, it is clear that he does not see any benefit for society, himself or for the prisoner in a sentence of imprisonment. ([1998] Unreported District Court Auckland T.971545 (Thorburn J) (para. 4))

The judge was of the view that the relative seriousness of the offence did warrant a term of imprisonment of two years (which legislation provided was the maximum period that could then be suspended). The then operative *Criminal Justice Act 1985* (NZ) required the judge in cases of serious violence offences to impose a full-time custodial sentence, unless otherwise satisfied that there were 'special circumstances' to depart from this (s.5). The judge reached the view that the outcome of the conference did provide such 'special circumstances' and so suspended the sentence of two years, imposed a community service order and a reparation order of $15,000 intended to facilitate plastic surgery for facial scars ($5,000 had been paid at the time of sentence and an installment order was made for the balance). The judge made specific reference to the statutory purposes of sentencing, saying that 'for the prisoner before this court, the issue of deterrence is almost non existent ' (para. 7) and thus, 'the only purpose served in this particular case by an unsuspended sentence of imprisonment, would be to satisfy that perceived community need for the court to be punitive' (para. 9). At the time the decision was reached there were no specific restorative purposes of sentencing, save that the provisions of the *Criminal Justice Act* required courts to explore 'reparation' possibilities (s.11), to take into account any offer of compensation and to consider whether such offer had 'been accepted by the victim as expiating or mitigating the wrong' (s.12). These provisions were read in a restorative light by the sentencing judge. The prosecution appealed the decision on the basis that a non-custodial sentence was an inadequate response to such serious offending. The New Zealand Court of Appeal considered the sentence imposed and reached the view that the sentencing judge had erred, saying that 'by no process could the appropriate starting point [of penalty] properly have been reduced to a sentence of 2 years imprisonment so as to permit suspension' (at p. 654). The court set the starting point instead at five years, the effect of which was to mandate a custodial sentence. Applying the existing s.12 considerations, the court was of the view that 'substantial weight should be given to this dimension, in particular because Mr Cowan [the victim, who had addressed the Court of Appeal] was prepared to accept that offer as expiating the wrong' (at p. 660). As a consequence, the court reduced the period of imprisonment substantially from five to three years. Because the offender was as a consequence sent to jail immediately, the court also reduced the reparation order to the $5,000 already paid. In an oft quoted passage, the Court made these comments about restorative justice as a sentencing consideration:

> We would not wish this judgment to be seen as expressing any general opposition to the concept of restorative justice (essentially the policies behind ss11 and 12 of the Criminal Justice Act). Those policies must, however, be balanced against other sentencing policies, particularly in this case those

> inherent in s5, dealing with cases of serious violence. Which aspect should predominate will depend on an assessment of where the balance should lie in the individual case. (at p. 661)

The Appeal Court's analysis of the restorative aspects was narrowly focused on reparation since at the time this was the only legislative licence available. These limited 'restorative aspects' were accepted as having 'a significant impact on the length of the term of imprisonment which the Court [was] directed to impose' by the legislation (at p. 661). The immediate response was to criticize the Court of Appeal for 'fail[ing] to seize the opportunity to fully consider restorative justice principles', particularly for giving scant attention to the 'personal deterrent element' of the restorative process (Bowen and Thompson 1999: 5, 7–8). The conference report had given particular prominence to its potential deterrent effect. It described the offender as being 'a basically law-abiding citizen who offends, however spectacularly, once or infrequently' and who 'by experiencing his victim's pain in the restorative justice conference, [has been] deterred by this experience' (as quoted in Bowen and Thompson 1999: 8).

A more recent analysis criticizes the original District Court decision for providing a false diminution of the objective seriousness of the harm caused. Davis (2007b, 2009: 13) interpreted the sentencing judge's remarks as in fact ill serving the development of a restorative jurisprudence because there was an attempt to diminish the objective gravity of the wrongdoing. Davis argued that the sentencing judge 'used Just World strategies to create an illusion of justice' so as to justify a more lenient sentence than appropriate. Davis's claim is that this original decision attempted 'to create the illusion that the facts themselves dictated a lenient sentence' which in her view they did not and that in fact the decision 'represents a lost opportunity to test restorative justice's power to transform the criminal justice system' (2009: 13).[4]

Nonetheless, this appeal decision, which reversed what the Court of Appeal considered a 'lenient sentence', has become a catalyst for some restorative development in New Zealand sentencing jurisprudence. Over the intervening 15 years restorative encounters and the commitments made in outcome agreements have gained acceptance as being capable of meeting some retributive

4 Davis provides a radically different analysis of the original *Clotworthy* decision, citing it as an example of Lerner's (1980) "Just World Delusion" being evident in judicial sentencing. She argues that the judge emphasized the subjective aspects of the offender and severely downplayed the objective seriousness of the offence (noting the behaviour as 'utterly bizarre, defying explanation, understanding or intelligent appreciation'), whereas the Court of Appeal noted the 'extreme and near fatal violence for the purposes of an attempted street robbery'. She said the judge in doing so was deluding himself that the decision was just. As a consequence, the judge missed the opportunity to 'explain exactly why a restorative approach should be fully incorporated into criminal sentencing and extended to serious cases like this one' (2009: 13).

aims (albeit limited mainly to facilitating expressions of genuine remorse and the denunciation of wrongful conduct), many restorative aims (by addressing both personal and normative harm) and even some consequential aims (particularly in terms of encouraging deterrence and rehabilitation and finding alternatives to full-time detention). These developments have resulted in some recognition of an obligation to balance restorative principles with more 'punitive' means when meeting sentencing aims. This legacy can usefully be traced through a series of post-*Clotworthy* sentencing decisions.

Post-Clotworthy Jurisprudence

The core principle abstracted from *Clotworthy* was that courts should always find 'where the balance should lie in the individual case' when sentencing offenders. This principle has been taken by some judges to mean that a court *must* strike a balance 'between retributive and restorative purposes on sentence'. As such, the decision has provided a vehicle for expanding the impact of restorative approaches within sentencing jurisprudence, rather than being dismissed as an appeal which spelled defeat or rejection for restorative principles or approaches. The appeal decision has instead been interpreted by some judges in positive terms, as providing the means to 'cement … confidence that restorative justice was a recognized concept that could be applied in serious offences' (Thorburn 2005: 4). More specifically, the decision can be seen as a growing acceptance of the ability of restorative approaches to deliver on each of the essential aims of responses to wrongdoing.[5] This can be illustrated by tracing a chronology of sentencing decisions post-*Clotworthy*.

In the 1999 decision of *D v Police* Unreported High Court Auckland AP 161/99 (Nicholson J), a successful appeal against the severity of an initial sentence was granted on the basis that insufficient regard had been given to the effect of a restorative encounter in meeting the need for personal and normative repair. The offender had confessed to serious sexual assaults on his two teenage daughters. The appeal judge gave particular emphasis to how the conference and its outcome agreement had addressed restorative aims, through the 'help that it gave to the victims in healing the hurt which the offending had caused them, particularly by helping with family difficulties to be healed for the benefit of all'. In the 2000

---

5 The Court of Appeal has not revisited the *Clotworthy* decision. Two matters have come before the court where restorative justice was mentioned, but in each case a conference had not been held. In the appeal of *R v Nikolao & Ors* [2005] Unreported Court of Appeal of New Zealand CA375/04; CA386/04; CA414/04 which involved a serious wounding, the court said, 'restorative justice appears to be raised for the first time on this appeal' (para. 38) and in *R v Wilcox* [2005] Unreported Court of Appeal of New Zealand CA14/05, involving assault with a rifle and threats to kill, the court noted that 'the appellant had contacted Restorative Justice Services with intention of seeking a conference with the victim' but that one was not held (para. 26).

decision of *R v Fletcher* Unreported District Court Auckland T 990070 (Gittos J), restorative principles were again considered. This case involved facts similar to *Clotworthy*, in that the offender had pleaded guilty to a malicious wounding offence where he had attacked and bitten off a large portion of the victim's ear in a bar room fight. The judge concluded that 'a prison sentence is an inevitable outcome of today's hearing' (para. 6) but suspended that sentence and ordered reparation of $25,000 to cover the victim's loss of earnings and medical treatment. The court was satisfied that the outcome agreement reached in the restorative encounter had sufficiently met the need for personal restoration and reparation. In the 2001 decision of *Police v Stretch* Unreported High Court Nelson AP 9/01 (Durie J), a Crown appeal was lodged concerning the adequacy of an 18-month-prison term for a charge of culpable driving causing death. In this case, while there had been no formal restorative conference, the court still considered meetings between the affected families as constituting restorative encounters. The appeal judge recognized that the sentencing judge had considered the capacity of these meetings in terms of addressing consequential aims:

> It appears the principles of restorative justice may stand in conflict with principles of deterrence which represent the norm, but if the recognition of restorative justice in *Clotworthy* is to have practical effect, then I think a balance must be sought, no matter how difficult it might be to find that balance. That is what the sentencing Judge sought to do. (para. 45)

On this basis, the appeals court was satisfied that such aims had been met restoratively and did not interfere with the original sentence.

Other decisions show the scope given to addressing retributive aims through restorative means. In the 2001 severity appeal of *Kalim v Police* unreported High Court Auckland A198/01 (Glazebrook J), the appeal court considered the penalty needed to express retribution for an offender who had carried out a violent road rage assault. The court accepted that the restorative conference had provided 'a valuable source to evaluate the depth and quality of [the expression of] remorse'. The appeal court rejected the sentencing judge's view that the restorative encounter 'did not achieve a great deal' and reduced the imprisonment term of four months (Thorburn 2005: 10). Similarly, in *Police v Carter* 2001 Unreported District Court Wanganui CRN 1083010524 (Becroft J), an offender had pleaded guilty to drink driving, causing the death of 'his lifelong best friend'. A restorative conference took place. The judge was described in an address by Carruthers J, a fellow judge on that court, as attempting to balance the recommendation of that conference with the then extant legislation that said an offender 'deserves to suffer punishment' in such a case (Carruthers 2005: 3). The judge departed from the strict requirement to impose a full-time custodial sentence by suspending it for a period of 18 months and imposing conditions to attend community service sessions involving addressing students on drink driving. Carruthers said the court was satisfied that some retributive aims had been addressed on the basis that:

> [T]he restorative justice process resulted in an agreement that went some way to redressing the harm caused to the victims, whilst also recognising the harm that the offender had brought upon himself [and the need for] denunciation. (2005: 5)

The 2002 case of *R v Castles* NZCA 109 involved a Crown appeal against a sentence of two and a half years' imprisonment for a serious sexual assault by a group of men on a fellow male, which was part of a pattern of bullying. The Court of Appeal accepted the sentencing judge's decision that the need for retribution had in part been met by one offender's attendance at a conference with the victim's parents, where the offender apologized to the victim and his family (para. 19). The court accepted that the apology provided partial satisfaction of the need for retribution and so mitigated the length of the punitive sentence imposed.

Following these early post-*Clotworthy* decisions, the 2002 *Sentencing Act* (NZ) had the effect of further 'crystalliz[ing] into one broad principle for sentencing' the varying accommodations already made in some sentencing decisions based on restorative principles (Thorburn 2005: 11).[6] In s.8, the Act specifically required courts 'to take into account any outcomes of restorative justice processes that have occurred, or that the court is satisfied are likely to occur'. As well, s.10 widened the list of specific purposes of sentencing, making it easier for restorative approaches to be used to satisfy a broader range of sentencing purposes. Courts were now *required* to take into account more specific purposes which could be interpreted restoratively, including (extract from s.10):

- any offers of amends,
- any agreement between the offender and the victim as to how the offender may remedy the wrong, loss or damage,
- the responses of the offender or the offender's family, *whanau*, or family group of the victim,
- any measures taken … to make compensation, apologise or otherwise make good the harm, and
- any remedial action taken … in relation to the circumstances of the offending.

These additional provisions were seen as cementing the *Clotworthy* requirement for courts to determine 'where the balance should lie' between restorative and punitive principles (Thorburn 2005: 11). The reforms were also seen as an indication that the 'paths of reasoning are now being carefully laid to demonstrate how conference outcomes [can be] taken into account' to address such wider sentencing aims (Thorburn 2005: 12). It is useful to trace the further jurisprudential accommodations that occurred as a result of this broader legislation.

---

6 There are concerns that 2012 amendments which add a series of additional aggravating factors to section 8 to the *Sentencing Act* might reduce the influence of the restorative-type provisions.

In the 2002 decision in *Feng v Police* Unreported High Court Auckland A127/02 (Salmon J), an appeal court reversed a refusal of home detention on a two-year term of imprisonment for dangerous driving causing death. The court in overturning the original decision was satisfied that the deceased's mother's remarks during the restorative conference that 'we are not here to punish you or judge you' indicated that a measure of retribution had been achieved in the conference other than by punishment (para. 18). In the 2003 case of *R v Cassidy* Unreported High Court New Plymouth T2/03 (Paterson J), the offender's 'willingness to partake in a restorative justice conference' was recognized as an acceptable means by which to express remorse. The offender was a staff member in a bar who had been convicted of manslaughter after striking and killing a patron while removing him from the premises. A restorative conference took place with the deceased's family. The judge addressed the offender about that conference:

> At it [the conference], it is to your credit that you accepted full responsibility for what happened and expressed your sorrow and deep remorse ... A facilitator of the conference noted [that this] would be a starting point for the healing process for all involved. (para. 10)

Though the offender was in fact imprisoned for two years, there was recognition that the requirement for retribution had been partly satisfied through the pain of expressing remorse in the conference and that this could be reflected in reduced time to be served.

A similar view was taken in the 2004 case of *R v Folaumoeloa* [2006] DCR 135 (Thorburn J), which involved a young offender involved in an aggravated robbery of a service station. In imposing a reduced period of imprisonment, the sentencing judge referred to the fact that the offender had expressed

> the sort of embarrassment and shame that is of a nature that engenders a deep desire to do better and not offend again for the sake of avoiding embarrassment for a family or close community. (para. 24)

In the 2006 case of *R v Sami* NZDCR 128 (McElrea J) involving a violent purse-snatching, the judge specifically expressed satisfaction that the necessary denunciation of the defendant's wrongdoing had occurred as a consequence of the restorative conference:

> I am sure that denunciation has already occurred through the defendant's family and the restorative process. [You have] been held accountable not just through the Court but in a direct, face-to-face way. (para. 34)

The judge considered imprisonment in that case was not warranted, and that retribution at the conference had provided denunciation, which could be sufficiently supplemented by community work, supervision and reparation. Similar acceptance was evident in the case of *Kingi and McEwen v. New Zealand Police* CRI-2007-483-4 High Court, Wanganui (Simon France J), cited by McElrea (2011: 50). In that case, the High Court on appeal set aside sentences of four and five months' imprisonment for assault with intent to injure where restorative justice outcomes had been agreed and implemented, including written apologies, community service, reparation payments and attending remedial counselling. The appellate judge commented that the role of the restorative process was more integral than in merely reducing the length of a prison term, noting (para. 55) that the conference was evidence that 'remorse was immediate and genuine [and] reconciliation had occurred'. In *R. v. Buttar* [2008] NZCA 28 (also cited in McElrea (2011: 50)), the Court of Appeal upheld sentences imposed in the District Court of imprisonment for 30 months and 42 months where reductions of 30 to 35 per cent were allowed on account of the restorative process undertaken (and in the light of evidence received concerning cultural factors affecting the offending). These discounts were not disturbed by the Court of Appeal, noting that the District Court judge had considered that the restorative processes had addressed many of the sentencing purposes including deterrence within the Sikh community to which the defendants belonged.

This small but developing selection of New Zealand sentencing decisions seems to reflect some growing judicial awareness that the relational aspects of wrongdoing must be addressed in criminal justice responses and that some of the requirements of responding to such aspects of wrongdoing are better met *through* restorative approaches. They also provide some evidence of a growing cognizance of the need to consider relational aspects of offending for the requirements of the harmonious social relationships standard of justice to be met. This progress is tempered by the sober words of Judge McElrea, who has sat in criminal matters for more than 20 years in these courts and who has lamented 'that progress is slow' (2007b: 102), offering as explanation:

> The adversary ethos is so deeply imbedded in our legal structures, the legal profession, and the judges, who (in common law countries) are drawn from the profession, that restorative justice is continually pushed to the margins, despite the encouragement of the legislators. (2007a)

Nonetheless, there is considerable evidence of this growing acceptance in its judiciary (including appeal courts). Restorative approaches are accepted as capable of providing not only restoration itself, but also of meeting some aspects of retribution (specifically the need to provide a forum in which offenders are accountable, their behaviour is denounced and self-censure is evident through remorse) and some elements of the consequential requirements (most notably deterring further offending). These accommodations have become more substantial as legislative provisions have required *courts*, as a compulsory step, to take into account what takes place at a conference and what can be achieved through outcome commitments agreed there. What can be seen to have begun in the New Zealand jurisprudence is recognition that restorative approaches can play a substantial role in achieving the essential aims of responses to wrongdoing. This recognition is routinely framed in jurisprudential language as meeting 'sentencing objectives' such as acceptance of responsibility, reparation and apology. The position is much slower with respect to recognizing the role of such approaches to meet retributive aims. which is confined largely to an acceptance that encounters can facilitate expressions of remorse and can denounce wrongful behaviour directly. Though these developments are small, it is instructive to compare the New Zealand experience with the different approach taken in Canadian jurisprudence.

The Canadian Jurisprudence

The Gladue Principle

For Canada, its extension to consider relational aspects in its sentencing jurisprudence began with the influence of the landmark decision of *R v Gladue* [1999] 1 SCR 688 (*Gladue*) and its subsequent review in *R v Proulx* [2000] 1 SCR 61 (*Proulx*),[7] the principles of which were later revisited in *R v Ipeelee* [2012] 1 SCR 433 (*Ipeelee*).[8] These cases were judicial responses to significant codified sentencing reforms introduced Canada-wide in 1996. The 1996 reforms added a new statutory statement of the purposes and principles of sentencing to the *Criminal Code*, principally in ss. 718 and 742. Section 718 provides for 'just sanctions' to meet certain objectives:

> The fundamental purpose of sentencing is to contribute, along with crime prevention initiatives, to respect for the law and the maintenance of a just, peaceful and safe society by imposing just sanctions that have one or more of the following objectives:
>
> a. to denounce unlawful conduct;
> b. to deter the offender and other persons from committing offences;
> c. to separate offenders from society, where necessary;
> d. to assist in rehabilitating offenders;
> e. to provide reparations for harm done to victims or the community;
> f. to promote a sense of responsibility in offenders, and acknowledgment of the harm done to victims and the community.

Section 718.2(e) forms part of a provision dealing with other considerations on sentencing, including the need to take account of mitigating and aggravating factors, consistency and concurrent penalties:

7 *R v Proulx* was heard together with the appeal of *R v Wells*.

8 A CanLII search shows the influence of these decisions, with *Gladue* cited more than 1,000 times and *Ipeelee* cited more than 250 times as of November 2013. *Ipeelee* has been cited in the High Court of Australia in *Bugmy v The Queen* [2013] HCA 37.

> A court that imposes a sentence shall also take into consideration the following principles:
>
> [.....]
>
> (e) all available sanctions other than imprisonment that are reasonable in the circumstances should be considered for all offenders, with particular attention to the circumstances of aboriginal offenders.

A further important element of the reforms was the creation of the intermediate sanction of a 'conditional sentence of imprisonment' in s.742. Section 742.1 provided (at the time the reforms were introduced)[9] certain conditions for the imposing of conditional sentences:

> Where a person is convicted of an offence, except an offence that is punishable by a minimum term of imprisonment, and the court
>
> a. imposes a sentence of imprisonment of less than two years, and
> b. is satisfied that serving the sentence in the community would not endanger the safety of the community and would be consistent with the fundamental purpose and principles of sentencing set out in sections 718 to 718.2,
>
> the court may, for the purposes of supervising the offender's behaviour in the community, order that the offender serve the sentence in the community, subject to the offender's complying with the conditions of the conditional sentence order made under section 742.3.

As this section of the legislation makes clear, the conditional sentence is 'a term of imprisonment that is served in the community'. As such, it is a hybrid measure so that the 'semi-separation' remains punitive, but 'serving' it in the community is seen as potentially restorative. The legislation was subsequently judicially interpreted in such a way that conditional sentences are seen as 'intermediate sanctions with the potential to impose restorative conditions on offenders who would otherwise be sentenced to jail' (Roberts and Roach 2003: 246).

These legislative reforms were given close judicial scrutiny in *Gladue*, most specifically the effect of s.718.2(e) which required that sanctions other than imprisonment be preferred particularly in the case of Aboriginal offenders. The case

9 As a result of reforms to the Code introduced in the *Conditional Sentencing Reform Bill* (2007), this section excludes 'a serious personal injury offence as defined in s. 752, a terrorism offence or a criminal organization offence prosecuted by way of indictment for which the maximum term of imprisonment is ten years or more'. Section 752 defines a serious personal injury offence as including an offence involving violence, conduct endangering the lives of others and certain sexual assault offences.

also considered the effect of the new sentencing objectives in s.718 more broadly. In *Gladue* the defendant was a 19-year-old Aboriginal woman who had stabbed and killed her partner during the course of an argument in which he had taunted her with his infidelities. She pleaded guilty to manslaughter and was sentenced to three years' imprisonment at trial. This sentence was appealed but confirmed by the Court of Appeal for British Columbia. On further appeal to the Supreme Court of Canada, the court did not interfere with the sentence imposed, saying it was 'not unreasonable' (and indicating in any event that 'the accused was granted, subject to certain conditions, day parole after she had served six months' (para. 98)). But the court did comment on the effect of the reforms on the satisfaction of the sentencing objectives. The court acknowledged that the legislative reforms represented a significant departure from existing sentencing jurisprudence requiring courts to accommodate this departure in their decisions. The court recognized that certain sentencing aims now included restorative requirements:

> Clearly, s.718 is, in part, a restatement of the basic sentencing aims, which are listed in paras. (a) through to (d). What are new, though, are paras. (e) and (f), which along with para. (d) focus upon the restorative goals of repairing the harms suffered by individual victims and by the community as a whole, promoting a sense of responsibility and an acknowledgment of the harm caused on the part of the offender, and attempting to rehabilitate or heal the offender. (para. 43)

Additionally, there was a recognition that 'restorative sentencing goals do not usually correlate with the use of prison as a sanction' (para. 43), and are better satisfied through community-based sanctions. In this particular case, the offender had not participated in a restorative encounter and as such none of the sentencing aims could be seen as being addressed through conferencing (as has been the case with the New Zealand judicial decisions). The court did not have the benefit of a conferencing report, though as a consequence of the decision the provision of a '*Gladue* report' on the offender's indigenous background had become routine (Roberts and Roach 2003: 247).[10] The expectation of the legislation was that judges themselves would include 'restorative components' in the sentences they imposed. This has meant that the new sentencing objectives have been largely confined to using 'less intrusive alternatives' in the sentence imposed, rather than seeing some sentencing aims achieved through a restorative encounter (Roach and Rudin 2000: 363). The Supreme Court noted in this regard (para. 48) that the principle objective of the legislation was 'expanding the use of restorative justice principles in sentencing', rather than licensing a form of non-judicial response

10 Such occurred in the case of offenders who had participated in the Ottawa Collaborative Justice Project, discussed in Chapter 8. Sentencing courts now routinely have the benefit of a 'Gladue Report' which provides some information on the potential for restoration and is 'a form of pre-sentence report tailored to the specific circumstances of Aboriginal offenders' (*Ipeelee*: para. 60).

through restorative conferencing. The *Gladue* decision provided important judicial recognition for the newly minted *Criminal Code* sentencing purposes of 'reparations for harm', 'responsibility' and 'acknowledgement of harm', recognizing that these were not 'neutral' provisions but were intended to open up potentially different responses to wrongdoing. These provisions gave restorative principles a focus previously missing (Roach and Rudin 2000: 362). At the time of its decision, it was predicted that *Gladue* would be 'a leading case whenever any offender asks a court to consider a sentence that has a restorative purpose' (Roach and Rudin 2000: 362). It is therefore interesting to trace the breadth of the subsequent influence of the *Gladue* principle.

Post-Gladue Jurisprudence

The 2000 decision in *Proulx* was a further appeal review by the Supreme Court of Canada where the focus of the court's decision was with the interpretation of s.742, specifically the provisions dealing with conditional sentences. The court reconsidered the effect of the new statement of purposes in s.718 as enunciated in *Gladue*. In its decision the court found 'punitive objectives' in s.742 where, at least on the face of it, there were none (Archibald 2005a: 252). The ultimate effect of *Proulx* was to narrow the scope that the *Gladue* interpretation of s.718 might have initially promised. *Proulx* was a case involving a recently licensed non-Aboriginal driver crashing his car after drinking alcohol, killing his passenger and seriously injuring another driver. He pleaded guilty to dangerous driving causing death and was jailed for 18 months at trial. The Court of Appeal allowed an appeal by the defendant and substituted instead a conditional sentence of the same term. This decision was then reversed by the Supreme Court which reinstated the original custodial sentence (though by the time of the appeal the accused had completed his conditional sentence). In considering whether a conditional sentence was in fact the appropriate response in the circumstances, the original sentencing judge had described such an option as a 'sort of a halfway house' through which 'both punitive and restorative objectives' could be achieved (as cited in Archibald 2005a: 252). On the appeal, the Supreme Court recognized that suitably fashioned restorative responses could provide the necessary 'symbolic, collective statement' of retributive denunciation (para. 109). It allowed that the 'objectives of rehabilitation, reparations, and promotion of a sense of responsibility in the offender' (para. 109) could also be achieved by restorative means. But it did not depart from the traditional view that punitive measures such as 'incarceration will usually provide more denunciation [and by implication more deterrence]' than restorative means (paras. 102, 107–108). When considering the objectives of sentencing in s.718, the Supreme Court essentially divided the provisions of the section into two sets. The first set were 'punitive objectives' (essentially denunciation, deterrence and separation s.718(a)–(c)), and these were seen as best carried out by responses that promoted traditional retributive means (that is punishment, particularly involving 'separation' in custody). The second set were 'restorative objectives' (rehabilitation, reparation and promotion of a sense of responsibility s.718(d)–(f)) which were seen as best achieved through restorative means (in the Canadian context through non-custodial 'conditions' on sentencing). This artificial division essentially curtailed the possibility that denunciation, deterrence and separation (in its 'semi-separation' guise) could be accepted as being attainable through restorative means. This was despite the acceptance in *Gladue* (para. 69) that potentially 'imprisonment will utterly fail to vindicate the objectives of deterrence or denunciation' in situations where grossly negative systemic factors are influential. The effect of these comments in the *Proulx* appeal judgment was to narrow the scope for restorative forms of response to simply meeting the consequential aims of rehabilitation, reparations and promotion of a sense of responsibility, and leaving (by implication 'more serious') retributive elements of denunciation, deterrence and separation to purely punitive means. Interpreted this way, *Proulx* provided at best a limited recognition of the potential for denunciation and deterrence to be gained from restorative means through the 'semi-separation' of a conditional sentence of imprisonment (para. 35). While the court did acknowledge the 'importance of reconciling, if not integrating, the restorative and retributive perspectives', the decision was seen to reinforce a conservative position that the legislatively created restorative device of conditional sentences could not deliver on most retributive aims (Roberts and Roach 2003: 247–248).[11]

It is also useful to trace the application of the *Gladue* principle in the decision of *R v Wells* [2000] 1 SCR 207 (*Wells*),[12] heard concurrently with *Proulx*. In *Wells* the Supreme Court's specific focus was again on the s.718.2(e) provision, specifically whether non-custodial sentences should be the first sentencing consideration for Aboriginal offenders. The court firstly confirmed that s.718.2(e) was intended to have 'a remedial purpose for all offenders [both Aboriginal and non-Aboriginal offenders], focusing as it does on the concept of restorative justice', but then narrowed that application in its judgment (Roach and Rudin 2000: 363). The Supreme Court upheld a sentence of 20 months' imprisonment for an Aboriginal offender convicted of sexual assault, categorized by the sentencing court as a 'major' or 'near major' assault (para. 48). The court said:

11 Conditional sentences have continued to draw the ire of public comment (typical court reports of such sentence proceedings in the *Winnipeg Free Press* edition of 12 June 2004, for instance, those headlined '*Slap* Angers Victim's Family' and 'Retribution, Punishment Missing: Crown', are indicative). This has led to pressure to exclude matters such as drink driving causing death and manslaughter from the conditional sentence option. The *Conditional Sentencing Reform Bill* (2007) amended the *Criminal Code* in 2008 to exclude the use of conditional sentences for a range of serious 'personal injury' offences.

12 Four other similar decisions were also handed down at the same time as *Proulx*: *R v L.F.W.* [2000] 1 SCR 132, *R v R.N.S.* [2000] 1 SCR 149, *R v R.A.R.* [2000] 1 SCR 163 and *R v Bunn* [2000] 1 SCR 183.

> *Gladue* does not mean that aboriginal offenders must always be sentenced in a manner which gives greatest weight to the principles of restorative justice and less weight to goals such as deterrence, denunciation, and separation. (para. 44)

In fact, it had been specifically argued in *Wells* that 'a healing-based community sanction [could] promote the difficult and painful process of denouncing unlawful conduct' just as effectively as imprisonment (Roberts and Roach 2003: 252).[13] The court rejected this argument and reverted to the traditional view that in cases of serious offending 'the goals of denunciation and deterrence are accordingly increasingly significant' (para. 42) and that these goals are best achieved (or at times *only* achievable) by punitive means involving total separation. The court equated meeting denunciation and deterrence objectives with imposing punitive measures and thereby 'discounted the ability of restorative justice to denounce and deter' (Roach and Rudin 2000: 367). This represented a major shift from the interpretation the original *Gladue* interpretation had allowed. *Proulx* (and *Wells*) certainly continued the development of a changed sentencing jurisprudence, albeit one more limited in scope than *Gladue*'s early promise.

The lost scope of the original *Gladue* interpretation was suggested in the outcome of an appeal decision of *R v Logan* [1999] CANLII 927 (ONCA) (*Logan*), which the Ontario Court of Appeal heard after *Gladue* but before the *Proulx* judgment was handed down. In *Logan*, the appeal court applied a reading of *Gladue* that gave judicial licence such that 'in many instances more restorative sentencing principles will gain primary relevance precisely because the prevention of crime as well as individual and social healing can occur through [such] means' (para. 414). In *Logan*, an Aboriginal defendant had been convicted of dangerous driving causing death and bodily harm with alcohol as a significant contributing factor. The sentencing judge imposed a period of 30 months' imprisonment which the defence appealed. The appeal court substituted a 20-month conditional sentence, including conditions that the defendant was required to perform 'community service' such as being involved in the counseling of young people on the dangers of drinking and driving. The imposition of such conditions in lieu of imprisonment was seen as signaling a recognition that such restorative devices could contribute to 'denounc[ing] and deter[ring] drunk driving' specifically, but also wider crime more generally (Roach and Rudin 2000: 377). This decision signaled a broader potential for using restorative means to meet sentencing aims, a scope that was substantially reduced following *Proulx*.

Outside of judicial decisions, there were indications that sentencing jurisprudence might be open to a potential change of direction. In a 1999 national survey of judges, more than 70 per cent (in a sample of 461 judges representing a third of the total Canadian judicial population) agreed with the proposition that conditional sentences

13 The Aboriginal Service of Toronto (ALST), represented by Kent Roach, were granted leave as intervener to appear in this matter (and also in *Gladue*) and made this and other arguments. ALST and Roach also had leave as interveners in *Ipeelee*.

were 'always' or 'usually' as effective as imprisonment in achieving rehabilitation (Roberts, Doob et al. 1999; Roberts and LaPrairie 2000: 8). Approximately one-third of these respondents also expressed some support for the effectiveness of conditional sentences to meet certain retributive aims, notably as a means to express deterrence (35 per cent) or denunciation (35 per cent) (Roberts and LaPrairie 2000: 7).[14] It was evident from the nature of the conditions actually imposed by many of the judges in their judgments in this sample that they were routinely using conditional sentencing to achieve treatment and separation aims through non-punitive means. Almost 90 per cent of respondents said they 'often' imposed treatment conditions (alcohol, drug, psychological, other counselling) in their conditional sentences. In terms of measures designed to meet consequential aims, judges reported 'often' imposing non-contact orders (85 per cent), curfews (70 per cent) and abstentions on alcohol consumption (74 per cent) and drug use (79 per cent) with these purposes in mind (Roberts and LaPrairie 2000: 12–13).[15] These conditions were accepted as placing restrictions on everyday behaviour (home detention, curfews, non-association orders, reporting requirements) designed to change offending behaviour and therefore onerous even if not 'punishment' as such. Given these apparently receptive judicial attitudes and the direction provided in *Gladue* and the Supreme Court's other appellate decisions, it is useful to try to discern change in the application of sentencing provisions in provincial court decisions.

Certainly the use of conditional sentencing options, seen as a 'restorative vehicle', has had an effect. In the first three years of their use (1996–99), nearly 43,000 such sentences were imposed (Roberts and LaPrairie 2000: viii). The rate from 2003 to 2004 onwards then settled into a pattern of approximately 13,000 sentences (about 5 per cent of all sentences imposed Canada-wide (Canadian Criminal Justice Association 2006: 2)). Data from 2005–06 shows a decline to 11,154 (Statistics Canada 2006) and further reduction in view of the 2008 tightening of their offence application, but the conditional option continued to have an effect on the level of jailing. Research by Roberts and colleagues shows a discernible downward trend in the use of jail. In the period 1993/94–1997/98, they reported a 'national 13% reduction in the number of admissions to custody represent[ing] 53,990 individuals' (Roberts and Gabor 2003: 46). Allowing for some time overlap figures for the period 1996–2001 indicated a 22 per cent

14 Importantly, the evidence showed that judges who were more familiar with conditional sentencing (assessed as judges who had imposed at least 11 such sentences) were more optimistic about their effectiveness in achieving such denunciary and deterrent aims (Roberts and LaPrairie 2000: 8).

15 There was some concern that the onerous nature of these conditions would be likely to see high rates of breach (one estimate suggested that it might be as high as one-third) which, given the direction in *Proulx* that 'where an offender breaches a condition without reasonable excuse, there should be a presumption that the offender serve the remainder of his or her sentence in jail' (para. 39), might negate this sanction as a truly restorative approach (Roberts and Gabor 2003: 47).

reduction (for non-Aboriginal offenders) and a further 9 per cent reduction (for overall offenders) for the period 2001–2006.[16]

A review of sentencing decisions by provincial courts confirms a discernible departure from primarily punitive decision-making to an acceptance that 'restorative justice' is a legitimate sentencing principle that can stand beside and should be balanced against traditional principles like deterrence, denunciation, rehabilitation and protection. This is both a marked departure from traditional sentencing jurisprudence and a deviation from the New Zealand experience, where the requirement for any 'balancing' remains judicially contested. In the reporting of sentencing remarks by provincial and appellate courts there is a consistent acceptance of the need to balance 'restorative justice', though a reluctance remains with regard to giving it greater weight than other goals. A review of a small number of commonly cited decisions illustrates the level of acceptance of these principles in sentencing jurisprudence. In the 2006 decision of *R v Brizard* OJ No. 729 (*Brizard*), the Ontario Court of Appeal specifically described a non-custodial sentence as 'the *restorative approach* [which could] assist the appellant with his treatment for substance abuse and to upgrade his education so that he may obtain employment' (para. 4, emphasis added). The court also held that failure to give adequate weight to Aboriginal status in accordance with s.718.2(e) and *Gladue* amounts to an error of law (para. 3). However, as the review of the sentencing decision in *R v Kakekagamick* [2006] 214 OAC 127 (*Kakekagamick*) by the Ontario Court of Appeal suggests that provincial courts' adherence to these principles may be inconsistent. A 22-year-old First Nation resident of a remote community in northwestern Ontario had been sentenced to five years in jail for a domestic violence assault on his partner. While the appellate court dismissed his appeal, it noted the almost complete failure to reference the *Gladue* principle in the sentence hearing, noting 'defence counsel ... made no reference whatsoever to *Gladue*' (para. 29), and the principle was virtually ignored by the judge. The appellate court used the opportunity in strong judicial language to 'reiterate the duties they [s.718.2(e) and *Gladue*] impose when a court is dealing with an Aboriginal offender' (para. 32). The court said this amounted to a statutory *duty* on judges to consider the unique circumstances of Aboriginal offenders (para. 39, emphasis added). This has meant that courts must have specific regard for 'the types of sentencing procedures which may be appropriate ... because of his or her Aboriginal heritage or connection' (para. 40). 'Types of sentencing

16 There are two caveats to this apparently positive picture. Other research suggests that, given the 'extraordinary' breach provisions for such sentences (Roach and Rudin 2000: 370), it is likely that a substantial number of offenders (perhaps upwards of a third) will nonetheless end up in jail as a result of a breach of their conditions. Also sadly, the position for Aboriginal offenders is the opposite – in the period 1996–2001 as general jailing went down dramatically Aboriginal incarceration increased by 3 per cent and again by 4 per cent in 2001–06. The result was that in 1999 when *Gladue* was decided, Aboriginal jail admissions were 12 per cent but by 2005 the proportion had jumped to 17 per cent (*Ipeelee*: para. 62, citing Roberts and Melchers (2003)).

procedures' was a direct reference to the s.718.2(e) provision of 'all available sanctions other than imprisonment'. The appellate court equated these procedures with 'sentencing in a way that gives most weight to the principles of restorative justice', even though there is 'no general rule' that a non-custodial penalty should always apply (para. 42). In the l2011 decision in *R v Collins* ONCA 182 (*Collins*), the same court again attempted to remedy the scant consideration being given to *Gladue* in provincial court sentencing decisions. *Collins* involved an appeal by a 51-year-old woman from the isolated Fort William First Nation sentenced to 16 months in jail for her involvement in a major social security fraud in that community. She had lived as an outcast from her community as a child and as an adult had developed a long-term gambling addiction. The appellate court was not prepared to substitute a conditional sentence but did reduce the period of imprisonment to 10 months, while acknowledging the statement in *Gladue* (para. 69) that in some instances 'imprisonment will utterly fail to vindicate the objectives of deterrence or denunciation' and a non-custodial restorative justice–based sentence may be preferable (para. 33). The court strongly criticized the sentencing judge's reference to 'the so-called *Gladue* factors that have contributed to bringing Susan Collins before the court' and his conclusion that 'the evidence does not support the argument that systemic factors' had in fact contributed (para. 26). The appellate court restated the principle that the burden of proof to show that such a causal link exists is never with the accused but rather with the court, which has a statutory *duty* to take such factors into account (para. 32, emphasis added). It is noteworthy that in a decision from around the same time, *R v Martin* [2011] ONCJ 423 (*Martin*), the Ontario provincial court cancelled a conditional sentence imposed on a 31-year-old Mi'kmaq man for drug trafficking when he reoffended and imposed full-time jail, saying, 'denunciation and deterrence are the paramount factors in sentencing persons who are trafficking in drugs for profit' (para. 40), implicitly accepting that jail was the only way to achieve these aims.

The Restatement of Restorative Principles in Ipeelee

In *Ipeelee*, the Supreme Court also took the opportunity to reiterate important restorative sentencing principles from *Gladue* that had not been consistently followed in provincial and appellate courts. It expressly restated that 'restorative justice' is a sentencing principle which stands alongside 'traditional' principles of deterrence, rehabilitation and punishment such that Canadian courts have moved past the New Zealand position and there is no dispute of 'a balance to be struck'. More specifically, the Supreme Court's decision in *Ipeelee* was used to address the 'fundamental misunderstanding and misapplication of the laws found in *R v Gladue* and s.718.2(e) of the Code' (judgment per LeBel J for the majority allowing the appeals[17]). The court makes reference to Roach's critique

17 In *Ipeelee*, the court dealt with two separate appeals by Aboriginal offenders – Manasie Ipeelee and Frank Ralph Ladue – together.

that 'appellate courts have attended disproportionately to just a few paragraphs in these two Supreme Court judgments (*Gladue* and *Wells*)' (*Ipeelee*: para. 84). This narrowing of the interpretation that provincial and appellate courts have made of the *Gladue* decision is clear from a consistent coupling of two statements from the Supreme Court. Firstly, from *Gladue*:

> In describing the effect of s.718.2(e) in this way, we do not mean to suggest that, as a general practice, aboriginal offenders must always be sentenced in a manner which gives greatest weight to the principals of restorative justice, and less weight to goals such as deterrence, denunciation and separation. (para. 78)

And from *Wells* that

> in no way [was it] intended to suggest that as a general rule, the greater weight is to be given to principles of restorative justice. (para. 40)

The correction that *Ipeelee* makes is that the sentencing principles of restorative justice *are* particularly warranted for Aboriginal offenders. It reaffirmed that the purpose of s.718.2(e) as was stated in *Gladue* is to 'encourage sentencing judges to have recourse to a restorative approach to sentencing' (*Gladue*: para. 93). *Ipeelee* does more than affirm existing principles of sentencing; it calls upon judges 'to use a different method of analysis in determining a fit sentence for Aboriginal offenders' (para. 59). The background and situation of the two appellants in *Ipeelee* illustrate this restorative preferment well.

Mr Ipeelee was a 39-year-old Inuk man with a 'life story far removed from the experience of most Canadians' (para. 2), with a lengthy criminal history including spending 'a significant proportion of his life in custody' (para. 3). As part of his most recent sentence for sexual assault, he had been placed on a long-term supervision order of 10 years which became effective once he was released from jail following a 6-year sentence. The supervision order allowed him to live in the community and attempt to address the clear nexus between his alcohol abuse and offending. One of the conditions of this order was that he not consume alcohol. In the early period of this supervision, he committed breaches which brought him back into custody for short periods. About 18 months after his initial release, he was found (for the first time) intoxicated and was charged with breaching the alcohol condition of his order. When the breach came back before the court he was sentenced to return to jail for a further 3 years. He appealed and lost to the Ontario Court of Appeal and then appealed to the Supreme Court which quashed the 3-year jail sentence and substituted a period of 1 year. Mr Ladue was a 49-year-old member of a small indigenous community at Ross River in the Yukon Territory with abusive 'life experiences [which] may seem foreign to most Canadians, but … all too common in Ross River' (para. 21). He had a long history of alcohol-influenced offending and drug use but had had a 6-year period of sobriety in his 20s, during which he was offence-free. In 2003, he was convicted of sexual assault and given a 3-year sentence and placed on a 7-year long-term supervision order. The supervision order came into effect in 2006, when he was released from custody. He breached the order numerous times and was returned to jail. On the last occasion on his release from jail, he had a placement to a culturally appropriate rural-based halfway house. Because of delay by jail authorities, this placement was lost and he was released to a halfway house in downtown Vancouver. He was breached again on his supervision order, when a urinalysis returned positive for cocaine. When he came back before the court on the breach, he was sentenced to 3 years in jail. He appealed this and the sentence was reduced to a year. A Crown appeal against that reduced sentence was dismissed by the Supreme Court.

In dealing with each of these appeals, the court made clear that it was not intended by *Gladue* that Aboriginal offenders needed to trace a causal link between systemic and background factors of abuse and their individual offending. This is because 'the operation of s. 718.2(e) does not require such a connection … [because these] factors do not operate as an excuse or justification for the criminal conduct' (para. 83). But the court said they do provide the necessary context to enable a court to determine an appropriate sentence, and it is this sentence that needs to focus on 'restorative justice'. The line of reasoning the court engaged is set out in paragraph 73 of the judgment. Systemic and background factors are seen as having a potential bearing on the culpability of offenders to the extent that they may shed light on moral blameworthiness. The reality of constrained circumstances as a consequence of these factors may diminish their culpability.[18] The court cites remarks in the decision in *R v Skani* [2002] ABQB 1097 concerning such factors in the life of one offender to the effect that 'few mortals could withstand such a childhood and youth without becoming seriously troubled'. The consequence the court saw was that punishment made would be an ineffective response to persons with such backgrounds. It noted with approval the remarks of Cory and Iacobucci JJ in *Gladue* that

> [i]n cases where such factors have played a significant role, it is incumbent upon the sentencing judge to consider these factors in evaluating whether imprisonment would actually serve to deter, or to denounce crime in a sense that would be meaningful to the community of which the offender is a member. In many instances, more restorative sentencing principles will gain primary relevance precisely because the prevention of crime as well as individual and social healing cannot occur through other means. (para. 69)

In spite of this lack of consistency in the application of restorative justice principles by sentencing courts which the Supreme Court in *Ipeelee* and other

18 For example, the Canadian Mental Health Initiative's finding that most residential school survivors had grown up in circumstances that left them bereft of 'the skills, knowledge, or emotional strength to parent their own children', leading to severe dysfunction and abuse in their future families (cited in *Martin*: para. 9).

appellate courts have sought to address, Roach's conclusion in 2000 immediately post-*Gladue* continues to have strong resonance:

> It is now no longer possible to understand the jurisprudence of sentencing without understanding restorative justice as understood by the Supreme Court. (2000: 3.3)

Roach's qualification of 'restorative justice as understood by the Supreme Court' is an important rider. Canadian sentencing jurisprudence has reached a clear acceptance of 'the use of restorative justice principles in sentencing' (*Proulx*: para. 48), though not one that equates to giving consideration to the effect of pre-sentence restorative engagements. The Canadian approach remains predominantly judge-centred and -directed. Provincial and appellate courts have in the main come to accept the appropriate judicial interpretation of 'restorative justice' as the direction in *Gladue* that 'as a general matter restorative justice involves some form of restitution and reintegration into the community' (para. 43). This direction has been variously seen as recommending 'a community based sentence … in recognition of the community's involvement in the healing of the accused' in *R v T.C.* [2009] SKPC 80, 'returning people to the community where possible, and to focus on the human beings affected by the crime', as in *R v Jeff* [2010] BCSC 1800, or requiring the offender 'to give something back to the community that he has wronged', as in *R v Myke* [2010] ONCJ 160. 'Restorative approaches' in this guise have been interpreted to mean courts needing to be cognizant of what is achievable in sentencing terms through a focus on restoration as well as punishment. The absence of conferencing involving 'all those affected' has meant that some of the New Zealand acceptance that retributive aims (accountability, denunciation and the self-censure of remorse) can be met through such engagements is missing. The Canadian jurisprudence has also recognized that restorative principles can be mixed in some proportion with non-restorative principles when responding to wrongdoing. The mixture as narrowed in *Proulx* may tend to return priority to punitive approaches, particularly as the seriousness of offending increases such that in those cases 'restorative objectives cannot dominate in a conditional sentence and they cannot be given equal weight either' (Healy 2000: ii.1). But the decision in *Ipeelee* seeks to correct the erroneous view that restorative justice has no place in serious offences (para. 84). There is also a limit to the 'restoration' in the Canadian jurisprudence – the offender is still 'told' of the imposition of sanctions rather than being a party to any negotiation of their terms. The message that may reach the offender is that he or she is being given 'a limited opportunity of rehabilitation and restorative justice while being punished' (Healy 2000: ii.2). Nonetheless, there is sufficient movement in sentencing jurisprudence that allows restorative justice principles to coexist alongside traditional punitive principles as a means to achieving the essential aims.

Conclusion

The sentencing jurisprudence in these jurisdictions shows some indications of an acceptance of restorative principles and approaches. There was some accommodation that restorative practice could meet some of the essential aims of responses to wrongdoing. This was particularly so with respect to the restoration of personal harm, and partly so for the consequential aims of deterrence and rehabilitation. There was, however, only limited acceptance that retributive aims could also be delivered via restorative means. What can be gleaned from this is evidence of a slow (and varied) judicial acceptance that restorative justice has considerable potential to meet some of the essential aims of responses to wrongdoing. There is recognition that they offer an additional means to potentially 'lessen the very difficult task of judges to ensure these goals and requirements are met through sentencing' (Shy 2006: 17). However, this is well short of any substantial accommodation. Part of the reluctance stems from the mistrust largely borne of lack of knowledge as to how restorative practices work. How these methods can generate a sense of justice remains a comparative mystery. The next section seeks to dispel some of this mystique. Part III explores examples of restorative practice, seeking causal links between the generative mechanisms which are used in these practices and the sense of justice created. Chapter 8 explores diverse sites of practice in New Zealand, Canada, Australia and Europe with a keen eye to restorative justice practice. Chapter 9 reports on the view of practice facilitators about what mix of generative mechanisms work together to deliver this unique experience of justice.

Conclusion

PART III

Chapter 8
What Happens in Restorative Justice Practice?

Introduction

The next two chapters turn the spotlight on restorative justice to examine the nature of its distinctive practice. This analysis looks at both its departures from legal justice identified in Chapter 5 and its similarities. The first chapter in Part III gives an overview of the inner workings of a number of restorative programs in different jurisdictions to provide some insight into how they work to generate justice. In doing so, it seeks to remove some of the mystique and mistrust about such practices which in part helps remove the reluctance among mainstream responses as to the role these practices can play in responding to criminal wrongdoing. The chapter that follows records how facilitators and others involved in these programs describe its particular justice-generating methods. There is a dearth of data focused on judicial attitudes towards restorative practice. Fellegi (2013) has canvassed the attitudes of criminal justice practitioners (judges and prosecutors) about restorative justice, particularly victim-offender mediation prior to its implementation in Hungarian criminal law in 2007. She found positive attitudes, with practitioners seeing such mediation as a potential tool for making the criminal justice response less rigid, as well as concern as to the effects of allowing 'parties' discretional input into sanctioning (see, for example, Cashman 1985; Canadian Sentencing Commission 1988; Mack and Roach Anleu 2008).[1] The analysis and descriptions here may help to dispel some misconceptions. While they show that restorative approaches distill a different

---

1 This scarcity of data is nothing new. Even in the case of analysis of mainstream judicial attitudes, most of the studies are based on US data. As Mack and Roach Anleu (2008: 6) point out, US empirical legal research into judicial attitudes is aided by substantial empirical databases (see, for example, those accessible from the Empirical Legal Studies blog at http://www.elsblog.org/the_empirical_legal_studi/courts_judges/index.html, accessed 14 April 2009). There are emerging studies relating to legal practice in the three jurisdictions examined here. In Canada, there are studies from the late 1980s (Canadian Sentencing Commission 1988; Roberts, Doob et al. 1999); in Australia from the early 1980s (Cashman 1985) and Mack's and Roach Anleu's own work from 2007, but nothing similar was found for New Zealand. Carter (1974) and Johnson (2002) have researched legal justice attitudes from the perspective of prosecutors (respectively American and Japanese) and Landau (2004) has examined attitudes towards' restorative forms of response (which in summary is reported as 'generally positive' (2004: 143), based on the perspective of legal professionals in Canada (Toronto)).

approach to the generation of justice when compared with criminal practice, there are nonetheless similar concerns with regard to responsiveness to the essential aims. The overview of programs is drawn from modern Western, largely common law, legal systems where restorative practice has gained either modest or significant foothold in institutional responses. Each site is described using information from primary sources (supplemented by some site visits) and from evaluative and reporting data.[2] In an attempt to discern consistency of practice, where possible programs are assessed in terms of their 'restorativeness' using Roche's (2003) value prescriptions (participation, personalism, reparation and reintegration), and in terms of their 'responsiveness' using the essential aims identified in Chapter 1 (retribution, restoration and consequential outcomes). The focus is on programs in Canada, New Zealand and Australia and in Europe, both continental and in the United Kingdom. New Zealand practice is important because it is the Southern Hemisphere 'birthplace' of restorative justice as well as because of its significant use of community-managed programs, many of which are informed by indigenous practices. New Zealand also provides a good model of mainstreaming restorative practice in its juvenile jurisdiction. Likewise, Canadian practice is important as the respective Northern Hemisphere birthplace of restorative practice and again because of the strong indigenous influence evident in its programs. Australia has a long history of varied institutional experimentation with different programs in a number of its federated states and territories which can provide good examples of institutional experimentation. Australian researchers have also made significant contribution to the development of restorative practice and theory. Programs in continental Europe (most notably Norway, Belgium and the Netherlands) and in the United Kingdom (specifically England and Northern Ireland) are important as examples of newer jurisdictions in which restorative practices have gained some foothold in criminal justice practice where there was previously no historical or institutional foundation.[3]

2 Programs were analyzed using primary source data including print and web-based materials for each program, descriptive and promotional material, and practice and procedure guidelines and manuals. Statistical, evaluative and descriptive reports were also reviewed where available. This content was collected from websites, government sources and independent evaluators and, in the case of New Zealand, Canada and Australia, during site visits as well. Enabling legislation, particularly provisions allowing or restricting restorative referrals based on offence type, seriousness of offending or likely penalty was also reviewed. Many programs have comprehensive practice handbooks, including those in New Zealand (Hayden 2001), Canada (for example, the Nova Scotia program) (Nova Scotia Department of Justice 2005c) and Australia (such as the Victoria program) (Condliffe 2006).

3 By contrast, programs in the US do not lend themselves to a comprehensive analysis. This is because it is difficult to gain any sense of a national direction given that most programs (a 2005 national survey reported in McCorry 2010 identified some 773 such programs) exist locally, operating only within local communities. On the face of it, many of these programs appear to be juvenile restorative programs (Bazemore and Schiff 2005).

Restorativeness and Responsiveness

Not all of these programs are restorative in the McCold and Wachtel (2003) sense of 'mostly' or 'fully' restorative, nor are they all 'responsive' in the sense of being focused on addressing each of the essential aims of criminal wrongdoing responses. To highlight programs that are, the measures of restorativeness and responsiveness provide a useful means to rate programs. These criteria allow comparison of the foothold each has established in the mainstream criminal justice system.

'Restorativeness'

Recall that 'restorativeness' is a way of assessing the extent to which programs facilitate 'fully restorative' encounters. Such 'restorativeness' can conveniently be assessed using Roche's indicia of participation, personalism, reparation and reintegration (Roche 2003: 27–30):

1. 'Participation' assesses interventions on a restorative continuum based on their capacity and intent to engage three broad affected groups – victims, offenders and communities. Where all three groups are involved, a process can be identified as 'fully restorative' or 'mostly restorative' (McCold and Wachtel 2003).
2. 'Personalism' assesses interventions on the basis that wrongdoing is first and foremost seen as a violation of people and their relationships. Programs are seen to be more restorative if they value relational repair above a focus on violations of the law.
3. 'Reparation' assesses interventions on the basis that the practice emphasizes repair of harm caused by wrongdoing over an emphasis on sanction or penalty.
4. 'Reintegration' assesses interventions on the basis that a practice focuses on assisting offenders to rebuild ties with their community rather than emphasizing penalty.

These indicia can help to identify programs that best exemplify programs that are 'fully restorative' or 'mostly restorative'.[4]

4 A number of programs do not satisfy this criterion because of their format or structure. For example, the work of the Restorative Resolutions Project in Winnipeg, Manitoba (visited on 4 June 2004), while highly valuable, seemed to manifest more a process of restorative probation which routinely did not involve any persons affected other than the offender (Richardson and Galaway 1995; Bonta and Gray 1996; Bonta, Wallace-Capretta et al. 1998).

'Responsiveness'

Recall, too, that 'responsiveness' is a way of assessing programs by the extent to which they exhibit a broadly based response to criminal wrongdoing. The essential aims of responses to wrongdoing are used as a means of assessing this degree of responsiveness by the extent to which they meet:

1. The aim of retribution requiring interventions to address violations of the moral standard implicit in the rule of (criminal) law by giving people what they deserve.
2. The aim of restoration requiring interventions to seek to restore personal and normative damage caused by wrongdoing.
3. Consequential aims requiring interventions to seek to protect the community by deterrence and rehabilitative measures.

These indicia are applied to individual programs to identify those which can be assessed as highly or less responsive. In some instances, there was an absence of data on which to assess programs based on these criteria, and in these programs the degree of seriousness of offences was used as a proxy measure. The alternative of 'offence range' assessed responsiveness highly where there was legislative or other capacity to respond to a broad range of offending, particularly serious offending.[5]

New Zealand Restorative Justice Practice

Context: Juvenile Family Group Conferences

Restorative practice in New Zealand has 'an ancient history through its connections with traditional Maori forms of conflict resolution' (NZ Ministry of Justice 2005b: 1.3.1). In its more modern formulations, the New Zealand justice system has engaged with restorative practice beginning at its earliest with juvenile offenders from the late 1980s. The Youth Justice provisions of the *Children, Young Persons and Their Families Act 1989* (NZ) provided a framework for 'responsibilizing' the care and protection of young people. The core of its approach was to require young people who had come to the notice of police for offending behaviour to attend a compulsory family group conference (FGC) prior to the possibility of any arrest or court proceeding being considered. Attendance at a FGC is by way of police diversion. Even if this step is missed and police

5 A number of programs were significantly restricted in this regard. As well, a considerable number of potential programs only responded to juvenile offenders (this was particularly the case in Australia). Programs were not assessed as 'unresponsive' solely on the basis of this criterion if there was still evidence of a broad scope of juvenile offence level and type.

charging of a young offender has in fact occurred, a 'court ordered FGC' is still likely to be ordered.[6] Usually, the outcome of the FGC provides a voluntary plan for the young person to undertake and if this is agreed and completed, no charge or further court sanction results (Becroft 2003: 14–15; McElrea 2005: 13–14). In this sense, the FGC is a complete diversion. The effect of this form of response has been a fundamental shift from the use of court intervention as the default form of response, to instead engaging with young offenders in conferences as the default. This shift produced a systemic change in the New Zealand response to young offending, a shift that has grown and developed since the late 1980s (Carruthers 2005: 10). The change in the form of youth response has also had a profound effect on responses to adult offenders as is evident from the developing restorative jurisprudence discussed in Chapter 7.

Adult Community-managed Programs

Restorative forms of response were gradually and at the outset informally expanded to cover adult offenders from the mid-1990s onwards. The sentencing provisions in the then extant *Criminal Justice Act 1985* (NZ) mandated only one requirement – to 'take into account offers to make amends' and their 'acceptance by victims' as evidence of mitigation (s.12) that could conceivably be seen as having a restorative focus. This small legislative licence was exploited in order to introduce and develop informal restorative responses for adult offenders in increasingly broad terms influenced by the developments in youth justice. From the early 1990s adult conferences were facilitated by the Te Oritenga Restorative Justice Group in Auckland, a large city on the North Island, with cases referred from courts or police (Bowen and Boyack 2003; Carruthers 2005: 11). The first conference was facilitated by Revd Douglas Mansill of Auckland's St Giles Church in 1994. In 1995, the New Zealand government began to provide funding support to develop this and other restorative community-based programs. Three programs dealt solely with adult offenders – Project Turnaround, Te Whanau Awhina and the Community Accountability Programme. Each of the programs was funded as pilots by the New Zealand Crime Prevention Unit in 1996.[7] By 2000, this funding support had been expanded to cover more than 20 diverse restorative programs, which were either administered directly by the then Department of Justice or more often

6 The use of FGC's should be viewed against the backdrop that 'far more young offenders are dealt with by the police *without* using the conference procedure at all' in any event. Some 76 per cent are dealt with by warnings, written cautions or police-organized informal diversions outside the FGC system (McElrea 2005: 14). At the other extreme, about 12 per cent of all youth offending is handled by actual arrest and charging through the courts (Becroft 2003: 14).

7 Project Turnaround operated in Timaru in the South Island, Te Whanau Awhina in West Auckland and the Community Accountability Programme (Second Chance Restorative Justice Programme) in Rotorua in the North Island.

through private providers, such as the Auckland-based Restorative Justice Trust (Morris and Maxwell 2003). Since 2004, these programs have been delivering more than 900 adult conferences annually (Maxwell and Hayes 2006). This form of response developed to be seen as 'an established service in many district courts and communities throughout New Zealand' and as a commonplace way to respond to adult wrongdoing (Paulin and Kingi 2005; Paulin, Kingi et al. 2005; NZ Ministry of Justice 2005b). As we have seen, the acceptance accelerated in 1998 when the New Zealand Court of Appeal gave recognition and overt approval to the use of restorative practices in responses to adult wrongdoing in the *Clotworthy* decision.

A number of programs operated more in the form of 'community panels' rather than as anything that could be strictly identified as 'fully restorative' responses, particularly when there was only small-scale victim involvement (Maxwell and Hayes 2006: 134). However, each of the original pilot programs had other strongly focused restorative elements. The Te Whanau Awhina program, for instance, operating in Waitakere City in suburban Auckland, had a strong Maori community presence, with its meetings held on the *marae* (a communal Maori meeting place) before a panel consisting of local *marae* members and with the offender accompanied by their *whanau* (extended family) and friends (Smith and Cram 1998; Webster 2000). Similarly, the Community Accountability Programme (subsequently renamed the Second Chance Restorative Justice Programme) operated in a similar way in the large rural community of Rotorua in the North Island. Second Chance used a more strictly victim-offender model but still with provision for a strong 'communities of care' presence in the form of family and community-based victim or offender supporters (Maxwell and Hayes 2006: 131 n110). There were several positive early evaluations of these pilot programs in terms of their effect on reducing reoffending, and this helped to cement their standing in the criminal justice system. Maxwell et al. (1999) compared the reconvictions of 200 participants in the Project Turnaround and Te Whanau Awhina programs, with control samples of offenders taken from the same district courts with the same charges. Results indicated that reconvictions for those participating in the restorative schemes were 'significantly less' than the matched control groups.[8] Results from this and similar evaluations gave impetus to moves to place adult restorative programs on a more formal footing within the mainstream system.

8 Project Turnaround showed reconvictions of 16 per cent as compared with 30 per cent for the matched control sample and Te Whanau Awhina showed 33 per cent of participants being reconvicted as compared with 47 per cent of the controls. Morris and Maxwell's analysis of the data (2003: 267 n223) suggests that for the greater proportion of the Te Whanau Awhina participants (and their matched controls) reoffending was 'most likely due to the fact that they were more serious and persistent offenders'. In comparison, a separate evaluation of the Rotorua Second Chance Restorative Justice Programme (Paulin, Kingi et al. 2005) showed that the one-year reconviction rate for a sample of conference participants was very similar for a matched comparison group of offenders (42 per cent as compared with 43 per cent).

Adult Court-annexed Referral Programs

The idea of formalizing an adult court-referred program was first explored in April 1994 by leading restorative advocate District Court judge Fred McElrea in a presentation to the National District Court Judges Conference entitled 'The New Zealand Youth Court: A Model for Development in Other Courts?' The proposal he outlined to introduce restorative practice into adult courts was referred to the Ministry of Justice and a pilot court-annexed program was quickly recommended, though funding was not made available for it to commence until 2001 (Hayden 2001: 9). The conferencing model used in the pilot was a version of the juvenile program redesigned to address some of the perceived deficiencies in the FGC model. Some criticisms of FGC's in evaluations had expressed concern that conferences were often too offender-focused,[9] unnecessarily mandatory[10] and failed to locate and invite the widest possible 'community' group to participate.[11] By the time the adult pilot commenced, there had also been lengthy experience with the 'community panel' response to adult offenders and this experience was drawn upon. These modifications raised high expectations that the victim and 'community' component of adult restorative encounters would be strengthened and expanded.[12] The court-referred adult model began as a pilot in September 2001 and positive results from the evaluation in 2005 encouraged the New Zealand government to expand it as a permanent form of response in district courts throughout the country (initially in central Auckland and Waitakere in the City of Auckland, in regional Hamilton and in Dunedin in the South Island and subsequently in more than 30 other courts) (NZ Ministry of Justice 2010; McElrea 2011; Bowen, Boyack et al. 2012: 128).

The integration of restorative practice for adult offenders was given additional impetus by the legislative change introduced in 2002. As well as the *Sentencing Act 2002* (NZ), parallel changes were introduced in the *Victims' Rights Act 2002* (NZ) and the *Parole Act 2002* (NZ). As a consequence of these changes, courts for the first time were obliged to consider the effect of restorative process outcomes when dealing with adult offenders. It was Section 8(j) of the *Sentencing Act* in particular which provided a requirement that

9 From a low participation base, 51 per cent of victims were reported to be participating in FGC's by 2003 (Becroft 2003: 34).

10 'The striking feature about the earlier [youth] legislation is that there are no gate keepers. The FGC process was made mandatory in virtually all cases in where an offence is admitted' (McElrea 2005: 8).

11 'In some cases, FGCs are being held with only the police, YJC, young person and one parent (usually the mother) attending. This is not seen as a "true" FGC by those connected with the program' (Becroft 2003: 39).

12 A 2005 'stocktake' of community-managed programs showed that of 19 providers, only six were using solely a community panel model (NZ Ministry of Justice 2005b: 4).

> [i]n sentencing or otherwise dealing with an offender the court … must take into account any outcomes of restorative justice processes that have occurred, or that the court is satisfied are likely to occur, in relation to the particular case.

Evaluation of the court-referred adult program in its pilot stage (2001–2004) confirmed earlier findings of a small but significant reduction in reconviction rates for conferenced cases (32 per cent reoffending in the subsequent two years) as compared to matched comparison groups of court-processed offenders (36 per cent reoffending) (Triggs 2005).[13] Also important was the finding that when conferenced offenders did reoffend, the offences for which they were reconvicted in a two-year follow-up period were reported as 'significantly less serious' than those committed by non-conferenced offenders (NZ Ministry of Justice 2005b: 8). Given these positive results in terms of recidivism, the adult scheme was continued past the pilot period stage. It was expanded to cover all of New Zealand's 32 district courts (which deal with the vast bulk of criminal offending in New Zealand) in 2010–11 (Ministry of Justice 2010). The Ministry funds 26 provider organizations (which include the existing networks of 'community-managed' programs) to offer 1,282 conferences across these courts in 2010–11 (Ministry of Justice 2010; see NZ Ministry of Justice: Crime Prevention Unit 2008 for details of these earlier programs). Examining the restorativeness and responsiveness of these adult programs – both community-based and court-annexed – provides a useful assessment of New Zealand restorative practice.

New Zealand Adult Programs

Restorativeness

As examples of New Zealand practice, both the Auckland Restorative Justice Trust, a community-managed program operating in Auckland,[14] and the court referral programs prioritize strong community involvement. Each has an indirect community presence through the external provider groups, drawing trained facilitators and convenors from local communities and networks.[15] As to more direct community participation for those affected by the wrongdoing, the court-

---

13 McElrea disputes suggestions that these reductions are not statistically significant. In a recalculation of the raw data, he suggests a '9% reduction in reoffending measured after 2 years, together with a 50% reduction in the seriousness of offences where participants did reoffend' (2007b: 102).

14 See Restorative Justice Aotearoa; http://www.restorativejusticeaotearoa.org.nz, accessed 20 August 2013. The Trust, which formed in 1999, is an umbrella group of restorative justice services contracted by the New Zealand Ministry of Justice to respond to referrals from the North Shore District Court in Auckland.

15 During the pilot evaluation period, six community providers conducted conferences in Auckland and Waitakere, four in Hamilton and two in Dunedin (NZ Ministry of Justice 2005a: n20).

referred program evaluation reports that more than half of conferences have up to five participants, with 14 per cent having ten or more participants which included the offender, the victim and their respective support groups. In the 91 conferences observed for the pilot, the vast majority of conferences had victim presence. Of these conferences, only five had no victim presence at all and in those cases a victim's representative had participated as a substitute (NZ Ministry of Justice 2005b: n137). In both the community-managed and court-annexed programs, there was also evidence of close attention to developing practice standards that would meet many of the indicia of restorativeness. A training program on restorative justice skills was delivered in a large number of locations in New Zealand in late 2000 with a view to promoting consistency in practice and procedure. The practice guide for this training emphasized principles similar to participation, personalism, reparation and reintegration (Hayden 2001). Consistency in adhering to these standards has since been maintained by ongoing training, some of which was provided by Auckland Restorative Justice Trust personnel (Bowen and Boyack 2003: 3). A consultative process produced a set of 'Principles of Best Practice for Restorative Process in Criminal Cases' and a 'Statement of Restorative Justice Values and Processes', both of which were implemented and which specifically endorsed participation, reintegration and reparation as important practice values (NZ Ministry of Justice 2004).

Responsiveness

Using the proxy of offence responsiveness, the type and seriousness of offences dealt with in the community-based programs is controlled in large measure by the range of cases referred by courts or police. These referrals generally involve a high degree of offence seriousness, but are subject to mandatory exclusion of cases involving family and sexual violence. It is noteworthy that a number of community-managed providers do include family violence offences in their intakes, reporting that 'a significance proportion of its intake involves such cases' (Maxwell and Hayes 2006: 134). Rotorua Second Chance, Taupo's 'Making it Right' and the Whakamana Tikanga Program in South Waikato have all reported high proportions of offenders with family violence offences (in 2005 they respectively reported these as 30 per cent, 40 per cent and 39 per cent of the referrals they accepted) (NZ Ministry of Justice 2005a). The offence range is similarly broad for the court-annexed programs. In these programs offenders must first plead guilty to an 'eligible' offence which can include all property matters with maximum penalties of two years' or more imprisonment, 'almost all' other *Crimes Act* offences where the maximum penalty is between two and seven years' imprisonment, as well as more serious driving offences causing death and 'more serious' firearm offences. Drug offences and domestic violence offences are currently excluded from referral (NZ Ministry of Justice 2005b: 1.5.3, 2010). In this overview, both the community-managed and court-annexed programs assess well against the criteria of restorativeness and responsiveness. The data available for both programs show a strong commitment to the indicia of restorativeness (participation, personalism, reparation and reintegration). This was also evident from observations made at site visits and during court attendances.[16] A number of facilitators and others involved in these programs were interviewed, and their perspectives about how these practices generate a sense of justice are reported in the next chapter.

Canadian Restorative Justice Practice

Context: National Legislative Framework

Unlike New Zealand, Canada does not have a nationwide form of restorative response. Though Canada's constitutional structure gives the federal government exclusive legislative authority in criminal law, this has never resulted in any essential consistency of response to criminal wrongdoing (Archibald 2008).[17] This is partly because the *Constitution Act 1982* envisages the sharing of legislative and administrative regulation of policing, courts and corrections between the federal and provincial governments.[18] What this has meant in practice is a wide variety of local and regional forms of criminal justice practice. The introduction of the *Canadian Charter of Rights and Freedoms 1982* saw a further push towards greater provincial autonomy in forms of response which has led to still greater variety (Archibald 2008).[19] Against this background of diversity, a number of inquiries have highlighted disproportionate incarceration of Canada's Aboriginal peoples, both in terms of relative numbers and more pointedly in terms of specific provincial locations.[20] Reviews also found the regime of responses to youth offending in the then extant national *Young Offenders Act* of 1985 was unnecessarily punitive, with a 'very high use of custody as a sentence, particularly for less serious and non-violent offences'

16 The Auckland District Court was observed on 7 July 2005. During the court session observed, a number of referrals for family group conferences were made under s.246 of the *Children, Young Persons, and Their Families Act 1989* (NZ) which is the trigger for the 'decline to deny' referrals, allowing FGC's to be held without an explicit acceptance of responsibility.

17 The provinces are Alberta, British Columbia, Manitoba, New Brunswick, Newfoundland and Labrador, Nova Scotia, Ontario, Prince Edward Island, Quebec and Saskatchewan. The territories of Nunavut, Yukon and the Northwest Territories were added to the federation but only exercise such legislative powers as are delegated to them by the federal government.

18 Schedule B to the *Canada Act 1982* (UK), c.11.

19 The Canadian *Charter of Rights and Freedoms* forms Part I of the *Constitution Act*, proclaimed on 17 April 1982.

20 A large number of commissions and inquiries had investigated the excessive incarceration of Aboriginal peoples in Canada, especially in the 1990s with the Public Inquiry into the Administration of Justice and Aboriginal People (1991) and the Royal Commission on Aboriginal Peoples (1996).

(Department of Justice Canada 2002: 8).[21] In response to this provincial governments began to develop various 'alternative measures', most pressingly to address the high levels of indigenous and youth incarceration. An important consequence of at least some of these alternative approaches was the recognition of indigenous conceptions of justice emphasizing reintegrative approaches. However, as Roberts and Roach (2003: 240) caution, 'the forms of Aboriginal justice are as diverse as Aboriginal peoples themselves, and should not be reduced to, or assimilated within the restorative justice paradigm'. Nonetheless, some Aboriginal justice responses such as initiatives with circle sentencing have developed as an established alternative sentencing process and these draw from traditional peacemaking circles with some distinctive elements of restorativeness (Stuart 1997a).[22]

It was from these responses that a number of provinces established distinctly restorative type programs, particularly programs for juvenile offenders.[23] These programs are very broad in scope and varied in terms of their accessibility, variety and breadth of application but many have clear elements of restoration.[24] Three of these programs measure particularly well in terms of their restorativeness and responsiveness and were selected for closer review:

- The Toronto-based Community Council Project which operates as a diversionary response for indigenous offenders through a referral scheme from the Gladue Aboriginal Court;
- The Ottawa-based Collaborative Justice Project which has operated as a program for serious offenders from referral from the Ottawa Provincial Court; and

21 These included 'A Review of the *Young Offenders Act 1985* and the Youth Justice System in Canada', Report of the Federal-Provincial-Territorial Task Force on Youth Justice (1996); 'Renewing Youth Justice', Report of the House of Commons Standing Committee on Justice and Human Rights (1997) and 'A Strategy for the Renewal of Youth Justice', Report of the Department of Justice Canada (1998).

22 Examples of circle sentencing programs in Canada include the Carcross Circle Program in Yukon Territory and, in a different form, the Four Circles of Hollow Water (Aboriginal Corrections Policy Unit 1997).

23 Quebec retains its strong emphasis on rehabilitation programs instead.

24 Other programs include the Victim-Offender Mediation Project Langley (Roberts 1995) and the Fraser Valley Community Restorative Justice Programs Network (Beebe, Williams et al. 2003), both in British Columbia; the Restorative Resolutions Project in Winnipeg, Manitoba (Richardson and Galaway 1995; Bonta and Gray 1996; Bonta, Wallace-Capretta et al. 1998) which provided a form of restorative probation; the adult victim-offender mediation program in Saskatoon, Saskatchewan (Nuffield 1997); the Toronto-based Community Council Project (Aboriginal Legal Services of Toronto 2007) and the Ottawa-based Collaborative Justice Project (Rugge and Cormier 2003; Rugge, Bonta et al. 2005), both in Ontario and both dealing with serious level offences and, lastly, the Nova Scotia Restorative Justice Program (Nova Scotia Department of Justice 2005a, 2005b, 2005c), dealing with juvenile offenders.

- The Nova Scotia Restorative Justice Program which operates a province-wide program for juvenile offenders through a network of community justice agencies from referral from police and juvenile courts.

Toronto Community Council Program

Since 1992, the Aboriginal Legal Services of Toronto (ALST) has administered a community council program (CCP) dealing with referrals from city-based courts in that city.[25] The CCP provides restorative-type diversionary programs for both adult and juvenile criminal offenders who identify as Aboriginal (Aboriginal Legal Services of Toronto 2007). When an Aboriginal offender is assessed as appropriate for the program, prosecution consent is sought for diversion from court on condition of an admission of guilt. If the diversion is agreed, charges are then stayed or in some instances withdrawn. Offenders charged with serious assaults and robberies where jail is a distinct possibility form the core target group for this program. Those charged with domestic violence or sexual assaults are excluded from the program. A CCP 'hearing' first takes place with the offender, two or three elders (drawn from a panel of some 30 to 40 traditional elders) and an indigenous caseworker. The offender and his or her support group attend. While 'every effort is made to encourage victim participation', there is in fact small victim involvement (Aboriginal Legal Services of Toronto 2007). The number of community panel meetings held for each offender varies between two and three sessions, but these sessions are usually followed by continuing caseworker contact over varying ongoing periods. The successful completion of a program is marked with a 'graduation' ceremony conducted before community groups, judges and other court officials involved in the program. While the CCP operates solely as a diversionary program, the court from which the majority of its referrals flow also uses restorative approaches in its own sentencing practice. This was as a direct consequence of the decision in *R v Gladue* mandating a departure from traditional sentencing jurisprudence in the case of Aboriginal offenders. The *Gladue* decision was the catalyst for the creation of the first Aboriginal-specific Gladue (Aboriginal Persons) Court by the judges in the downtown Toronto District Court in 2001 (Knazan 2003). The development of this court was seen as an explicit move to a practice of 'sentencing within a restorative justice paradigm' as prescribed by *Gladue* (Turpel-Lafond 1999). This designated 'Aboriginal Persons' court has since expanded in terms of court time (up from two half days to two full days per week) and in terms of its influence on the use of restorative sentencing principles in

25 The function of ALST is not primarily to offer legal representation but to strengthen the capacity of the Aboriginal community to deal with justice issues and to 'provide Aboriginal controlled and culturally based justice alternatives' (Aboriginal Legal Services of Toronto 2007). Its representational role is essentially confined to intervening in major Supreme Court of Canada cases, and assisting in deaths in custody inquests and appearances in test case sentence appeals, such as *Proulx* (2000).

courts more broadly in Toronto and across Canada (see Knazan 2003, 2005). The guiding principles of the Gladue Court are to make the court as Aboriginal-specific as possible. This is done both by 'identification' (accepting self-identification as Indian, Metis or Inuit from offenders); through targeting 'resources' (specifically identifying and drawing upon Aboriginal social services agencies for sentencing options) and by creating a particular court 'atmosphere' that provides for a respect for Aboriginality in court protocol. This respect is exemplified through the exercise of care in the use and pronunciation of Aboriginal names and place names, through ensuring an Aboriginal 'presence' in court in terms of court personnel and through providing time for the offender to be heard and have his or her Aboriginal presence specifically acknowledged (Knazan 2003: 5–15). Ongoing evaluations of the court over three-year cycles shows an increasing caseload (assessed against the number of reports prepared by caseworkers) rising from approximately 50 matters in 2005 to 75 in 2006 and continuing to increase annually, with most referrals (80 per cent) coming from requests by defence counsel. Recommendations in community conference reports for restorative-type outcomes are reported as being 'completely' or 'mostly' accepted by courts as a substitute for usually more punitively based sentences (Campbell Research Associates 2006a, 2006b). Examining the restorativeness and responsiveness of the CCP program provides one assessment of Canadian restorative practice.

Toronto CCP's restorativeness

The CCP's focus on establishing or reestablishing indigenous community ties by drawing upon Aboriginal social services agencies to 'provide offenders with realistic and meaningful dispositions' aims to support the achievement of outcome obligations by offenders (Aboriginal Legal Services of Toronto 2007). While the process 'encourages' victim attendance, it is seen as 'giving little [real] scope for victims' interests' or participation, with its major focus being on integrating offenders into their particular Aboriginal community (Roach 2007). Roche's work (2003: 269) confirmed that while victims are invited to attend they rarely do, and if they do attend they often prefer to participate in separate meetings with the community panel rather than together with the offender. There is nonetheless a strong emphasis on personalism, particularly in terms of encouraging offenders to use the opportunity to strengthen their Aboriginal community values and thereby allow 'the Aboriginal community of Toronto to take a measure of control over the manner that the criminal justice system deals with Aboriginal offenders' (Aboriginal Legal Services of Toronto 2007). In deciding how best to accomplish this healing, 'the Council make[s] a decision requiring the individual to do certain things ... [aimed at beginning] the healing process' which then forms part of an outcome agreement (Aboriginal Legal Services of Toronto 2007). Common 'requirements' for the offender to meet may include reparation, attendance at counselling, community service or treatment programs. The performance of these agreed outcomes is monitored by indigenous caseworkers. and their monitoring records indicate 'successful completion figures are extremely high, even for individuals with long-term interactions with the criminal justice system' (Drumgold 2004: 37). Data reported by Proulx (2003) from CCP records confirmed full completion rates in 65 per cent of cases and partial completion rates in an additional 13 per cent of matters. This emphasis on community participation, though without virtually any victim participation, and on addressing personal elements of offending and integration suggest a relatively high level of restorativeness in the program while allowing for a low level of victim participation.

Toronto CCP's responsiveness

As regards responsiveness, there is a much stronger emphasis on restoration than retribution in the CCP's responses. There is also a clearer emphasis on addressing particular consequential goals, especially in attempting to reduce offending through treatment and long-term rehabilitation but without resort to separation or imprisonment. At the same time there is no statutory basis for the CCP, and as such no legislative schedule of 'eligible offences' to which the scheme is bound. Referrals are simply based upon a practice protocol between ALST and the Crown Attorney's Office. The types of offences which are usually diverted do, however, cover a wide range of offence type which are open to further extension by agreement between ALST and the Crown Attorney (Aboriginal Legal Services of Toronto 2007). For instance, a history of success in reducing reoffending with prior participants has seen 'increasingly complex matters being diverted' (Drumgold 2004: 36) so that diversion now includes serious offences of robbery and violent assaults. This has 'resulted in gradual erosion of the pool of excluded charges', making the potential offence range quite broad (Drumgold 2004: 36). On this basis, the CCP is assessed highly in terms of its responsiveness.

Ottawa Collaborative Justice Project

The Collaborative Justice Project (CJP) in Ottawa has had a long history of applying restorative approaches to objectively 'serious offending'. The CJP completed in excess of 300 cases in its 'serious offending' mode from 1998 until 2007, when its rate of serious referrals lowered due to funding changes.[26] While the program excludes sexual assaults and domestic violence, it does include most other serious offence categories, such as robbery, aggravated assault, break and enter, impaired driving causing death and various serious frauds. Case referral is by the Ottawa Provincial Court following a guilty plea and is subject to consent of the prosecution and defence. Charges are adjourned for a number of months to allow the intervention to take place, after which the offender returns to court for reporting and final sentencing. The desired outcome of the program is to reach a 'resolution agreement' (which may or may not be the result of a face-to-face

26 Since 2007, government funding has been earmarked for post-sentence youth cases and diversionary programs for young adult offenders. Private funding is used to maintain a now-limited serious offender program.

encounter with the victim) which contains provisions with respect to apology, agreed attendance at various treatment programs (violence, anger management, drug or alcohol counselling), restitution, agreed future behaviour and certain forms of reconciliation gestures (apologies, reparation, community service) (Collaborative Justice Project 1999). Resolution agreements are made available to the court and the agreement provisions more often than not form the core terms of probation orders set. For instance, a typical court order is a conditional sentence with the agreed outcome provisions providing the court-imposed conditions. Examining the CJP's restorativeness and responsiveness provides another useful assessment of Canadian restorative practice.

Ottawa CJP's restorativeness

Bringing the offender, the victim and affected community members together in a face-to-face encounter is viewed by the CJP as one way to address its aims of 'support, accompaniment and empowerment' for those affected by wrongdoing (Collaborative Justice Project 1999). This is characterized as a restorative process though it can proceed without victim participation, provided consent is given for the process to take place by the victim in their absence. An option of indirect contact is also available as a form of communication between the victim and offender using a caseworker as an intermediary. About half (47.3 per cent) of all victims contacted by the program participate in either direct or indirect form. The most common reason for non-participation is that victims already feel a sense of closure and so lack the desire to communicate further with the offender (Rugge, Bonta et al. 2005: 37). Conversely, the most common reason for participation is to obtain information about the offence, to 'hear' the offender's explanation and to communicate the impact the offence has had on them to the offender and his or her supporters. An additional aim of the CJP is to empower victims, 'allowing them to decide the nature and degree of contact with the offender' (Rugge, Bonta et al. 2005: 40). In the absence of direct victim participation, the process continues with the offender, their social supports and 'engaged community members such as community volunteers, a police and a probation officer' as participants (Rugge, Bonta et al. 2005: 5). The philosophy of the CJP is 'to demonstrate how an approach that promotes healing and repair in cases of serious crime can deliver more satisfying justice to victims, the accused and the community' than a traditional form of response (Collaborative Justice Project 1999). In this sense, there is a clear emphasis on personalism and direct involvement. Resolution agreements also show a strong emphasis on reparation, both symbolic and material. Symbolic reparation in the form of apology is reported in more than 87 per cent of matters evaluated, either in face-to-face meetings or communicated by letter (Rugge, Bonta et al. 2005: 22). Resolution plans also typically include provision for monetary restitution. Additionally, there is a strong emphasis on reintegration through rehabilitative measures, including performing community services, attendance or continuance of treatment programs and maintaining or finding regular employment (Rugge, Bonta et al. 2005: 22).[27] Data on completion of resolution agreements suggests that successful reintegration occurs more often when a direct face-to-face meeting has taken place (Rugge, Bonta et al. 2005: 22). Some victim reintegration is also suggested in reports of slightly lower levels of fear of further offending following face-to-face meetings (Rugge, Bonta et al. 2005: 26). Victims who have participated report their heightened suspicion of strangers and unease in public places had been alleviated as compared with a control group of victims whose offenders were dealt with in the traditional justice system (Rugge, Bonta et al. 2005: 27). From the analysis of the program's primary data and from a site visit and courtroom observations when matters were referred,[28] the Ottawa CJP was assessed highly against the indicia of restorativeness. There was a particularly strong emphasis on participation (though focused primarily on offenders) and on personalism. The program's website notes this view on offending:

> [T]he application of a restorative approach in cases of serious adult or youth crime, [provides] for a more satisfying experience of justice for all parties involved, for the victim(s), offender(s) and the community. We recognize that serious crime usually involves a greater degree of impact and therefore contributes to a greater need for a restorative approach.[29]

Ottawa CJP's responsiveness

As regards responsiveness, the focus of offending in the CJP is on 'serious criminal matters' of a kind that would normally be dealt with by a court and would typically result in imprisonment of the offender. Offenders who have participated in the program are assessed as having committed a 'fairly serious crime, with 70.8 per cent of offenders committing crime against the person' (Rugge, Bonta et al. 2005: 38). This finding was moderated to some extent by analysis of data showing that 'although crimes against the person are certainly serious, results indicated that over half of offenders were [in fact] first time offenders and less than one third of victims reported physical injury resulting from the crime, ([though] seven cases involved a death)' (Rugge, Bonta et al. 2005: 38–39). Program offenders are therefore more likely to be persons who have committed serious crimes rather than necessarily being 'serious' offenders in the sense of being habitual criminals themselves. This is confirmed when offenders are assessed against the risk of reoffending, with the CJP participants 'scoring as low to medium risk' of reoffending. At the time of referral, many offenders certainly face the prospect of a period of imprisonment for their offending, though less than 20 per cent eventually receive a full-time

27 When the case returns to court for sentencing the Crown is reported as supporting the vast majority of plans (85.4 per cent) and the court itself generally endorses those plans (in 79 per cent of cases) (Rugge and Cormier 2003).

28 The Ottawa Provincial Court was observed while in session on 1 October 2007.

29 Http://www.collaborativejustice.ca/EN/who-we-are.php, accessed 20 August 2013.

custodial sentence (Rugge, Bonta et al. 2005: 39).[30] Offenders have reported their own objectives from the program in restorative terms as 'needing' to apologize, provide an explanation for their actions and have the opportunity to repair the harm they had caused (Rugge and Cormier 2003: 9). In this analysis, the Ottawa CJP also assesses well in terms of responsiveness.

Nova Scotia Restorative Justice

The Nova Scotia Restorative Justice (NSRJ) program commenced as a provincial government 'alternative measure' initiative in 1997. The program developed from a lengthy consultative process involving all 'the criminal justice services [seen as making] vital discretionary decisions in relation to offenders and victims' (Archibald 2008).[31] The province's justice system has been particularly amenable to innovative approaches, given that 'alternative measures other than judicial proceedings' have been used to divert adult and youth offenders from as early as 1986.[32] Since the mid-1990s, the Royal Canadian Mounted Police (RCMP) has also conducted a diversionary program for adult and youth offenders in that province called Community Justice Forums (CJF).[33] Additionally, Community Corrections has had a parallel adult diversionary program covering offenders charged with 'low end offences' since the mid-1980s.[34] Nonetheless, some of these programs have been criticized as being essentially stigmatizing and narrow in their reach and purpose and hardly restorative in any strict sense. The NSRJ therefore sought to introduce an explicitly restorative program (see Montgomery 1997; Archibald 2008: 301). Guidelines to introduce the NSRJ initiative province-wide

---

30 A common penalty is a conditional sentence (served in the community) where the offender is subject to a range of liberty-reducing conditions imposed under Section 741.1 of the *Criminal Code*. Conditional sentences have been interpreted by some (see Roberts and Roach 2003: 246) as 'restorative sentences', but this was not a view shared by the CJP staff itself (Mann 2007).

31 Archibald relates a story of just how serendipitous this was in his and Llewellyn's (2006: 301) review of the history of the program. He says, 'a critical turning point for restorative justice in Nova Scotia was an airplane conversation in early 1997 between the then provincial Minister of Justice and a prominent criminal defence counsel who were both returning from Vancouver after attendance at one of the first large restorative justice congresses ever held in Canada'.

32 Section 717 of the *Criminal Code* (1985) provides for the program's authorization of alternative measures for adults, and the now repealed *Young Offenders Act* (1985) under s.4 provided similar authorization for young persons.

33 This is based on the Australian Wagga Wagga restorative justice model (Archibald 2008).

34 A post-charge Adult Diversion Program is in place pursuant to Section 717 of the *Criminal Code* (Nova Scotia Department of Justice 1998: 10). Clairmont estimates that this program, which in some instances involves victim-offender mediation, diverts up to 1,500 offenders per annum (2007).

were negotiated in the form of a protocol under the then extant federal *Young Offenders Act 1985*.[35] The NSRJ program for young offenders initially commenced as a pilot in November 1999 in four communities, and by 2001 was extended province-wide on a permanent basis (Archibald 2008: 298).[36] It remains today as an established program, focused on juveniles. The NSRJ program involves conferencing delivered through a network of regional nonprofit agencies. These agencies have significant prior experience through their involvement in the earlier youth 'alternative measures' programs. The NSRJ program is also closely aligned with two existing and continuing province-wide restorative programs – the indigenous Mi'kmaq Customary Law Program[37] and the RCMP-run Community Justice Forums, both of which are now seen as 'dovetail[ing] closely with the NSRJ in protocol and administration' (Clairmont 2005: 4). The program is designed to provide for a 'continuum of options', only some of which would qualify as 'fully' or 'mostly' restorative in the McCold and Wachtel sense (Nova Scotia Department of Justice 2005a: 11–13). For instance, the preexisting individual or group 'accountability sessions' and 'adult diversions' (which do not involve victim participation) were incorporated into the new scheme and while now classified as 'alternative measures', are not restorative in a strict sense (Archibald 2008: 318).[38] More specific 'restorative justice' processes which do emphasize encounter and which include 'victim-offender conferences, restorative conferences and sentencing circles' are much more akin to 'fully' restorative options. The scheme's operational protocol for these processes mandates that 'an agency shall not conduct a 'restorative justice process' [without] the victim or a representative from the community of harm' being present (Nova Scotia Department of Justice 2005a: 12).

35 See *Restorative Justice: A Program for Nova Scotia* (Nova Scotia Department of Justice 1998). The *Program* (1998: 19) provides that 'implementation of the Initiative will be multi-phased', and at the time of review had not extended past 'Phase 1 targeting youth between the ages of 12 and 17', firstly in the pilot areas and subsequently province-wide. The Nova Scotia Attorney General's authorization for the youth-focused phases was reissued in April 2003 under the *Youth Criminal Justice Act 2002* as 'extra-judicial sanctions' and extra-judicial measures' pursuant to s.10.

36 The original four communities were the Cape Breton Regional Municipality and the Halifax Regional Municipality (both urban), and the Cumberland County and the Kings/Annapolis/West Hants Region (both rural).

37 The Mi'kmaq Customary Law Program is part of the Aboriginal community development activities of the Mi'kmaq Legal Support Network, which has recognized government status for the conduct of treaty rights and constitutional rights claims and provides a voice on indigenous justice development (see Clairmont and McMillan 2001; Archibald and Llewellyn 2006: 311).

38 As well, Archibald and Llewellyn (2006: 320 n98) report that 'victims were present at a significant number of accountability sessions', which is borne out to some extent by data indicating that of the 391 accountability sessions conducted in 2003–04 'victims or victim representatives' participated in 86, or 22 per cent of the sessions (Nova Scotia Department of Justice 2005b: 12, Chart 18).

Two examples of the program's operation illustrate how the NSRJ works in practice.[39] The Valley Restorative Justice (VRJ) agency delivers the program in three primarily rural-based communities (Annapolis, West Hants and Kings Counties). VRJ deals with up to 10 per cent of the overall province referrals for young offenders (Nova Scotia Department of Justice 2005b: 6, Chart 2). The vast majority of offences handled (in fact, more than 70 per cent) involve 'property offences', with a small proportion of 'violent offences' (approximately 5 per cent) making up the largest part of the remainder (Valley Restorative Justice 2007: Appendix 4). The most common form of response is a 'community group conference', and in almost two-thirds of these sessions, victims (or victim or community representatives) are present. A further indirect community presence is built into the program as the convenors who co-facilitate the restorative encounters and supervise the completion of outcome agreement commitments are all local community members undertaking the convening work on a voluntary basis. A second example is the Halifax Community Restorative Justice (HCRJ) which operates in the predominantly urban area of Halifax. The HCRJ deals with up to 45 per cent of the total province-wide referrals, including two-thirds of all post-charge referrals in the province.[40] The effect of this high referral rate is that HCRJ conducts a large volume of what its facilitators describe as 'high harm files' in many of its referrals. This has resulted in the scheme becoming 'a very major option for dealing with young offenders', used by both police and prosecutors as a commonplace alternative to the court process (Clairmont 2006: 14). The HCRJ's most typical restorative response is 'accountability sessions' which are conducted in the absence of a victim by a community volunteer facilitator.[41] Assessing the HCRJ in terms of the restorativeness and responsiveness criteria provide one further means to gauge the quality of Canadian restorative practice.

---

39 The agencies cover both urban (Halifax Community and Island Community) and a range of rural areas (including The Valley, Southwest Community and Cumberland County). The HCRJ was visited on 3 October and the VRJ on 4 October 2007. No court observations were conducted in Nova Scotia.

40 In 2006, HCRJ staff report that they accepted 692 referrals and of these 57 per cent were post-charge (Interview comments of HCRJ staff 3 October 2007). In Nova Scotia, as distinct from the practice in other provinces, police lay charges rather than the Crown. Where the Crown refers a matter to restorative justice, the charge already laid by police is either dismissed outright or stayed until outcome agreement commitments are completed.

41 HCRJ staff report that they would 'do' victim-offender sessions in about 20 per cent of matters (Interview comments of HCRJ staff 3 October 2007). 'Accountability sessions' are described as 'an accountability meeting where the youth, accompanied by parents/ guardian, is required to explore the offence and its impact with trained facilitators and develops and commits to a reparation plan which forms the Restorative Justice Agreement' (Nova Scotia Department of Justice 2005b: 11).

Nova Scotia RJ's restorativeness

Particularly in those forms of responses explicitly categorized as 'restorative' including victim-offender conferences and sentencing circles (conducted by the Mi'kmaq Customary Law Program), active personal participation is an important value of the program. This emphasis on personalism is enhanced by the use of community volunteers to conduct conferences and afterwards to manage agreement commitments. The NSRJ philosophy is driven by an explicit 'relational conception of justice' which has strong resonance with the value of personalism. 'Criminal wrongdoing' is seen as behaviour which disrupts social equilibrium and requires 'social dialogue that includes victims and perpetrators and involves concrete consideration of the needs of each for restoration' in order to address that disequilibrium (Llewellyn and Howse 1999: 375). The program therefore rejects a purely criminal violation focus in favour of 'a restorative approach [that] invites the participation of communities in achieving reconciliation between offenders and those harmed through the commission of an offence' (Nova Scotia Department of Justice 2005a: 6).[42] This emphasis on 'community' participation has a number of practical dimensions. The delivery mode of the program is through not-for-profit agencies which combine paid staff with 'high calibre volunteers [who operate] at the facilitator and board levels' in conducting conferences and in managing outcome agreements (Clairmont 2005: 5). For this reason, the programs are seen as being 'clearly rooted in the communities which they serve' (Archibald 2008: 311). The NSRJ program also reflects an explicit emphasis on reparation and reintegration. Reparation is emphasized as one means of bringing together 'the victim, offender and community members [to] actively participate in a process which identifies how the offender may begin to repair the harm'. More specifically, the process is designed to put in place 'reparation plans to respond to the harm done' (Nova Scotia Department of Justice 2005a: 2–3). This analysis suggests that the NSRJ program clearly assesses well in terms of the restorativeness criteria.

Nova Scotia RJ's responsiveness

Referrals to the NSRJ program are subject to an 'offence level' restriction which regulates the stages at which offences of various levels of seriousness can be referred. Moratoria remain in place for certain offence types, including serious sexual assault and family violence (Nova Scotia Department of Justice 2005a: Appendix B; Archibald and Llewellyn 2006: 315).[43] There is a standard categorization of offence types which determines the level and timing

42 The NSRJ Coordinator in interview on 4 October 2007 expressed the view that 'one stated goal of the program is "building stronger communities", but we need language for, and evidence of, what this means in practice. If we just use anecdotes of successful encounters, this looks like our concepts are underdeveloped or uncertain'.

43 The Protocol notes, 'there is currently a moratorium in place restricting the referral' of three classes of offences: sexual offences (summary), spousal/partner violence offences (both Level 3) and sexual offences (indictable), which are a Level 4 offence (Nova

of restorative referrals.[44] This schema of 'offence level' referral has the effect that while most offences are potentially open to restorative intervention, judicial oversight is retained as the gateway for those charged with more serious offences.[45] There is some evidence of a reduction in reoffending in the referral category offenders. In the HCRJ scheme, self-reported reoffending by young persons (in the six-month period after their first restorative session) showed reduced levels of reoffending (self-reported at only 9 per cent) (Clairmont 2005: 175–176).[46] Data from a wider 'window of opportunity' (the two-year period post-session) confirms a similar pattern of reduced offending. The commitment by justice officials to a restorative response seems to remain intact even when reoffending does occur, as more than 20 per cent of those who have had a previous 'restorative justice experience' again referred to 'another RJ experience' by police or prosecution in relation to fresh reoffending in the evaluation sample (Clairmont 2005: 185–186).[47] Indirect evidence of reintegration is clear from the effect the program has had on reductions in the use of imprisonment for young offenders in Nova Scotia. A review of the federal *Youth Criminal Justice Act 2002* changes showed significantly decreased use of custodial sentences for young persons following years of depressingly high youth incarceration rates in most provinces (Department of Justice Canada 2005). Nova Scotia was no exception. Significantly, its reduction in rates of youths 'jailed' became evident from 1999, when the pilot was introduced and was again seen to spike further downwards from 2001, when the scheme became province-wide (Clairmont 2005a). There was other confirming evidence that young offenders were being diverted from court-based responses. The rate of 'youth *not* charged (but otherwise dealt with) per a 10,000 of population rose from 164 to 641' in the period 1999–2003. This suggests a substantial uptake of

---

Scotia Department of Justice 2005b). This moratorium was imposed in April 2000 and remained in place at the time of review.

44 Only minor property and assault offences ('Level 1 offences') are referable for pre-charge caution. 'Level 2 offences' (such as break and entering, some fraud and theft-related offences) are referable at all entry points of police, Crown, court and Corrections. 'Level 3 offences' (which include more serious fraud and theft-related offences, summary sexual offences, aggravated assaults, dangerous driving causing death, and manslaughter) are referable only at the court and Corrections entry points. 'Level 4 offences', which are the most serious category (currently only murder), can be referred only at post-conviction.

45 This may explain why the allocation of offence levels was an exacting process involving 'lots of stuff that had to be fought through involving the four levels of offences and the four entry points' (Interview comments of the Crown Attorney, representative on the 'Police' and 'Crown Entry Points' subcommittees 4 October 2007).

46 Clairmont (2005: 176) expresses caution concerning this sample of 359 youths, saying the follow-up sample may not be representative since only 53 per cent of the original young offenders consented to reinterview.

47 This sample of 854 young offenders came from the four 'founding' restorative justice agencies (Halifax, Sydney, Amherst and Kentville) involved in the initial pilot project which commenced in November 1999, and thus were drawn from both urban and rural communities.

diversionary alternatives amongst police and youth courts acting as an alternative to the use of traditional 'charging' and court attendance (Clairmont 2005: 27). This diversionary uptake was not reported as 'net-widening' but more as evidence that a semi-formal alternative intervention could be 'beneficial for both the youth and the larger community' where court processing would otherwise occur (Clairmont 2005: 13). The net effect on courts was that 'judges were seeing fewer young people aged 12 to 17 in their courtrooms', and fewer of those whom they did see were being jailed (Statistics Canada 2000). In addition, the 'requisite attention to the needs of victims, offenders and communities' in order to effect reintegration was also reported as being significantly increased through restorative responses (Archibald 2008: 329). This analysis also assesses the NSRJ program highly in terms of the responsiveness criteria.

Each of these Canadian programs rate relatively highly against the criteria of restorativeness and responsiveness. Primary source material and observations confirm the programs as 'mostly' or 'fully' restorative and rate them well in terms of responsiveness. They provide good examples from which to draw insights about how a sense of justice is generated in restorative processes. Comments from facilitators working in these programs about how this sense of justice is generated are reported in the next chapter.

Australian Restorative Justice Practice

Context: Early Experimentation

The Australian development and implementation of restorative justice has in large measure been influenced by the New Zealand experience coupled with some of its own experiments involving reintegrative shaming theory. Australian programs have since expanded from a discrete focus on the dynamic of reintegrative shaming (as used in the now superseded Wagga Wagga and RISE experiments[48]) to embrace more diverse practice approaches, though these are still mainly focused on juvenile offenders (Braithwaite 1989; Sherman and Strang 1997a). Each Australian state or territory now has a legislatively-based restorative program of some kind (see Maxwell and Hayes 2006).[49] Of particular interest are those

48 RISE continues as an experiment with longitudinal data currently being collected from participants in original referrals.

49 Statutory programs on a state-run or territorial basis include the Queensland Youth Justice conferencing operation (since 1997) (Hayes, Prenzler et al. 1998; Hayes and Daly 2004); the conferences administered by the Tasmanian dual system of police (since 1994) and the Department of Health (since 2000 with the proclamation of the *Youth Justice Act 1997* (Tas)) (Pritchard 2002, 2004); the West Australian Restorative Justice Conference program for young persons (since 1994) (Cant and Downie 1998); the Northern Territory police pre-court diversion program for young people (since 1999 under amendments to

programs which use varied models of family group conferencing as well as those programs with some (albeit limited) application to young adult offenders. From the breadth of operational programs, four were selected as sites for closer review to give a snapshot of the breadth of current practice (for more detailed description of Australian practices see the recent collection of Bolitho, Bruce and Mason (2012):

- The New South Wales (NSW) Juvenile Conferencing Scheme which operates as an adjunct to that state's juvenile justice system;
- The Australian Capital Territory (ACT) Restorative Justice Scheme which operates as a territory-wide program for young persons;
- The South Australian Family Conference Scheme which operates as an adjunct to that state's Youth Court;
- The Victorian Youth Justice Group Conferencing Program which operates as an adjunct to that state's Children's Court.

NSW Youth Justice Conferencing

The Youth Justice Conferencing scheme was established under the *Young Offenders Act 1997* (NSW) (YOA) and commenced operation in 1998. Since then, an average of 1,600 conferences are conducted each year throughout NSW (Wengert 2008).[50] The scheme was deliberately designed to provide 'an alternative process to court proceedings for dealing with children who commit certain offences' (Shaw 1997). The legislative framework provides for three different levels of intervention, beginning with police warnings and cautions and graduating to Youth Justice Conferences (YJC's). The use of diversionary options is not mandatory, but the regulated sequence of responses is deliberately designed to direct the exercise of police discretion away from court appearances for young people towards alternative forms of response. This has been successful to a significant degree (Chan, Bargen et al. 2004). In common with other jurisdictions, there are statutory limits on the type of offences that may be referred to each of the three levels of diversion. A Youth Justice Conference, which is the peak diversionary option, operates as a 'decision-making body' to the extent that it can make recommendations about the young person and determine an outcome plan regarding them (s.34(2)YOA). In doing

---

the *Juvenile Justice Act* (NT)) of 1997 (Wilczynski, Wallace et al. 2004); the New South Wales Juvenile Conferencing Scheme (since 1998) (Trimboli 2000); the Australian Capital Territory Restorative Justice Scheme (since 2005); the South Australian Family Conference Scheme (since 1994) (Daly, Venables et al. 1998) and the Victorian Youth Justice Group Conferencing Program (since 1995) (Markiewicz, Lagay et al. 1997, 1997a). Victoria was the last to have a legislative backing when the *Children Youth and Families Act* (Vic) of 2005 conference provisions were extended to all Children's Courts in 2007 following an initial Melbourne-based pilot.

50 Maxwell and Hayes reported an average of 1,373 conferences in the period 1999–2004 (2006: 137).

so, conference participants are specifically directed to make recommendations which provide some form of relief to the victim (s.34(3)(e)) to meet 'the need to make reparation' while at the same time reintegrating the offender into their family and community in a way that 'strengthens the family or family group' (s.34(1)(a)(ii). There is a clear intention to provide developmental and support services which will 'enable the young person to overcome the offending behaviour and become a fully autonomous individual' (Trimboli 2000: 1).

It is noteworthy that in 2005, the YJC model was used for a pilot to extend conferencing to young adult offenders (aged 18 to 24 years).[51] The Community Conferencing Program for Young Adults (CCYA) program was established under the *Criminal Procedure Act 1986* (NSW) and was designed to give courts additional sentencing options for young adult offenders likely to be facing a sentence of imprisonment (People and Trimboli 2007: 1). The program commenced in two Local Courts in Liverpool in suburban Sydney and on the New South Wales north coast Tweed Heads circuit in September 2005. Though the CCYA scheme gave the conference group some limited decision-making power in ways similar to that of the YJC, its primary function was to develop a 'draft intervention plan' through which the young adult offender could show commitment to 'undertake activities or attend programs which aim at promoting rehabilitation and reducing re-offending' (NSW Attorney General's Department 2005). The program accepted a wide range of serious offenders (statutory exclusions include sexual assaults and domestic violence offences). Disappointingly, more than half the referrals in the initial pilot period were for traffic or drug-related offences. This understandably resulted in low victim participation rates (36 per cent) which were predicted to increase if the range of offence types were expanded (People and Trimboli 2007: 20). However, in 2008 the CCYA was 'repositioned' to operate more as a 'sentencing initiative' (and renamed 'Forum Sentencing') with a consequently much lessened restorative capacity. Though it has been extended to other Local Courts in New South Wales (now located in more than 50 courts), the young adult program has shifted significantly from a restorative form of response to operating simply as an additional sentencing input process.[52] However in a recent report Hart and Pirc, managers in the program, suggest that Forum Sentencing exhibits considerable restorative potential (2012). Assessing the restorativeness and responsiveness of the YJC scheme provides one measure of the quality of Australian restorative practice.

---

51 NSW also has a post-sentence program operated since 1999 by the NSW Department of Corrective Services. Its Restorative Justice Unit (RJU) facilitates victim-offender family group conferences with offenders in custody where victims have requested or agreed to a mediated encounter (Milner 2012).

52 The press release from the NSW Attorney General announcing this repositioning was titled 'Victims of Crime to Assist in Sentencing' and promised that under the program 'offenders will be '*ordered* to sit down with their victims' and '*might be forced* to make an apology, pay compensation or undertake drug and alcohol treatment' (Hatzistergos 2008, emphasis added).

NSW YJC's restorativeness

YJC's fare moderately well when assessed against the restorativeness criterion.[53] The YJC scheme (and the CCP scheme in its pilot mode) was 'designed to open up participation in criminal justice processes to families, victims and "communities of care" in arguable restorative ways' (Bargen 2003: 2). The scheme provides an 'entitlement' to a young person and members of his or her family or extended family to attend a conference, and this is also the case with the victim (or victim representative) and their support persons (s.47(1)). Additionally, the convenor has the capacity to build a 'community of care' for the offender by inviting 'a respected member of the community', a representative of any school the young person attends and the young person's care worker together with 'any other person requested by the child's family or extended family' (s.47(2)). Trimboli found in her evaluation of some 400 conferences that in 90 per cent of matters at least one member of the young person's immediate family did attend, and that in 18 per cent of cases at least one member of the extended family (for example, a grandparent, aunt or uncle) also attended (2000: 61). Also in three-quarters of conferences, at least one victim was present (2000: 28). The preparation for and conduct of conference is in the hands of paid conference convenors recruited from the local community. The hiring of convenors on a fee-for-service basis is seen as 'a deliberate move to de-bureaucratize the operations of the conference, to avoid burnouts as experienced in other jurisdictions, as well as to involve members of local communities' (Chan, Bargen et al. 2004: 80). Since the start of 2005, the number of active convenors has stabilized at approximate 370 who are based in metropolitan Sydney and in regional communities (Chan, Bargen et al. 2004: 80). However, the notion that crime is primarily a response to law breaking remains at the heart of the scheme. There is little evidence of a move to prioritize more personal effects of wrongdoing. In reaching decisions, participants are specifically directed to have regard to 'the need to make reparation to any victim' (s.34(3)). Evaluations suggest some dissatisfaction with how well this is met in practice. In response to an evaluation question – 'What are the *worst* features of the outcome plan?', the most frequent comment made by victims (23 per cent of victims) and their support persons (17 per cent of support persons) is that compensation is not seen as commensurate with the harm caused by the offending (Trimboli 2000: 48–49). By contrast, reintegration does appear as a strong principle of the YJC scheme in that young persons are seen as best 'dealt with in their communities in order to assist their reintegration and to sustain family and community ties' (s.7(e)). The impact of YJC attendance also shows a positive effect on reduced levels of reoffending with an evaluation which compared the experience of conference and court pathways indicating that conferencing resulted in up to a 20 per cent greater reduction in the rate of reoffending as compared to the court process, albeit for only certain categories of offences (Luke and Lind 2002). Allowing for some qualifications, the YJC is assessable as showing a significant

53 The Queanbeyan regional YJC unit was visited on 3 January 2008.

commitment to restorativeness, in particular in strongly emphasizing participation and reintegration.

NSW YJC's responsiveness

There are statutory limitations on the type and seriousness of offences that may be diverted to conferencing (s.8(2)). The stated intention is that conferencing is not to be used for minor offences, which are instead to be dealt with by way of 'warnings' or 'cautions'. Warnings can be used for a wide range of minor offences, provided those offences do not involve violence (s.13); and cautions can be used for a still wider range of offences eligible to dealt with by police response alone, subject to considerations of seriousness, degree of violence involved and harm caused (s.20(3)). The range of offences that can be conferenced include property and personal violence offences below a certain ceiling, with serious violence offences, serious sexual assaults, domestic violence offences and serious drug offences excluded (s.8(1a–b)). The statutory scheme's provision for three levels of response (warnings, cautions and conferences) has meant that more serious offending comes before conferences. In this sense it assesses well in terms of the responsiveness criterion. Additionally, the program's approach incorporates strong due process protections designed to 'facilitate the protection of children's rights through weaving procedural and other safeguards into the fabric of the scheme' (Bargen 1996: 235).[54] On the basis of its current and potential offence breadth, the YJC is assessable moderately highly in terms of its responsiveness.

The ACT Restorative Justice Scheme

A statutory scheme of restorative practice was introduced into the Australian Capital Territory (ACT) in 2005, underpinned by the *Crimes (Restorative Justice) Act 2004* (ACT). Prior to this, a pre-court diversionary conferencing scheme had been delivered by ACT Policing since 1994 for juvenile and adult offenders.[55] For part of that period (1995–2000), the effectiveness of this diversionary form of conferencing was subject to detailed evaluation as part of the Reintegrative Shaming Experiment (RISE) project.[56] The ACT statutory scheme has two phases.

54 Bargen (1996, 2001) had been strongly critical of the absence of these protections in police run conferences prior to the implementation of the 1997 *Young Offenders Act* (NSW) scheme in 1998. She was then appointed to the new position of the Director of YJC in NSW which he held for some time and facilitated the interweaving of procedural protections to a significant degree.

55 By 2004, the number of diversionary conferences conducted by ACT Policing had fallen from 500 at its peak to fewer than 50 per year (Legislative Assembly for the Australian Capital Territory 2004: 2).

56 The RISE project gathered data about diversionary conferences including 900 adult drink driving offenders, 470 juvenile property offenders (some with a personal victim and others without a personal victim such as shoplifting offences) and 110 violence offenders under the age of 30. A central hypothesis of the experiments was that there would

Phase One commenced in January 2005 and focuses specifically on young offenders aged 10 to 18 years of age who have accepted responsibility for certain 'less serious' offences. Phase Two is yet to commence, but could potentially expand the scheme to include adult offenders, and 'more serious' offences, for both juvenile and adult offenders (possibly including family violence and sexual assault offences) (ACT Department of Justice and Community Safety 2006: 7). The operation of the Restorative Justice Scheme is closely regulated by its governing legislation, the *Crimes (Restorative Justice) Act* of 2004. Section 6(a) of that statute specifies the object of the scheme as:

> to enhance the rights of victims of offences by providing restorative justice as a way of empowering victims to make decisions about how to repair the harm done by offences.

The scheme's further stated purpose is to make a constructive impact upon the offender by enabling him or her 'to express contrition or remorse in a meaningful way' (Legislative Assembly for the Australian Capital Territory 2004: 5).[57] The key means to achieving both these aims is through a facilitated conference. The scheme is administered by the ACT Restorative Justice Unit (RJU), created under the Act which operates as part of the ACT Justice and Community Safety Directorate. Referrals for participation in the program are made to the RJU by various criminal justice system actors, and the RJU then makes assessments of suitability based on considerations such as power balances and safety to determine whether participation is likely to be a constructive or a negative experience for victims. The scheme 'requires' that certain parties take part in a conference and this includes 'a suitable victim or parent' (s.42(1)(a)). The Phase One review (completed after the first year of operation in 2005) showed that the vast majority of referrals assessed as 'unsuitable' for conference were either because no suitable victim could be contacted or because the victim did not consent to participate (ACT Department of Justice and Community Safety 2006: 14). A total of 63 per cent of victims participated in the first year (2006: 15). The most common reasons for non-participation were 'not feeling personally affected by the crime', 'not wanting to have contact with the offender' or simply 'wanting to move on and put the matter behind them' (ACT Department of Justice and Community Safety 2006: 16). More

be less repeat offending after a conference than after court. This was borne out primarily in the case of the violence offenders, with no significant differences seen in the case of property offenders (except for a subgroup analysis involving 23 Aboriginal offenders where reoffending was exacerbated by conferencing) and a small increase for drink drive offenders that proved transitory (Sherman, Strang et al. 2000; Sherman and Strang 2007).

57 'However, these other positive aspects of restorative justice are not outlined in the objects of the Act because the starting point of the scheme is victims' (Legislative Assembly for the Australian Capital Territory 2004: 5).

extensive external evaluations are not yet publicly available.[58] A review of the RJU's restorativeness and responsiveness provides another measure of the quality of Australian restorative practice.

ACT RJU's restorativeness

As well as offender and victim attendance, the scheme provides that convenors may invite supporters of both the offender and victim to a conference as 'community participants' (ACT Department of Justice and Community Safety 2006: 35).[59] In addition to these supporters, relevant police and 'persons acting for participants in a professional capacity' (lawyers, 'victim/offender intercessors' and the like) are seen as part of the community that can be 'constructed' by the facilitator (s.44(3)). The scheme is positioned so as to 'augment' rather than replace offence-based notions of criminal justice. This is reflected in the stated intention to address 'victims' needs ... without distorting the prosecution of a crime' (Legislative Assembly for the Australian Capital Territory 2004: 5). The primary aim of a conference is to reach an outcome agreement which includes measures 'intended to repair the harm caused by the offence'. Such measures routinely include apology, plans to address the offending behaviour, work plans and provisions for material or symbolic reparation. The scheme specifically excludes measures which require the offender to be detained, humiliated or made to endure duress. The first phase review indicates that outcome agreements consistently showed a trend towards victims demonstrating that 'they want young people to undertake some type of program that assists young people to address their offending behaviour' (ACT Department of Justice and Community Safety 2006: 46). The types of tasks identified as beneficial in this regard were seen as 'attendance at residential rehabilitation programs', 'drug and alcohol counselling', 'anger management course attendance' and 'sport and recreation programs'. Any outcome agreement is made available to all parties and to the referring entity and the court. A very high compliance rate (98 per cent reported in the first year) with the terms of individual agreements was reported, due in large measure to the strict monitoring by the RJU (ACT Department of Justice and Community Safety 2006: 21). The extent to which victims and offenders have been able to resume their normal lives after the effects of wrongdoing was viewed as a measure of their 'reintegration'. Using self-reporting assessments of level of anger, fear and anxiety before and after conferences, both victims and offenders expressed significantly reduced feelings of distress.[60] Most victims reported a shift

58 The ACT RJU was visited on 6 and 13 September 2006 and an RJU-facilitated conference was observed on 12 April 2006.

59 Over 95 per cent of both victim supporters and young person supporters were reported as finding the process 'helpful' and 'fair' and indicated that they would 'participate in a process again' and 'recommend it to someone else' (ACT Department of Justice and Community Safety 2006: 35–38).

60 Victims' level of anger with the person responsible for the harming was reported to have dropped from 44 per cent before the conference to 16 per cent after, and similarly

in negative attitudes towards the offender (falling from 66 per cent of victims reporting antipathy before the conference to 43 per cent after the process). In a similar vein, more than three-quarters of victims anticipated that they would have no difficulty in meeting the young person again (ACT Department of Justice and Community Safety 2006: 40–41). Reintegration of offenders measured in terms of the pattern and type of any reoffending behaviour indicates 'no particularly high rate of recidivism' during the initial 'window of opportunity' of up to 18 months post-conference (ACT Department of Justice and Community Safety 2006: 44). Based on this data, the RJU assesses well against the criterion of restorativeness.

ACT RJU's responsiveness

Consistent with the intention to 'augment the criminal justice process' rather than replace it, two different 'triggers' operate for different levels of offences to be engaged by the Act (Legislative Assembly for the Australian Capital Territory 2004: 5). For 'less serious offences', the trigger is 'an acceptance of responsibility for the commission of an offence' (s.20) which opens up the conferencing option as an ancillary form of response. For 'serious' offences (e.g., offences against the person which hold a penalty exceeding 10 years jail), the trigger requires a formal plea of guilty with the availability of conferencing options regulated by the stage in the criminal process at which the plea is entered. Essentially, opportunities for referral diminish as the case proceeds upwards through the criminal process.[61] The RJU program provide a significant response to criminal wrongdoing with a deliberate focus on addressing victims' needs while still retaining a strong focus on offender needs. Based on these assessments the RJU also fares well in terms of the responsiveness criterion.

South Australian Family Conference Scheme

The South Australian Family Conference Scheme has operated as an adjunct to that state's Youth Court since 1994 under the provisions of the *Young Offenders Act* (SA) of 1993. The program operates state-wide, with approximately 70 per cent of referrals coming from police and most of the balance from the Youth Court. Some 1,800 conferences are held each year, representing about 18 per cent of all youth offending subject to police action in South Australia (Daly, Venables

---

with level of fear (dropping from 12 per cent to 2 per cent) and level of anxiety (dropping from 29 per cent of victims who were anxious to 13 per cent) (ACT Department of Justice and Community Safety 2006: 38–40).

61 'Less serious offences' include a very wide class of matters where the penalty is below the statutory maxima (10 years' imprisonment for offences against the person and 14 years for other offences). As the second phase has not yet commenced, all domestic violence and sexual offences remain excluded.

et al. 1998: 7).[62] Conferencing has also been pursued (in 2005) for pre-sentence young adult offenders but its extension to such offenders has not continued past the pilot stage principally because of small referral numbers (Goldsmith, Halsey et al. 2005). Young offenders referred to the scheme are required to attend conferences accompanied by 'such other persons [who are] invited to attend', usually one parent, invariably their mother. About half of victims also attend (Doig 2008). Wider participation than offenders and victims in conferences is reported as small, with the average number participants in more than two-thirds of conferences being three or fewer, excluding the facilitator and police youth officer (Daly, Venables et al. 1998: 8). The program does not require a broader community attendance as its legislative basis specifically confines the referral to 'family' conferences. The Family Conference Team which facilitates all conferences is part of the SA Courts Administration Authority and is co-located with the Youth Court.[63] Assessing the restorativeness and responsiveness of the South Australian scheme provides a further measure of the quality of Australian restorative practice.

South Australian FCS's restorativeness

The SA program has been subject to substantial evaluation, predominantly as part of the South Australian Juvenile Justice Project (SAJJ), since 1998. One of the objectives of that research is to assess the degree to which participants involved in the process experience a sense of 'restorativeness' as a consequence of their involvement. SAJJ's measures of restorativeness have sought to 'tap the degree to which offenders and victims recognized the other and were affected by the other', focusing on signs of 'positive movement between the offender and victim and their supports during the conference' as indications of this (Daly 2002: 207). As part of the evaluation, SAJJ researchers have observed up to 90 conferences in which more serious offending was being addressed and which were seen as having the type of 'high emotional intensity for victims (and offenders)' likely to provoke some 'positive movement' (Daly, Venables et al. 1998: 16, 26). Participants in the conferences have been assessed by SAJJ researchers for evidence of 'movement' suggestive of restorativeness (Daly, Venables et al. 1998: 10). Results have indicated high levels of perceived procedural justice, though fewer participants reported feeling 'restored' in terms of the relational measure used (Daly 2002: 206–207). The indicators of restorativeness include specific behaviours, such as displays of remorse and offers of apologies and less defined signals, such as 'the degree and quality of interactions' in terms of 'positive movement (or mutual understanding) between the victim and the young person' (Daly, Venables et al. 1998: Appendixes 1, 4, 5;

62 Estimate supplied by Marnie Doig, Family Conference Team (2008). Maxwell and Hayes's (2006: 136) finding of an average of 1,669 finalized case referrals for the period 1999–2003 based on Office of Crime Statistics Reports confirms this estimate.

63 The SA FGC program at the Youth Court was visited on 18 August 2009.

Daly 2001, 2006: n4).[64] 'Restorativeness' measured in this way was seen as present 'in 30 to 60 percent of conferences' and solidly present 'in about one-third of cases' (Daly 2002: 207; Daly 2006: 138).[65] Daly suggests that 'restorativeness' is less easily achieved than procedural fairness because the relationship from which this renewal needs to emerge is necessarily more personal and more a factor of the interaction between parties rather than an atmosphere that could be created by a facilitator. As it is the personal relationship most likely to have been damaged by the wrongdoing, pathways to repair and renewal are therefore likely to be significantly weaker (Daly 2006: 138).[66] Assessment of the South Australian FGC program suggests significant evidence of 'restorativeness'.

South Australian FCS's responsiveness

The objective seriousness of the range of offences dealt with in this scheme is substantial. As Maxwell and Hayes (2006: 136) point out, '[o]ne important jurisdictional feature of family conferencing in SA is that there is no schedule of offences that may be referred to conference'. The legislation provides on its face that a conference referral may be made 'if a youth admits to the commission of a *minor* offence' (s.7(i)). However, the standard of 'minor' as provided for in police operational protocols allows for a much wider scope than what might otherwise be considered 'minor' in an objective sense. Police practice has also been influenced by the decision in *R v Police* (2002) SASC 403 (Gray J), where the South Australian Supreme Court considered the interpretation of legislative provisions which restrict court diversion. The Supreme Court held that while the referral power of police might itself be specifically limited to 'minor offences', 'there is no reason in principle to limit the court's [own] power to refer only minor matters' (para. 24). A broader capacity for courts to refer was accepted as necessary to allow diversion to a 'family conference [where it] may be appropriately used as an alternative to traditional sentencing' (para. 25). The practical effect of the decision has been that courts could refer even if the police did not. As a consequence, police discretion itself has been exercised widely and covers a variety of objectively 'serious offences'. Types of offences routinely conferenced include major indictable matters ranging from serious organized shoplifting to arson and

64 Facilitator responses were obtained from self-completed surveys, while offenders and victims were separately interviewed face-to-face.

65 Interestingly, Daly speculates that it is in jurisdictions where conferences are routinely used (as in South Australia) that we should not expect to see 'restorativeness' emerging most of the time. By comparison, in other jurisdictions where conferences are used selectively (perhaps for matters seen as ripe for relational repair) restorativeness may be more likely to be evident (2002: 210 n210).

66 In contrast, in the adult conferencing pilot 'restorativeness' was assessed in terms of 'emotional well-being as well as tangible compensation' coupled with the effect on participants of 'a genuine display of remorse', and this was seen as more easily achievable (Goldsmith, Halsey et al. 2005: 25, 37).

dangerous assaults to serious sexual offending, including rape where committed by juveniles.[67] The program's exposure to this broad range of objectively serious offending clearly rates well in terms of responsiveness.

Victorian Group Conferencing Program

Since 1995, restorative programs have operated without legislative backing in Victoria. These operations began with group conferencing conducted by Anglicare Victoria as a private provider for a small number of juvenile referrals by Victorian Children's Courts. This developed further into a more formal Group Conferencing Program (GCP) dealing with offenders who face supervisory order (such as a probation, youth supervision or youth attendance order) in those courts (Maxwell and Hayes 2006: 143).[68] This program was later expanded to other areas of Victoria and other providers. In 2006 the scheme was given statutory recognition under the 2005 *Children, Youth and Families Act* (Vic), and in 2007 conferencing was expanded to cover all Children's Courts in Victoria.[69]

A wider role for restorative responses has also been proposed for young adult offenders, and such a pilot commenced in 2008 (Bassett 2007).[70] This pilot was situated at the Collingwood Neighbourhood Justice Centre (NJC), which is an innovative court operating in the form of a 'multi-door court' since 2007 under the *Courts Legislation (Neighbourhood Justice Centre) Act* (Vic) of 2006. The NJC court has an explicit mandate to 'apply therapeutic and restorative approaches in the administration of justice' (s.1).[71] The target number for the two-year trial period was set at a relatively low 15 to 25 conferences per year (Bassett and Walker 2008: 5). Despite these modest aims, the young adult program was not continued beyond the pilot due to low levels of referrals. The aim of conferencing in the juvenile program was seen as 'improving decision making with young

---

67 SAJJ data suggest that serious matters were routinely conferenced, with, for instance, more indecent assault offences by youths (carrying up to 10 years' imprisonment) in fact being finalized by conferencing rather than in court in the period 1995–2001 (59 per cent as compared with 35 per cent) (Daly, Curtis-Fawley et al. 2003: Table 2a).

68 There were about 500 young offenders potentially facing such an order each year.

69 Group Conferencing provider organizations were expanded from Anglicare (whose area was moved to Gippsland) to include Jesuit Social Services (Metropolitan Melbourne) and the Salvation Army (Hume).

70 Rob Hulls, the Victorian Attorney General at the time, was reported as considering restorative justice for adult offenders more generally; http://www.crikey.com.au, accessed 8 May 2009.

71 The Collingwood NJC has been in operation since 2007 and is designed to house a wide range of services from which the court can draw. The services available on-site include community corrections, Aboriginal justice, alcohol and drug case officers, mediation, crime and violence prevention, legal aid, financial counselling, victim support, mental health, emergency relief, accommodation services and family violence support (Lim and Bassett 2008).

offenders, as well as reducing the rate of juvenile offending, and diverting young people away from state programs' (Markiewicz, Lagay et al. 1997: vii). This aim has been addressed by 'utilising the resources of the family and significant others, and empowering them in the decision making process' within the criminal justice system (Markiewicz, Lagay et al. 1997: 1). The scheme requires that conferences be attended by the young person, by his or her lawyer and by the police informant (s.415(6)). A conference may also be attended by members of the young person's family and 'persons of significance' to him or her and by the victim or a victim representative (s.415(7)). In practice, this has resulted in the young person being accompanied by his family and supporters, together with the arresting police and a youth lawyer, and in some instances the victim or a victim representative (Spencer and McIvor 2000: 7).[72] Victims are reported as participating directly in approximately half of conferences (Bassett and Walker 2008: 31). The young adult pilot similarly emphasizes restorative encounters with victims attending where possible, as this is seen to 'strengthen the integrity of the conferencing process by requiring offenders to face their victim' and therefore may 'improve victim satisfaction with and participation in the justice process' (Bassett and Walker 2008: 30). The Victorian GCP was reviewed from primary source material and from the observations made at site visits.[73] Assessing the restorativeness and responsiveness of the GCP scheme provides a further measure of the quality of Australian restorative practice.

Victorian GCP's restorativeness

The conferencing program extends the response to criminal wrongdoing from primarily a breach of the law to encompass its effects as a violation of people and their relationships. Participants in the process are asked to 'provide suggestions about how [the young person] might repair the harm caused to the victim'. These suggestions, in turn, 'set ... the expectations for the outcome plan' (Victorian Department of Human Services 2007). Informational material from provider agencies conducting conferences explicitly emphasize this aspect of repair. One provider's promotional pamphlet asks, 'Would you like the chance to say sorry and make amends?' (Jesuit Social Services 2005). The young adult pilot similarly 'aims at transformative outcomes' that promote 'the healing of the victim and the reintegration of the offender, not simply a focus on penalties that punish past wrongdoing' (Young Adult Restorative Justice Group Conferencing

---

72 The lawyer is present at each conference not to 'represent' the young person 'but to advise with respect to the content of plans and ensure that due process is observed' (Spencer and McIvor 2000: 7). Bargen (1996) saw this legal representation aspect of the Victorian model as important in ensuring procedural safeguards absent in some other Australian models.

73 The Collingwood Neighbourhood Justice Centre where the Young Adult Restorative Justice Group Conferencing program was being piloted was visited on two occasions – 13 May and 1 October 2008.

Program 2008: 5). The Group Conferencing scheme identifies two explicit 'strands' in any conference outcome plan. The first 'strand' is specifically directed at 'making reparation to the victim for the offence' and this may include apology, making financial reparation or carrying out unpaid community service (Spencer and McIvor 2000: 7). The young adult pilot has a similar emphasis on increasing 'offenders' awareness of the consequences of their offence for victims and the community and encourag[ing] them to make reparation' (Bassett and Walker 2008: 3). The second 'strand' identifies activities which the young person can undertake. These activities are designed to prevent further offending and assist in his or her rehabilitation (Spencer and McIvor 2000: 7). One agency's factsheets describe these aims as 'providing a community rehabilitation intervention' that diverts the offender from more intensive supervisory court outcomes and 'effectively integrate [him or her] into the community' (Victorian Department of Human Services 2007). If the court accepts the proposals made in the outcome agreement, the convenor engages with the young person and an identified community representative to implement the plan and provide follow-up. In a formal evaluation prior to rollout of the statutory scheme in 2006, 90 per cent of conference plans were assessed as fully or partially implemented, with those monitored by agencies more likely to be fulfilled than those monitored by family members (Markiewicz, Lagay et al. 1997). Young persons were seen to need external assistance in implementing outcome plans (Condliffe 2006: 29). The evaluation also compared conference participants with a comparison group of young persons given court-imposed probation in terms of reoffending rates. However, the results showed little appreciable difference as regards the offending between the two groups over the two-year period post-conference or court (Markiewicz, Lagay et al. 1997a). This review assesses the Victorian GCP well on the restorativeness criterion.

Victorian GCP's responsiveness

Referrals to group conference for young offenders are reserved for those offences in which the court is 'considering imposing a sentence of probation or a youth supervision order' (s.415(1)). This equates to moderate to serious levels of offending.[74] There are standard exclusions such as wrongful death, sex offences or serious violence offences. Sentencing is deferred following referral, and conference reports become a key factor in determining whether a supervision order with restrictive conditions will in fact be imposed (s.414). If the outcome plan is accepted, it may be substituted for the imposition of a strict supervisory order (s.576). The likelihood of a strict order (most generally, a probation order)

74 In the case of the young adult pilot, the program provides for multiple referral points (via police, courts and corrections) designed to capture offenders who might not normally be diverted to conferencing, with the hope of capturing more serious forms of offending than is the case with the juvenile program (Young Adult Restorative Justice Group Conferencing Program 2008).

increases if the young person has appeared before the court on previous occasions. A 2008 evaluation indicated that a pool of approximately 500 young people per year fell into the category of potential recipients of a supervision order. From that pool, an increasing number now attend conferences (rising from an initial 20 per year prior to the legislation to about 200 each year since the program went state-wide), with a significant resulting decline in the number of supervisory orders being imposed in Children's Courts (Griffiths 2008). Additionally, the program structure addresses many of the procedural critiques made of other juvenile programs (Bargen 1996). These protections (assured to a degree by the availability of legal advice at all stages in the process) are legislatively mandated. The process covers offenders facing a restrictive supervisory order as a consequence of moderately serious offending. The GCP program also assesses well against the responsiveness measure.

What makes these Australian programs distinctive is the substantial consistency of practice across different modes of delivery even allowing for clear evidence of difference in focus and operation. For instance, the ACT scheme's primary focus is on victims' needs as compared with the South Australian program's emphasis on engaging with young persons who have committed serious offences. This diversity provides for a wide scope of opinion from its facilitators about what works to generate a sense of justice in restorative processes and these views are reported in the next chapter.

European Restorative Justice Practice

Continental Europe

The standout examples of the implementation of restorative justice programs in continental Europe are in Norway and Belgium and, to a lesser extent (at least as regards responses to criminal wrongdoing), in the Netherlands. From these countries, a number of particular sites are particularly illustrative of restorative-focused practice:

- The *Konfliktråd* (National Mediation Services) in Norway;
- The HERGO (*Herstelgericht Groespsoverleg*, or 'Recovery-Focused Group Discussions' adapted from the translation of FGC) scheme which operates as a program for young persons in Belgium; The HALT (*Het ALTernatief* – the 'Alternative') scheme which operates as a diversionary program for young persons in the Netherlands.

Norway

Interest in restorative practice in Norway can be traced back at least to the 1970s, prompted by Nils Christie's critique that criminal justice institutions were 'stealing the conflicts' (Christie 1997). Victim-offender mediation (VOM) was introduced as a supplement to criminal proceedings in the 1990s and conferencing was more widely adopted beginning in the early 2000s (Zinsstag, Teunkens et al. 2011). Mediation and conferencing are now provided by the same agency – the *Konfliktråd*, or National Mediation Services (Hydle and Kemény 2010). There is a legislative base for offering the service (seen as a service 'offered' to citizens rather than as a program imposed on them (Zinsstag, Teunkens et al. 2011: 276)) under the provisions of the *National Mediation Service Act* of 1991 (with new legislation proposed at the time of review), with the procedures for both mediation and conferencing also regulated by the *Criminal Procedure Act* and the *Criminal Code* of 2003. The purpose of such mediation is expressed in the 1991 Act as 'intended as an alternative to ordinary criminal proceedings and to the resolution of other conflicts'. Mediation services now operate in some 22 regions throughout the country, broadly following police district boundaries (Kemény 2005). Mediation (both VOM and mediation in civil disputes) is more widely used, with Vanfraechem reporting figures of 9,000 mediations per year in 2007 (Van Doosselaere and Vanfraechem 2010). According to Hydle (2008), approximately half of these are for criminal cases, though a large number of the civil cases are offences where the offending parties are under the age of consent (15 years) and thus are essentially 'criminal' in nature. Hydle reports that FGC has been taken up on an experimental level since 1999 and is now regularly used (Hydle 2008). The Ministry of Justice's stated aim is to also increase the use of FGC with a view to conducting at least 250 conferences annually across the country (Zinsstag, Teunkens et al. 2011). The *Konfliktråd* program can be assessed against the restorativeness and responsiveness measures as one test of the quality of European restorative practice.

Konfliktråd

Restorativeness

As noted above the *Konfliktråd* provides mediation and conferencing, and no clear distinction is drawn here between the two services. The seriousness of the case, the resultant need for supporters and the number of persons affected by the wrongdoing are seen as the main factors in deciding between conducting conferencing and holding victim-offender mediation. When the conferencing model is used the offender is present, and 'most victims will participate' (Zinsstag, Teunkens et al. 2011: 279) together with their 'networks'. Hydle (2008) reports that in 69 per cent of cases referred, mediation or an FGC took place, with at least both victim and offender present in a face-to-face meeting. Additionally, a police officer attends in about half the cases (Zinsstag, Teunkens et al. 2011: 281), as do other professionals (on occasion a social worker, youth worker or school representatives, but not a lawyer). Particularly when the service provided is conferencing (which essentially equates to peace-making circles and which is increasingly introduced (see Fredriksen and Andersen 2008), its structure satisfies many of the measures of restorativeness.

Responsiveness
Both mediation and conferencing are used in response to a referral, with 85 per cent of referrals coming from police or prosecutors. The range of offence types can vary from low-level offending up to quite serious offending, such as burglary, but the majority of referrals involve offending for minor violence, destruction of property, shoplifting, bullying and some financial offences (Hydle and Kemény 2010: 209). Hydle (2008) separately provides a breakdown, giving percentages of violence (18 per cent), destruction of property (17 per cent), shoplifting (15 per cent), theft (11 per cent), bullying, defamation and menace (12 per cent) and economic offences (6 per cent). Police or prosecutors act as gateways for referral, and therefore the 'seriousness [of offending] very much depends on [their] willingness to pass on such a case' (Zinsstag, Teunkens et al. 2011: 279). A prerequisite for referral is an initial acknowledgement of the main facts alleged and an acceptance of responsibility, but a plea or finding of guilty is not necessarily required. The usual form of outcome from a conference is an agreement providing for payment of compensation, completion of work, apology or some form of reconciliation (Hydle and Kemény 2010). Given the potential offence range for referrals for moderately serious offending, the *Konfliktråd* rates reasonably well on the responsiveness measure.

Belgium

The federated political structure in Belgium, with three main language communities (Flemish, French and German) and three economic regions not directly corresponding to those language communities (Flanders, Wallonia and Brussels-Capital), means that criminal justice policy has evolved as a shared responsibility among federal and regional governments and community actors (Zinsstag, Teunkens et al. 2011: 259). This shared involvement has affected the engagement with restorative justice initiatives, with federal legislation setting the framework and establishing the requirement that prosecutors consider mediation in all juvenile cases (Vanfraechem, Aertsen et al. 2010). By contrast, implementation is in the main carried out by NGOs recognized and funded by communities (Zinsstag, Teunkens et al. 2011: 259). Since 1994, federal regulations have provided for 'penal mediation' facilitated through prosecutors' offices for adult offenders following their acceptance of responsibility, and this form of response now appears as an accepted part of its criminal justice system.[75] The birth of restorative conferencing can be traced to an initiative and a subsequent pilot scheme which introduced conferencing in Flanders in 2000. The pilot initiative saw restorative conferencing being provided by agencies that had previously offered mediation for juvenile criminal justice interventions, in some cases since the early 1990s. The pilot scheme consisted of the option of an FGC being made available on referral from Youth Courts for mostly serious offending, provided the young offender had

75 Comments of Judge J. P. Geske on restorative justice in Belgium on Restorative Practices eForum; http://www.restorativeworks.net/eforum, accessed 20 August 2013.

admitted or declined to deny responsibility (Vanfraechem 2001). This pilot ran for three years, from 2000 to 2003, with just over 100 conferences being conducted in that period (Zinsstag, Teunkens et al. 2011: 261). Because of positive evaluations (Vanfraechem 2003, 2005, 2006), a permanent conferencing service was established under the new *Youth Protection Act* of 2006. This service continues in Flanders, though principally only in the cities of Brussels and Leuven. Referral numbers for conferencing remain small, with one NGO, ALBA (http://www.alba.be/bal_index.php), conducting between 10 and 25 conferences per year in each city (Zinsstag, Teunkens et al. 2011: 264). Locally known as HERGO, the program is described as 'a conference, which focuses on searching [for] constructive solutions to the consequences of a crime' (Vanfraechem, Aertsen et al. 2010). Alongside these numbers is a larger exposure to mediation (often indirect mediation), with over 4,000 young people referred for mediation, 37 per cent of which proceeded. The HERGO program can be assessed against the restorativeness and responsiveness measures as a further indicator of the quality of European restorative practice.

HERGO

Restorativeness

The service design is strongly based on an FGC model, with core emphasis on the young offender's family and not on victims or the community. While indicated that 'the victim is not obligated to attend in order to participate … it is desirable, since results are generally better if a victim is physically present'; however, attendance is relatively low (Zinsstag, Teunkens et al. 2011: 260). Vanfraechem, Aertsen and Willemsens (2010) report that victims attended about 50 per cent of conferences in the pilot. Also present at a conference are police officers, who begin the process by offering 'a version of the events and the offender has to agree with what is being told … [otherwise,] the proceedings have to stop' (Zinsstag, Teunkens et al. 2011: 261), and youth lawyers and other professionals, who attend to ensure that procedural safeguards are observed.HERGO's conference structure suggests that it rates reasonably well on the measure of restorativeness.

Responsiveness

On the face of it, most wrongdoing can be referred to HERGO (save for homicide offences). With referral rates being very low, conferencing is more commonly seen by prosecutors as best reserved for more serious cases, including serious sexual assaults (Vanseveren 2010). The focus of the conference outcome agreement is then threefold – addressing reparation to the victim, acknowledging the harm done to the community and putting in place measures to prevent further offending (Zinsstag, Teunkens et al. 2011: 261). Given this focus on repair and prevention, HERGO conferences also rate reasonably highly on the responsiveness measure.

The Netherlands

Though the Netherlands had a promising pilot conferencing program in criminal matters in cooperation with police in the early 2000s this has been discontinued, and conferencing is no longer an option in criminal matters (Zinsstag, Teunkens et al. 2011: 267). However, there are a number of continuing programs which conduct conferencing-related programs in non-criminal matters. The *Elgen Kracht Centrale* (EKC) (http://www.eigen-kracht.nl) began operation in 2001 based largely on the FGC model and facilitated more than 3,000 conferences its first ten years (Zinsstag, Teunkens et al. 2011: 269). The focus of its activities remains on assisting individuals in resolving their own social and personal problems (*Elgen Kracht Centrale* literally translating to one's 'own strength') [and not on criminal wrongdoing. Traditionally, referrals most often occurred in child protection matters, but more recently this has been expanded to encompass conflicts arising from 'disturbed development of children, neighbourhood conflicts, a lack of security in the social environment, or domestic violence' (Blad and Van Lieshout 2010: 60). The domestic violence referrals, for instance, arise in situations where a period of separation has already taken place and a conference is organized where the assaulted partner has either decided to return home or to make the separation permanent (Joanknecht 2004). EKC has extended its work throughout the Netherlands and now operates in all provinces (Zinsstag, Teunkens et al. 2011: 272). A second scheme, *Slachtoffer in beeld* (SiB) (http://www.slachtofferinbeeld.nl), has existed since the 1990s and continues to conduct victim-offender mediations as a complementary adjunct to criminal proceedings (Zinsstag, Teunkens et al. 2011: 274). Approximately 1,000 such mediations are conducted per year dealing with quite serious offending, including where the offender is serving a term of imprisonment (Zinsstag, Teunkens et al. 2011: 274). The remaining program where a conferencing-type diversion occurs is the HALT program, founded in Rotterdam in 1981, which recently had 18 offices throughout the Netherlands. It provides a diversionary program for young people aged 12 to 18 years who are offered diversion or 'an alternative' by police when arrested for 'low level' offending such as vandalism, shoplifting or street offences and where they admit responsibility (Zinsstag, Teunkens et al. 2011: 273). If this 'talk' session, as it is referred to, and an outcome plan (which may include 'damage compensation and/or working or learning up to 20 hours') (HALT 2008: 2) are successfully negotiated, any criminal proceedings against the young person are dismissed. The HALT program can be assessed against the restorativeness and responsiveness criteria as further measures of the quality of European restorative practice.

HALT

Restorativeness

The service design for HALT is based closely on the FGC model, with the emphasis on the young offender and his family and the obligatory presence of parents. There is little victim or community participation. The program is therefore at the lower end in terms of restorativeness.

Responsiveness

As only minor wrongdoing can be referred to HALT, its focus is primarily with first offenders. Its main goals are to encourage offenders to take responsibility, to make reparation for the harm done and to serve as a means to involve (or reengage) parents in the young person's life (Zinsstag, Teunkens et al. 2011: 273). As with restorativeness, it rates at the lower level in terms of responsiveness.

The United Kingdom

In the United Kingdom the outstanding example of institutionalized restorative practice is the Northern Ireland Youth Conferencing Service (YCS), which has operated as an adjunct to the Northern Ireland juvenile justice system since the early 2000s. In addition, a small number of restorative pilot programs and some ongoing schemes have or continue to operate in England and Wales.

England and Wales

The UK (particularly England and to a much lesser extent Wales as well as Scotland, whose programs are now largely abandoned[76]) showed great early advances in introducing initiatives and experimental programs to gauge the efficacy of restorative practices throughout the 1980s and 90s and again in the early 2000s. However, many of these initiatives faded or were discontinued when funding was withdrawn. The lack of any overriding statutory basis, particularly where there were statutorily imposed pressures for speedy case management, saw low levels of judicial support and uptake and hence very low levels of referral and opportunities for restorative programs to gain prominence (Zinsstag, Teunkens et al. 2011: 283; Strang 2012). It had been hoped that the refocusing of criminal justice policy foreshadowed in the 2010 Green Paper 'Breaking the Cycle: Effective Punishment, Rehabilitation and Sentencing of Offenders' would include restorative processes as part of the formal justice response (Ministry of Justice 2010a, 2010b). This debate still continues with, for instance, the Restorative Justice Council advocating the use of restorative processes as 'better justice' in their response to the Green Paper (Restorative Justice Council 2011).

76 The largest provider is Sacro (Safeguarding Communities Reducing Offending), visited in July 2007; http://www.sacro.org.uk.

In England and Wales, some early piecemeal legislative provisions had the potential to encourage restorative practices. Section 6 of the *Youth Justice and Criminal Evidence Act* of 1999 provided for the possibility of a 'contract' being negotiated between the parties affected by juvenile offending. This approach developed in the form of youth offender panels which used a conferencing model to conduct meetings among offenders, their parents and supporters, victims and their supporters and members of the community (Crawford and Newburn 2003). Meetings were arranged for young offenders who had been made subject to a referral order and they were designed to continue for the length of the order. However, in practice little or no victim representation meant the panels largely lacked any real measure of restorativeness (Crawford and Newburn 2003). The other indirect legislative warrant was section 201 of the 2003 *Criminal Justice Act* which allowed a 'community sentence' imposed on an adult offender to include 'activities involving contact between offenders and persons affected by their offences'. Though this was seen by some as 'officially encouraging RJ initiatives', its wider use did not prove to be the case in the absence of ongoing agency funding to monitor contact activities (Zinsstag, Teunkens et al. 2011: 286).

There were a number of waves of early innovative and well evaluated initiatives which were not maintained. The first wave comprised a group of pilot schemes for both adult and young offenders in Leeds, Coventry and Essex, funded by the Home Office in 1984–85. The second consisted of an additional group of pilot schemes for adult offenders, funded by the Home Office (later the Ministry of Justice) in 2001–2005 and operated by three agencies, CONNECT and REMEDI (primarily mediation) and the Justice Research Consortium (conferencing). Evaluations of the initiatives essayed in the 1980s and 90s were invariably positive. The Coventry scheme began in 1985, focusing on young offenders and involving indirect mediation. High levels of victim satisfaction were reported (Umbreit and Roberts 1996) but referral rates remained stubbornly low, with 'a lack of will to participate [shown] by some criminal justice authorities' (Zinsstag, Teunkens et al. 2011: 289; see also Strang 2012: 236). The pilot was abandoned as a consequence by the early 1990s (Miers 2001). The focus of the Leeds pilot was direct mediation between offenders and victims pre-sentence, with an emphasis on determining whether alternatives to prison sentences could be substituted. The pilot was evaluated favourably by Marshall and Merry (1990) and again by Wynne (1996), but also lost its funding in the absence of a clear decrease in custodial sentencing. The Essex pilots were court-based schemes developed in three regional towns but once again, despite the strong cooperation of courts, the programs suffered from lack of referrals and were discontinued (Marshall and Merry 1990).

A renewed attempt was made to mainstream programs from 2000 onwards. The CONNECT project began in 2001 with the aims of reducing reoffending, allowing victim responses and reparation and having offenders accept responsibility (Shapland, Atkinson et al. 2004; Shapland, Atkinson et al. 2006; Shapland, Atkinson et al. 2007; Shapland, Atkinson et al. 2008). The project initially provided restorative services to the Camberwell Green Magistrates Court in South London but again, in the face of low or unsuitable referrals, a second court was added at Tower Bridge Magistrates Court to increase referrals, with staff attending court hearings and drawing judges' attention to potential suitable referrals (Shapland, Atkinson et al. 2006). The focus of these programs was upon adult offenders where sentences could be deferred to allow referrals to be completed. The most common process used in referrals was indirect mediation followed by direct mediation, but there was little or no conferencing (Shapland, Atkinson et al. 2004). The scheme was not refunded when the initial funding ceased (Shapland, Atkinson et al. 2006). The REMEDI scheme existed prior to pilot funding, providing services to areas in South Yorkshire, mostly in the form of post-sentence mediation (Shapland, Robinson et al. 2011). These services were expanded to cover all of South Yorkshire, with the Home Office funding injection (Shapland, Atkinson et al. 2004). The program serviced juvenile offenders who were subject to a final court warning (and then facing jail), and adult offenders who were completing community or custodial sentences. The scheme suffered in the absence of a clear legislative framework (which could have mandated or at least encouraged judicial referrals), and the initial time-limited funding was not renewed. However, today the REMEDI program continues to offer more limited services (Shapland, Atkinson et al. 2006).

The Justice Research Consortium (JRC) began as an attempt to introduce randomized controlled trials in a number of sites in London, Northumbria and Thames Valley. The JRC provided for randomly assigned conferences between court or conference referral with varying levels of offences and referral sources. JRC London initially began with 'assault, street crime and burglary' drawing upon two police districts, but was soon (again, in the face of a paucity of referrals) expanded to cover all Crown Courts in Greater London and also to draw referrals from cases of 'robbery/street crime and burglary of a dwelling' (Shapland, Robinson et al. 2011). JRC Northumbria dealt with less serious offending (assault and property crime), initially from a confined geographical area which soon expanded to draw on wider courts amidst a lack of referrals. JRC Thames Valley essentially duplicated the REMEDI model, focusing more on those subject to a community penalty or probationary supervision or in prison and due for release within a year (Shapland, Atkinson et al. 2004; Shapland, Robinson et al. 2011). Referrals were relatively low given the range of referring probation offices and prisons, but 723 referrals did reach the point of randomization (where consent from offenders and victims to conferencing had been obtained), with about half then proceeding to the conferencing stage (Shapland, Atkinson et al. 2006). At the end of the pilot period, the JRC continued to offer some of its conferencing services in the expanded drawing areas.

In summary, these restorative justice initiatives in England and Wales show a pattern of sporadic development, with innovative schemes being dependent on seed or pilot project funding; therefore, when that funding ceases the programs tend to disband, with the consequent loss of important skill and abilities (Shapland, Atkinson et al. 2006).

Northern Ireland

Significantly, and as a consequence of its troubled history, Northern Ireland has been the site of community-based restorative projects since the 1990s (Payne, Conway et al. 2010).[77] As the Independent Commission on Policing for Northern Ireland (1999: 2) recognized, there was considerable community mistrust of policing to the extent that 'the issue of policing is at the heart of many of the problems that politicians have been unable to resolve in Northern Ireland'. The effect of this mistrust, combined with the community's reluctance to engage with the traditional criminal justice system, was a long-standing use of community-based programs to fill the gap. While throughout the Troubles these alternatives were centred on paramilitary punishment violence, with the advent of the peace process restorative programs became the driving force for the more widespread adoption of restorative justice (Feenan 2002). Two community-based programs were significant – Community Restorative Justice Ireland (CRJI), founded in 1994 and predominantly servicing Catholic/Nationalist areas, and Northern Ireland Alternatives (NI Alternatives), set up in 1997 and operating largely in Protestant/Loyalist areas. Both programs began with a focus on diverting young offenders but were soon also involved with adult offenders (Payne, Conway et al. 2010: 20). Referrals first came from respective paramilitary groups but as these referrals dwindled, community members came to access both organizations directly by self-referrals (McGloin 2006). The programs used a number of innovative approaches, such as large community meetings run by CRJI and more focused intensive restorative support (aimed at reintegration) and community restorative assistant panels (providing training in resolving conflicts) run by NI Alternatives (Payne, Conway et al. 2010: 20–22). Nonetheless, both programs remained for a long period on the margin of institutional interventions in criminal wrongdoing. On the one hand, there was reluctance from the organizations themselves to encourage community members to report offences to the police, given the continuing community mistrust of the Royal Ulster Constabulary (RUC) (McEvoy and Eriksson 2008). In addition, their own history and perceived connection with paramilitary organizations meant that there was state suspicion and reluctance to accept their involvement as being appropriate beyond low-level neighbourhood disputes (Payne, Conway et al. 2010: 65–66). Nonetheless, both programs continued to address community justice issues throughout the early 2000s and following the conclusion of a government protocol in 2007 (Northern Ireland Office) these programs began finally to engage more formally with the criminal justice system. Both programs were then formally accredited by the government, NI Alternative in 2007 and CRJI in 2009. This provided access to funding and the opportunity to develop formal partnerships with criminal justice agencies, including the newly created Police Service of Northern Ireland (PSNI) (Payne,

77 This analysis benefits greatly from a conversation with Dr Derick Wilson, University of Ulster 11 September 2013.

Conway et al. 2010: 18). These community-based programs remain firmly entrenched in Northern Ireland society today. CTJI (now through its eight offices; see http://www.crji.ie) continues to deal with an average of 1,000 new cases annually, the majority of which remain neighbourhood- or youth-based self-referrals, with few, if any, referrals from police or the prosecution service. The majority of disputes are dealt with by mediation, usually indirect mediation. As well as these community-managed projects, institutional programs targeted specifically at juvenile offenders have been mainstreamed within the criminal justice system since the early 2000s. 'Restorative justice' was officially recognized as a response to criminal wrongdoing in the *Justice (Northern Ireland) Act* of 2002. The Youth Justice Conference service was established under that act and became operational in late 2003, first in Belfast and then expanding to other regions from 2004 onwards (Zinsstag, Teunkens et al. 2011: 249). More than 1,000 conferences are now conducted with juvenile offenders each year (Independent Commission on Youth Crime and Antisocial Behaviour 2010).

Northern Ireland Youth Conference Service

The youth conferencing service is part of the Youth Justice Agency (YJA). The service became operational in 2003, the result of a long period of gestation and part of the response to the cessation of sectarian violence to improve outdated institutions, particularly in the criminal justice system (Zinsstag, Teunkens et al. 2011: 245). In particular, justice authorities were looking for innovative ways to address high levels of juvenile offending. In searching out alternatives, authorities drew on the New Zealand family group conferencing model (FGC) (Campbell, Devlin et al. 2005) and its model of fully integrating restorative justice (Dignan and Lowey 2000). The YCS delivered significantly on this agenda for integration, with youth conferencing now being the means through which most youth offending is handled. Approximately 1,800 referrals (amounting to about 15 per cent of all young offenders) are made to conferencing each year. For these reasons, it provides the best example to assess UK practice against the indicators of restorativeness and responsiveness.

NIYCS's restorativeness

Although the design of the NIYCS was specifically drawn from the New Zealand FGC model, the Northern Ireland adaptation places more direct emphasis on victims than simply a primary focus on offenders and their families. Campbell et al. (2005) describes the result as a 'balanced model' which gives more equal emphasis to those affected by the wrongdoing, victim, offender and community. In a conference, a young person (the majority of whom are male, ages 14 to 16) is accompanied by an 'appropriate adult' (parent, friend or a professional) (Zinsstag, Teunkens et al. 2011: 250), with victims present in person in about half of the cases with the remainder attending through victim or community representatives (an overall 'victim participation' level of 74 per cent 'taking part in conferences' is reported) (Beckett, Campbell et al. 2005). Generally, there is a police officer present as well as other professionals, sometimes a community representative and on occasion a youth lawyer (Zinsstag, Teunkens et al. 2011: 253). There appears to be little connection between the YCS and the community-based projects, which negates the potential for fuller restorative collaboration (Chapman 2012). Nevertheless, on the available evidence the YCS appears to rate well on the restorativeness criterion.

NIYCS's responsiveness

There are two main sources of referral to the NIYCS, either by the prosecution service before a matter reaches court, or through a court-referred order where the young person has pleaded or been found guilty and required to 'participate in a conference' as part of their sentence (Youth Justice Agency 2007–2008, 2009–10). On the face of it, all types of offending (other than homicides) can be referred to conferencing, but the majority of referrals are for 'intermediate offences against person and property' with a majority involving first-time offenders (Campbell, Devlin et al. 2005). The standard outcome of a conference is a negotiated outcome agreement which may include commitments such as an apology, reimbursement, community work and attendance at therapeutic or educational programs (Zinsstag, Teunkens et al. 2011: 256). Again, the YCS rates well on the responsiveness indicator.

Conclusion

This chapter has sought to paint a picture of restorative practice to dispel myths about its capacity to respond appropriately to criminal wrongdoing. In doing so, it highlights features of programs that clearly suggest a capacity to serve purposes complementary to those of mainstream criminal justice practice. There is also evidence of those features that set it apart. This sketch provides a context for understanding the unique ways in which restorative practice generates a sense of justice in its operations. Interviews were conducted with a range of conference convenors and others such as police, lawyers and judges involved in the programs to draw a further narrative picture of how restorative justice works. Those interviewed were asked to turn their attention to how justice is generated in their programs. For many, this was a novel exercise. But the value of the exercise is that their views allow us, in turn, to form our own view of the capacity for restoration to be integrated within mainstream responses. The picture their words draws suggest how restorative practice might best complement mainstream practice if we are to meet the deficiencies identified in traditional responses.

Chapter 9
How Does Restorative Practice Generate Justice?

Introduction

This chapter draws a narrative picture of how a sense of justice is generated in restorative processes. It is based on the views of those involved in such practices as to which generative mechanisms their programs use to engage this sense of justice. It aggregates the views conveyed concerning the influence of each of the generative mechanisms explored in Chapter 4. The level of agreement expressed about what mix of practices, behaviours, approaches and principles most effectively generates a sense of justice was high, even when different weight and emphasis were given to certain practices. To put these views into context, recall that it was argued in Chapter 2 that certain harm-related benefits and burdens need to be distributed in response to wrongdoing for justice to be delivered. Certain burdens need to be removed or imposed to address the wrong done and certain benefits need to be distributed to right the wrong in some positive fashion. There is a set of social mechanisms which have the power to act as catalysts for such distributions to occur. Restorative processes employ a distinctive mix of these mechanisms which may help to explain their differences from criminal justice practice in terms of creating a sense that justice has been achieved.

Generating a Restorative Sense of Justice

The following narrative thread of responses concerning each of the generative mechanisms emerged from a series of interviews conducted with restorative justice practitioners (convenors, facilitators, program managers and the like) and with others such as lawyers, judges or magistrates either involved directly in the programs or who had knowledge of their outcomes as part of a formal criminal justice sentencing process.[1] Their responses concerning the importance of each mechanism are presented in pairs or groups in the same way they were introduced in Chapter 2, which is consistent with their perceived similarity of effect.

1 The methodology and the schedule of questions used in the interviews are detailed in the Appendix. Direct quotes from interviews are italicized.

Accountability and Responsibility

Accountability

It was consistently reported that accountability in the formal sense of being 'held accountable' was not part of the restorative process. Rather, the view was that *restorative justice enables someone (if they wish) to accept responsibility themselves ... By deliberately staying in the 'telling the story' part of the process until the full story of the wrongdoing is brought out, a different sort of accountability is seen to arise.* This sense of accountability *comes out from hearing other persons' stories about the effect on them of the offending.* The conference process facilitates this by *asking the offender to account for their wrongdoing explicitly, and once the offender actively takes responsibility in that form, then they are accountable.* If this *baseline acceptance of responsibility occurs at the outset*, then there is no need for a more formal holding to account because the offender has already accounted themselves for their own wrongdoing. This is different from being *held accountable as an objective phenomenon* as is the case in legal proceedings. Because the restorative process is seeking to promote this different expectation of accountability, it was important that offenders are prepared for this new form before the conference – *an offender has [to be prepared] to make a [different] commitment to proceed with restorative justice and accept responsibility.* If they do this, then once offenders are in the conference *they cannot deny responsibility, it is [simply] counterproductive.* The effect is that *they must own up and admit to what they have done ... rather than saying that the victim is to blame ... or trying to rationalize or justify [their behaviour] in some other way.*

In a majority of instances, a 'statement of facts' (variously described) was read out at the start of the conference and certain 'accountability' questions were put to the offender. Typical formats included:

> *The offender is asked, 'Is that right?' or*

> *The offender has to acknowledge and agree with it [the statement of facts], then tell his version of events in a ten- to fifteen-minute rave.*

As well as this self-accounting, the offender is also expected to begin to consider how they will *meet the needs of the individual victim, [as another way of] demonstrating they are accountable.* It was emphasized that what victims need from the process is some externally recognizable sign of the offender's self-accountability. This sign can be as simple as the offender's offering to make amends in an *outcome plan that can demonstrate accountability in a very tangible way*. This self-accountability is an important trigger to generating a sense of justice in those involved. Tangible signs of the acknowledgement can come from the offender accepting a version of the events of the wrongdoing or accepting the necessity of making amends to meet the victim's needs. Accountability in the more overt sense of the offender being 'held to account' by external authorities is not seen as being part of the restorative process.

Responsibility

Having the offender actively accept responsibility for their wrongdoing is seen as *accountability going a step further – [with] the offender accepting 100 per cent that they were involved in the wrongdoing.* Substantial preparation was needed for an offender to reach this state of full acknowledgement since

> *Acceptance of responsibility is more than just 'I'll plead guilty' [and] more than simply 'I did the act'. Rather, it is an acceptance of a moral wrong, [which] is a larger concept than simply admitting guilt.*

To do this, an offender has to move from simply admitting in the sense of *'Yeah I done it, so what!' ... [which indicates] that it may be necessary to work with the offender to find out why they are so ambivalent* to some fuller acceptance of responsibility. This is often *teased out in the [preliminary] 'suitability' process ... so that the offender comes prepared to give a full account of what happened.* In some practices, this was described as accepting responsibility for *'the undisputed harm' to the victim.* The importance of the process itself in facilitating this acceptance was recognized:

> *It is the process that will bring this home to [the offender] or not ... and they are prepared [beforehand] to engage with the process by giving details of their offending.*

The conference encounter is seen to provide *the feeling that an offender must take [full] responsibility*, often because significant others, such as their parents and family, are present. The discourse structure of the conference lends itself *to getting a full account of what happened* as well as *sorting out the meaning of what happened for those involved.* It is the process itself that also encourages offenders to *show responsibility by telling their story and being truthful and honest and telling the group, 'This is what I was thinking at the time' and 'This is what I have thought since'.*

An acceptance of responsibility in this fuller sense is seen to have a number of positive benefits. It was seen as *extremely important for the substantial effect it has on the offender in terms of voicing responsibility* and as the means of *beginning their process of moral reform and [as commencing] the process of repair for the victim to see the offender taking blame for their part in what happened.* The acknowledgement the process provoked was described as *one step further along than accountability.* The restorative procedure acts as the catalyst for encouraging such expressions of acknowledgement. Any distinction between accountability and responsibility was seen as largely artificial. For most practices, the two elements of accountability and acceptance of responsibility simply run together as 'acknowledgement'. Most importantly, however, behaviour in which wrongdoing is acknowledged was seen as critical to justice generation.

Censure and Remorse

Censure

Similar to accountability, deliberately overt censure was not reported as a core justice-promoting activity in restorative practices. Instead, the process delivers censure *by adding the missing piece of 'impact on others' ... not [by] telling offenders how wrong they are, [but by] getting them to reach this view for themselves.* The trigger for 'taking on' this role of self-censure is through *being made aware of the harm caused to the victim*. This awareness can flow particularly in the presence of victims, but also without their physical presence, sometimes working effectively *even if a victim just sends an email which can be read out, that can have an effect, too.* When victims are present, the awareness comes from victims saying such things as *'I feel really angry because you have done this to me'* or from the presence of supporters, often the offender's own supporters or families. It is often their presence that *allows for censuring to occur*.

When this awareness is established, censuring for the wrongdoing flows from *the process itself, because someone has accepted responsibility for harm and because of the exchange of emotions that takes place around [such acceptance].* Censure in these terms is consistently seen as *having an effect on the offender ... which even though it is not public can be stronger than that provided in the criminal justice system*. Such censure affects the offender because it *gives him a sense of relief [and] is an answer to [his or her often] debilitating feelings of guilt. Such censure is not 'structured in' as a preconceived outcome – its beginning can be where the topic is raised by the victim [initially saying something like] 'I want you to know that what you did was totally unacceptable and wrong'.*

The timing of the censure is also crucial. In some cases, the perceived *need for censure may have already disappeared [for instance,] once the poor social circumstances of the young person have become evident*. In other cases, the shift from *the anger of censure to the understanding of compassion* occurs more slowly as the process unfolds. Feelings of self-censure were not seen to require the expression of any particular sentiment as a catalyst. *While a victim or others in a restorative justice meeting might express blame or moral disapproval, they may not need to do so* because the feelings of self-censure can arise without such overt behaviour. Also, *ineffective denunciation by police [or others] as de facto for the community* is more likely to be seen as *coming from outside, [and] imposed upon the offender, who does not have to buy into it* and so is likely to ignore it. Such overt censure is also more likely rejected because it *implies something being done to the offender as compared with the wrongdoer being involved as an active participant in a process*. Different conceptualizations of this behaviour other than describing it as 'censure' were seen to provide a better understanding of what is occurring in a conference – *a better description of what happens rather than censure may be 'reproach' in the sense of 'look what you've done!' ... offenders [are better at] buying into this* than into more direct censure or critique. The encounter can do this work itself to some extent because it *enables the offender to demonstrate, from the outset, that they themselves disapprove of their offending behaviour. They do not need to be persuaded of this basic moral fact within the context of an encounter with the victim ... though their sense of remorse may deepen in the course of the process.* Overt censuring in terms of 'publicly denouncing harmful behaviour' is not seen as a core justice-generating mechanism. Rather, in restorative practice the self-censure engendered by the reproach of 'look what harm you have done' is found to be far more effective.

Remorse

Remorse is implicit in restorative practice because its processes are *social rituals which allow the person responsible to say, 'I no longer stand by what I did'.* While it was accepted that genuine expressions of remorse *could not be manufactured,* identifying *what remorse actually 'looks' like* is accepted as difficult. One implicit indicator of remorse could come from *the offender's motivation to participate [in the process itself] ... and fully admit the wrongdoing ... [by] putting in place ways for this not to happen again.* More tangible indications could come from *saying such things as 'I do not want to continue along this path'* or, more simply, by signs such as *offering to shake hands in the conference or by going a bit further to do something to indicate their remorse.* A particular advantage of restorative processes is that such expressions of remorse can more readily be *validated or established* by the participants directly involved at the time. Many practitioners reported an expectation in participants *that the restorative process will ignite a remorse response.* When such expressions were forthcoming this tended to *act as a catalyst for opening a dialogue,* and it was this dialogue that *allows the victim to release emotions of defiance (such as anger and resentment) ... which assist them in their process of healing and recovery.* A number of practitioners also proposed different conceptualizations than 'remorse' to describe what occurs. They used variations such as *expressions of vulnerability, where people show their vulnerability instead of being defensive, which opens up opportunities for discussion.* As well, many offenders *do not have an enormous capacity to feel a lot of remorse* and therefore it is crucial to assist them *to build the capacity for empathy and understanding* so as to be able to express these feelings. The self-censure that the process engenders can bring with it the beginnings of repair. Expressions of remorse act as a catalyst to drain negative emotions from victims and others. Restorative practice assists this by providing a forum to express remorse and the presence to allow participants to gauge its genuineness. Such remorse is seen as essential to helping generate a sense of justice in all participants.

Punishment and Vindication

Punishment

Punishment is not seen as *a goal of restorative justice; [rather,] the goal is to restore relationships. Describing the difficult aspects of restorative justice processes as punishment is not productive of any new version of justice.* Respondents did report that people who come to conferences do bring to the process strong emotions, including anger, vindictiveness and hatred. But while *perhaps these emotions give grounds to form a view that punishment should be an outcome – that is not seen to happen often.* Victims may well have *punishment on their minds* at the outset, but these feelings perceptibly shift in the preparatory stages as *accountability, not punishment* is stressed by convenors. A common view was that *punishment by its nature is not merely a descriptor for something unpleasant, but of something imposed on someone with the intention of inflicting pain, [and that such] imposition is antithetical to restorative justice.* Restorative processes are not structured around punishment. The reason given for this is that *restorative justice is not primarily about the punishment of the perpetrator, but rather about the vindication of the victim.* What follows from this is that the justice 'business' of a restorative process is not about *the inflicting of pain but rather [about] attempting to give the moral lesson of respect.* But *'making up for what has happened' can still include reintegrative programs that require an effort* on behalf of the offender. The resolution plan arrived at in most programs is potentially onerous given that it *holds the offender accountable and he or she may agree [to do certain things] to make amends.* However, *these obligations are not seen as punishment* because of their voluntary nature. The crucial difference drawn between punishment and such 'burdensome amends' is *how this outcome or consequence or whatever you may want to call it is arrived at.* The key distinction drawn is that *an offender accepting a sanction voluntarily is not the same as [one accepting or facing] an imposed outcome.* Nonetheless, *the fact that burdens agreed to in an outcome agreement ... may be perceived as a burden by offenders ought to be recognized* as evidence of the difficulty of the process for offenders. It was recognized that to utilize punishment as a justice-promoting tool would mean that *all the panoply of proportionality, rights protection, legal representation, etcetera would then need to be brought into play [with the effect of] damaging the restorative process itself.*

Certainly, punishment *is* on the minds of participants when they begin the restorative process but it fades from any central role as a justice-promoting mechanism. When offenders take on onerous burdens, their acceptance of the burdens rather than their imposition on them means that much of the negative or harmful associations of punishment can be removed.

Vindication

Vindication is behaviour that says *a wrong has been done*, and, most importantly, says that *this wrong is not the victim's fault.* Vindicating behaviour provides a way for *the conference group to acknowledge that the victim has done nothing wrong. [So that victims] get satisfaction from hearing this, which assists with their feelings of safety that these events will not reoccur.* In this regard, *restorative conferences are forums designed for vindication; [they serve as] as the raison d'être for the conference because they offer an open acknowledgement that the victim's experience is regrettable and morally wrong.* The result described is that this restorative emphasis on *validation, vindication and voice [sees] the focus shift to victims – to what they would like the offender to do [when] the spotlight is on the harm caused.* This gives victims *a voice when they would not otherwise have one, in an environment where they are going to be cared for [and which] can help them heal and come out stronger.* The restorative process provides such relief as a consequence of *the people in the conference having the chance to provide vindication for the victim.* Such vindicating behaviour is seen to *meet the most basic needs that victims experience – acknowledging their harms and needs, combined with an active effort to encourage offenders to take responsibility, make right the wrongs, and address the causes of their behaviour.*

It is clear from these comments that punishment is not a core justice-generating tool for restorative practice. By contrast, vindication is very much so; indeed, vindicating behaviour is seen as critical to communicating to the victim that the wrongdoing was not of their making. This vindication provides relief from feelings of responsibility and self-blame so as to begin the process of justice for victims.

Deterrence and Proportionality

Deterrence

Deterrence of further offending by the person involved in the wrongdoing is seen by some participants as *a very important byproduct of what might happen in a conference [because] the victim wants a community where the sort of wrongdoing done to them does not happen.* Having a deterrent effect is more an indirect rather than a conscious focus of the process since *deterrence is not something we strive for, not something we routinely raise with victims and offenders.* Restorative practice achieves its deterrent effect because of its deliberate focus on *making communities of accountability stronger and on strengthening clear community bonds.* The intended effect is that *the acknowledgement of responsibility as an acceptance of the reality of the harm caused [will give rise to] a deterrent effect.* It is this potential to gain *a clear picture of the impact of what they have done ... by personalizing the offence may have an effect in terms of specific deterrence that is higher than in the criminal justice system.* The intention is that such a focus will *keep offenders from wanting to create that same harm again.* Deterrence was seen as achievable through *the involvement of communities so that clear bonds are strengthened and a sense of 'we are in this together'* is developed. This focus on reducing reoffending revolves around asking, *'How did we get here [to the wrongdoing]?' and 'How can we avoid getting here again?'* The reconnection with community (and with community resources) *can have the effect of reducing offending totally or reducing it to less serious offending.* The restorative process contains *deterrence talk* and *deterrence procedures*, both aimed at establishing measures that may support non-offending patterns. For instance, in the case of young offenders, *the conference may look for conditions that may help offenders to 'self-police' through curfews or non-associations, or abiding by house rules. These can be tough to monitor but can work to prevent reoffending.* Such measures equip *the young person so that they have 'excuses' they can offer to mates for staying away from them.* It is in these ways that restorative practice was seen to have a deterrent effect on offenders which is justice-promoting in the way that it acts to renew and reinforce the victim's and the community's collective sense of safety and security.

Proportionality

Proportionality is not described as a strong justice factor in restorative practice. Its core focus is *upon what needs to be done to repair the harm; and [what is required for] each person's response [to this] is very different.* Its place in restorative justice is minor because restoration is *a process which is about addressing harm and restoring relationships by focusing on respect, concern and dignity, [and this means that] some things are taken off the table. When the root of the process is in restoring the relationship and repairing the harm, then strict mathematical proportionality becomes less relevant.* Proportionality in the sense of 'censure proportionate to the severity of the wrongdoing' is not a restorative function, and so *ultimate oversight, by enforcement/variation of agreements ... stands [apart] under the control of the criminal justice system.* Comments from judges involved with restorative practice in particular explain how this external oversight function works:

> *I often look at a FGC [family group conference] plan and say, for example, 'This number of hours of community service is way over the top or way too inadequate' and I change it to something more appropriate.*

Within the process itself *there is no attempt to make a comparison with other outcome plans ..., [since the focus is] to make it case-specific.* As such, restorative practice *couldn't have anything like a punishment scale; [while] there needs to be consequences, it is different for different people.* In the same way, *proportionality even seen in terms of 'repair proportionate to the harm done' is tricky because restorative justice is a process where those directly involved come up with a decision, and that decision can be simply an apology made by the offender.* For this reason, *you can't have a scale; everyone is different. The requirements of the outcome agreement may appear minor, but following through on the commitments may be really tough for the offender. Its requirements have to be proportionate to the person, not to what society thinks is appropriate.* There is a risk to the core reparative functions of the process *if there was a requirement that any outcome agreement be proportionate. That would change the situation and maybe those involved would overstretch to try and find an outcome that is more prescriptive.* This is because in large measure *conferences are completely unrelated to one another ... Two conferences are never the same, so proportionality doesn't come into it as much. The emphasis is much more on individuality than proportionality.* As such, the primary focus *is not the offence but the offender, [unlike] the criminal justice system which compares charges with charges – restorative justice is the antithesis of that.*

Convenors often report seeking to 'guide' agreement provisions so that there is some minimum measure of proportionality by *stipulating what can and can't be done in an outcome agreement.* In some situations, participants also *look to facilitators for parameters or ask the police officer [or lawyer] if one is present.* There was skepticism expressed about the value of using any 'upper limits' criteria (such as legislative penalty scales) as a guide. It was not seen as *a helpful model at all, given that these limits are punitive, not restorative.* In many instances, outcome agreements were seen as *more substantial [in terms of their requirements] than what a court might impose, [because they were] deliberately more specific and individualized.* When proportionality was needed to *act like a protection mechanism, then it was important that this control be provided by the criminal justice system* and not within the restorative process itself.

Restorative practice provides a deterrent effect on offenders which can be justice-promoting purely as a consequence of the personal nature of the encounter. But restorative practice's emphasis on 'individualizing justice' means that ensuring proportionality of treatment between offenders is not part of its justice rationale. Proportionality in the sense of 'the degree of restorative effort required to put things right' is tempered by a focus on what is required to make good the harm. The proportionality principle (in either its 'sanction' or 'repair' senses) is not part of restorative practice's justice promotion.

Truth Telling and Reparation

Truth telling

Truth telling's *close tie-in with responsibility and accountability* means that it is seen as central to the full expression of an acceptance of responsibility. Victims and others affected by the wrongdoing consistently express the view that they want *the truth about what happened and about the decisions the offender made which led to the offence* to be made known. What the restorative process can deliver in this regard is:

> *a very high level of detail both as to what occurred – what happened and when? – and about the offender's motivation – What were you thinking? What have you thought about since? This level of detail of what happened is very important for the victim to know, for example in the case of a robbery – 'Was the car locked?' 'What rooms did you go into?' and so on and so on.*

The restorative process is more effective in allowing this level of detail to come out in response to victims' demands and as a way to meet *their crucial need to get the story as complete as possible.* It was conceded by those involved in the process that it may not *always be possible to get the full truth (for example, if there are disputed factors we tell the victim in preparation that there is a dispute as to the facts) ... However, we do not allow central facts to be disputed in a restorative justice process.* 'Non-dispute' (rather than 'agreement') about the core facts can become crucial even if *it may take some time to get to this stage of agreement ([and] this can be done by shuttle dialogue before the conference is held*), in some instances. As well, the manner of the disclosure adopted by the offender is important, in the sense *that they are being straightforward in how they deliver their story, and that they are not intent on self-justification. Even if their own version of what happened is actually different from the victim's in some respects*, the way they relate their version is important. This process of truth telling is aided by the deliberative nature of the process in that *the [offender's] story can be taken apart to get the full details out.* For many participants, the purpose of the deliberation was described as *the opposite of the criminal justice system because it is to [the offender's] benefit to be totally honest.* The deliberative structure *opens the process of truth telling up; it often adds the details via the victim's questions. [In this way,] it goes beyond just the admission to getting more of the truth out* and so provides satisfaction and relief to the victim. Restorative practice delivers this possibility of *a more open and comprehensive truth telling*, both because the rules of evidence constraint is absent and because *there is a direct role provided for victims who may have had at least partial knowledge of the facts of the incident themselves from which to draw.*

Truth telling is a core generative mechanism for restorative practice. The difference in its practice is that its deliberative nature is seen to often reveal more of the truth of the wrongdoing and its consequences than is possible through a strictly forensic truth-finding process such is at work in the criminal justice system.

Reparation

The explicit aim for many restorative practices is to address in practical and symbolic terms questions like:

> *'What can be done to make things right?'*
>
> *'What can be done to make sure this doesn't happen again?'*

Restorative practice addresses these questions by focusing on *three aspects of reparation – a spiritual aspect in terms of expiation, an emotional aspect in terms of 'satisfaction' and a material aspect in terms of restitution or compensation.* Because of this combination, there is *explicit 'talk about reparation'* to show participants *that the conference isn't just a conversation,* but a process that has as its purpose finding ways to redress the harm done. The reparation comes through symbolic and material means either in the conference itself or as a consequence of a promise to do something following the conference. Symbolic reparation comes *simply from an apology or from the victim hearing [the offender's] acknowledgement of responsibility*. Or it may flow from some other form of response that shows *the offender feels what it is like to be out of their comfort zone for a time.* Likewise, material reparation can mean agreeing to pay money to the victim, agreeing to give something back to the community (in terms of volunteer work or more formal community service) or committing to do something (such as undertaking a rehabilitative program). Both forms of symbolic and material reparation are described as *a key thing for victims – since such behaviour addresses their need for an answer to the question 'How can we get back what we've lost?'* For offenders, *there is a sense of being required to address the harm [themselves] but with their communities and victims having obligations and responsibilities in a similar vein* to support them in meeting their commitments. A core principle of restorative practice is that *the offender is not the only person who has to think about what needs to be done to repair*. Victims can also make a contribution by moving *their focus away from punishment to placing the onus on the [offender] to take responsibility for not offending again*. Communities also contribute to reparation by taking tangible steps that allow the offender to give back to the community and to be reintegrated into it as a consequence.

Reparation was described as an important justice-generating mechanism for restorative practice because it provides a tangible answer to the question about what can be done to make things right. The restorative process provides an opportunity to discover the particular forms of symbolic or material reparation needed to achieve this outcome in each individual case of wrongdoing.

Apology and Forgiveness

Apology

Apology is described as a central *moral ritual of restorative practice [in the sense that] to take responsibility 'means' apology, and if you haven't apologized you may not in fact be accepting responsibility*. Its power flows from *how it sums up vindication, acknowledgement, denunciation and repair of harm – it is the essence of all these things because it says, 'You're worthy of me'*. Apology in this sense is the core restorative means of expressing acceptance of responsibility because it provides *evidence that the offender [has been] confronted with the reality of what they've done*. Apology is seen as *a 'natural harm response' that only restorative processes could do with such immediacy*. Its force was explained in these terms – *once the reality of harm is realized, apology flows as a response which has enormous power to validate the trauma of the victim and convert the offender*. This power comes from its two key elements – *its unconditionality which leaves excuses behind, and its expression of a resolve not to cause pain again*. These elements together were seen as being able to *dissipate the angriest victim and shift something in the victim as a result ... so that they express an acknowledgement of the apology in some way*.

Good preparation is crucial since *apology may not come naturally to offenders*. Such preparation must be explicit:

> *We tell them there is a point in the conference where the convenor will say something like 'Is there anything else you would like to say?' and that is their opportunity to give an apology if they want.*

> *As well, the offender may need to be prepared to make an apology more than once because the first apology can often be heard but not registered and so needs to be repeated several times.*

Apology takes many forms, including verbal apology given in the conference and ideally *accepted there as genuine and coming from the heart*, or written later, sometimes in response to *the victim asking the young person to 'Write down what you heard me say about the effect of your offending on me'*. In other cases, apology may *not be articulated as such [but shown] instead by an apologetic attitude which expresses remorsefulness*. These expressions can be *simply offering a handshake or, in some specific cultural situations, offering a song or serving a meal*. The effect of apology, especially *when you do get an apology from someone who has had a 'deny always' attitude*, can be significant. Respondents emphasized that in spite of its powerful effects, apology *cannot be a 'requirement' of a justice process*. No consequential connection can be drawn between apology and forgiveness since *apology expresses the feeling that 'I hope that you can forgive me and trust me in the future', [but] it cannot be given with the expectation of forgiveness being given in return*.

Apology is a core justice-generating mechanism in restorative practice directed both at the personal harm and the normative harm caused. It sums up many of the other requirements of a justice response because by apologizing the offender acknowledges responsibility and provides vindication for victims that the wrong done to them was not their fault.

Forgiveness

A typically expressed view about forgiveness is that *the word 'forgiveness' itself can be an impediment to a restorative outcome with its many unhelpful connotations, [such as] the religious duty to forgive, 'blank slate' forgiveness, 'forgive and forget' and so on, [all] suggestive of a duty or an obligation to forgive*. These expectations can militate against the creation of a sense of justice. Nonetheless, there is evidence of forgiveness being on the minds of some in restorative processes:

> *Because [victims] want to move on with their lives, they want to be released from the emotions of defiance; they are open to communicating with and accepting the offender as a fellow human being ... If apology is a gift that is offered in the hope that it will be accepted, accepting the apology is at least part of what it means to forgive.*

But offering forgiveness is not seen as *a matter of justice. [Rather,] forgiveness is a matter of grace, that is to say, the unearned generosity of others*. There can be no necessary connection between forgiveness and apology since *victims can accept a non-apology from the offender and still give forgiveness – they are not mutual.*

Some bond builds up for the offender and there is something useful in the victim being able to put the events to rest through forgiveness.

Forgiveness, when it does occur, can provide substantial benefit to both the victims and offenders. For victims, the benefit is in *allowing them to dissipate emotions of defiance (such as anger) which can be so destructive.* The act of forgiveness provides them with an acceptance that *the other person is responsible, not that I as the victim am responsible.* The beneficial effects that flow from these insights can include *an expression of relief for the victim* and *for many victims this is helpful, [since] it releases them from their burdens.* Victims also move to self-forgiveness in this process in the sense of saying, *'I can rest easy myself', 'I can forgive my own self now'.* But it was recognized that *for a lot of victims, forgiveness is not the first or most important thing. It is not necessary that it occurs. Rather, it is more about understanding of what has happened and what is happening in the process.* Forgiveness also provides direct benefit to the offender, either by *getting the message across that it is about forgiving themselves* or through victims overtly offering forgiveness by *saying, 'I forgive you for what you did'.* For *some offenders and their supporters, culturally for them forgiveness is quite important. It is important for them to hear forgiveness* in this way.

Restorative practice accommodates expressions of forgiveness because its processes are *consistent with the dynamics of forgiveness; it can set a process in train ... where the legacy of the harm is finally put to rest.* Sometimes, forgiveness *may come at a later date but the process has begun. Sometimes victims will say, 'I sort of accept your apology. I'll want to see something concrete. Maybe when you attend a program or make a payment I'll know then it is genuine'.* In this way, the *seeds are planted ... and are the beginning of a process that has long-term meaning for the victim and the offender; the interchange itself presents the potential for change.* However, in *most conferences it is too early for forgiveness. [This can have the effect that] some victims disappoint offenders when they say, 'I won't respond to your apology just yet; I'll think about what I think of you in time and then decide how I feel'.* None of the programs saw forgiveness as a necessity for justice creation. The consistently expressed view was that *forgiveness shouldn't be an expectation of what is to happen.* Once again, a better conceptualization offered as to what was occurring at this stage of the victim's response was that their feelings were *one rung lower on the ladder – at understanding, not forgiveness.* What this often means in practice is *a movement towards understanding or a sense of why the action was taken or some other sort of reconciliation.* The benefit of the restorative process is that *most victims leave with an understanding of where the other person was coming from ... this doesn't quite fit into forgiveness, but may be the beginning of it.* Acts of forgiveness or acceptance provide real restorative benefits to those affected by wrongdoing. But forgiveness is a gift that cannot be demanded, and as such is not restorative practice's core justice-promoting means.

Justice Generation and Restorative Practice

Drawing together the threads of this narrative provides some insight into how restorative practice can generate a sense of justice in responding to wrongdoing. Rather than being strictly behaviours, the key mechanisms are more a mix of behaviours and guiding principles which together contribute to participants experiencing the sense that justice has been done.

An offender's active acceptance of responsibility for his or her wrongdoing and its effects on others is core to generating this justice sense. Participation in a restorative process can act as a catalyst to move the offender towards acceptance. The process's discursive structure acts to defeat attempts to deny wrongdoing or to downplay its harmful effects. Expressions of remorse act as a catalyst to opening up dialogue that can assist victims in their process of healing and recovery. It is through this process that remorse generates the necessary flow of harm-related benefits and burdens. Providing opportunities for vindication is similarly critical because vindication is behaviour that openly acknowledges that the victim is blameless. Vindication works to reinforce that the offending is socially and normatively unacceptable. This can assist victims to revive their perceptions and feelings of safety and security by giving them the normative affirmation needed. A sense of justice flows from this open acknowledgement that the harm experienced was wrong and reprehensible. The deliberate focus on deterrence is a further crucial element of restorative justice because it addresses both the victim's desire to reaffirm his or her sense of a community in which wrongdoing of this kind should not reoccur, while at the same time putting in place strategies to prevent its reoccurrence. Uniquely, however, the deterrent effect is achieved by focusing on creating stronger communities of accountability and by personalizing the offending and its effects. Additionally, the facilitation of truth telling is crucial to its justice generation because truthfulness can provide tangible recognition of the offender's acknowledgement of responsibility. It also activates the flow of harm-related benefits and burdens needed to achieve just outcomes. Reparation is another important justice-promoting element because it meets the need for tangible amends as well as providing feelings of expiation and emotional release. Reparation in both its practical and symbolic guises addresses the core restorative requirement that things must be made right if justice is to be achieved. Finally, apology is a core justice-promoting activity because when it is offered it can, through one act, answer the need for vindication, acknowledgement, denunciation and repair. Apology provides the tangible evidence that offenders have confronted the reality of their wrongdoing and have accepted responsibility for making things right in some measure.

There are generative mechanisms which are not seen as contributive in any essential sense to participants experiencing a sense of justice. Being held accountable in an overt external sense is not part of a restorative process's function. Rather than being *held* accountable, offenders were seen to be better able to account *for* their own wrongdoing through an acceptance of responsibility.

This self-accounting was demonstrated both by the acknowledgement and by external signs of accepting responsibility through agreeing to make amends or apology. Overt censure in the sense of 'publicly denouncing harmful behaviour and providing consequences for offenders' was not seen as a justice-generating means, although 'self-censuring' was. Overt censure implies denunciation coming from outside and being imposed upon the offender. Restorative practice seeks instead to substitute a form of reproach which can bring an offender to a state of self-censure. Restorative justice does not use punishment for justice generation. Though it was routinely recognized that punishment is on the minds of victims and their supporters at the outset of any conference, it is not the restorative means to express censure. Rather, restorative practice highlights its own expressive powers and the agreements for reparation and apology that can be reached to convey disapprobation of the offending behaviour. Adhering to principles of proportionality is similarly not its method for generating just outcomes. Determining sanctions commensurate with the severity of the wrong or determining the amount of restoration needed commensurate with the harm done are not the means to just outcomes. Neither basis of comparison is an important consideration in restorative practice. Instead, its focus is on repairing harm, with proportionate censure or proportionate repair not relevant to achieving the particular repair required. Finally, at none of the sites of restorative practice was forgiveness reported as an essential means of justice generation. A consistently expressed view was that forgiveness should never be an expectation. A more modest expectation was that victims would find relief from some of the harm inflicted on them and begin to move towards feelings of understanding and release. Drawing together the descriptions of practice captured in this narrative, the distinctive justice-generating power of restorative practices flow from the power and effect of these guiding behaviours and principles:

- acknowledgement of responsibility
- expressions of remorse
- vindication of the victim
- deterrence of reoffending
- truth telling
- material and symbolic reparation
- expressions of apology.

Conclusion

This chapter has considered views expressed by restorative practitioners and others about the mechanisms important for generating an experience of a sense of justice in their practice. Acknowledgements of responsibility, expressions of remorse and the vindication of victims were all reported as crucial in creating that experience. Actively seeking to deter reoffending, encouraging truth telling, providing reparation and facilitating offers of apology were likewise important factors. Conversely, holding offenders to account publicly, overt censure, inflicting punishment or highlighting proportionate responses were not deemed important. Acts of forgiveness were neither an expectation nor a means to generate justice. Justice creation is a deliberate (albeit, not necessarily conscious) part of the restorative process. The encouragement of certain types of behaviour and the adherence to certain guiding principles both act as catalysts for justice. The explicit emphasis given to factors like apology, reparation, remorse and vindication of victims shows a clear departure from criminal justice practice and its means of creating justice.

At the end of Part II, we raised two related expectations about restorative justice. Firstly, we suggested that since its practice displayed such different potentials as regards the evaluative standards of justice (measuring well in terms of the relationships and equality standards, but poorly in terms of desert and rights), there must be something distinctive in the way it generates its experiences of justice. The generative mechanism typology developed in Chapter 4 was used here to confirm this and to identify the clear differences described above. A unique and distinctive mix of generative mechanisms is clearly at work in restorative processes when compared with criminal justice practice. These differences contribute to the creation of a distinctive sense of justice. The second expectation was that the differences had within them the potential to encourage growth and renewal in traditional criminal justice practice through some form of integration. Analysis has revealed both a paradigmatic unity between the two forms of justice that in many respects makes them potentially compatible. At the same time, it has identified an important paradigmatic shift by restorative justice which provides a possible catalyst for change. Restorative justice utilizes some of the methods of criminal justice practice in the importance it places on responsibility, remorse, vindication and truth telling. However, it shifts markedly in the way it generates censure, using reparation and apology for repair and rejects punishment. Its key strength is to look to 'equal appropriateness' by individualizing responses rather than strict equality (Hudson 1998b). Criminal justice practice can learn much from integration. If the mirroring of adherences and non-adherences is so apparent, then some combination thereof has the potential for better justice practice. Offering restorative justice as a complete substitute would simply replace old deficiencies with new ones, although remaining the same leaves current deficiencies unanswered. The concluding chapter of this volume suggests a way forward.

Conclusion: Developing Restorative Jurisprudence: A Minimalist Approach

Introduction

This book has attempted to capture the urgency evident in critiques of criminal justice practice as it is pressed to fashion more just responses to wrongdoing. It has argued that fuller recognition of restorative approaches provides a clear means to fill the substantial gaps in law's ability to deliver justice. This final chapter suggests how restorative justice jurisprudence might be developed to support this. Current sentencing jurisprudence needs to engage with the capacity of restorative justice to more fully meet the essential retributive, restorative and consequential aims identified. It draws ideas from the practice examples canvassed in Chapter 8 about what institutional designs are possible. It draws heart from the analysis of sentencing jurisprudence in Chapter 7 that criminal justice can develop to accommodate restorative approaches and principles. But without integration, restorative practices are likely to remain on the periphery of responses to criminal wrongdoing. The form of integration promoted here is simple – adding a requirement that courts consider 'the restorative question' each time an offender is dealt with – but still effective in helping to develop a different approach to wrongdoing. The model proposed is a minimalist one. Certain categories of wrongdoing are excluded at the outset. A traditional criminal justice response should remain the mandated response where culpability is denied and needs to be established or dismissed by forensic means. A restorative form of response should remain the preferred option where issues of relational repair are overriding and paramount and where criminality is absent or unlikely to be provable before a court.

The Parameters of Integration

Retaining Current Approaches for the 'Extreme Edges' of Wrongdoing

The 'extreme edges' of wrongdoing are quarantined from an integrated model. These areas include circumstances where the need to meet either the desert standard or the harmonious relationships standard is so paramount as to exclude a combined justice response. In these situations, sometimes a purely criminal justice response is required and sometimes a purely restorative one. There are situations where issues of establishing responsibility, protecting rights and providing strong normative warnings are so crucial that a criminal justice response is mandatory. Conversely, there are circumstances where issues of relational or societal repair are crucial, and where the likelihood of establishing criminality is so slim that a restorative response is appropriate. More specifically, an exclusively criminal justice response is called for:

1. where the determination of criminal responsibility is required;
2. where rights protection is fundamental;
3. where a clarifying pronouncement on broader normative harm is required.

In such situations, only the protective architecture of legal justice can provide the necessary means to adequately determine liability, protect rights and pronounce on important normative standards. Similarly, an exclusively restorative justice response is called for:

1. where relationship repair (either individual or societal) is fundamental;
2. where risk to relationships is of larger concern than criminality;
3. where the criminality of wrongdoing is overwhelmingly likely to remain unprovable.

In these situations, only the open architecture of restorative justice can properly address the important relational requirements which override questions of criminality. These exclusions should be seen as presumptive rather than prescriptive. This will allow for exceptional cases to be dealt with integratively where circumstances demand. While criminal justice is the presumptive choice where determinations of responsibility are required, in some cases restorative justice's alternative means of establishing responsibility may be more appropriate, while not as forensically exact. This was the case in the community holistic circle-healing form of response adopted in the Hollow Water First Nation in Manitoba (Lajunesse 1993). In this indigenous community, a more deliberative method of truth telling was found effective in addressing situations of endemic family and sexual abuse. The restorative approach established an acceptance of responsibility more effectively than could ever have been achieved with a criminal justice response. Participation in healing circles encouraged admissions which conventional forensic truth-finding methods would have left unresolved (Griffiths and Hamilton 1996: 182–183; Aboriginal Corrections Policy Unit 1997; Green 1998).[1] Between these 'extreme edges' remains the vast 'middle ground of criminal wrongdoing', in which a combination of both forms of response can play

1 A similar example is the Bougainville transitional justice practice of replacing determinations of individual responsibility (in events of wrongdoing during periods of civil strife) with more traditional forms of community responsibility (Braithwaite, Charlesworth et al. 2010; Reddy 2012).

a significant responsive role in delivering justice. This provides the opportunity for criminal justice to be influenced and enriched by restorative principles and practices so that a restorative justice jurisprudence can develop.

Design Requirements for an Integrated Model

Five key design lessons can be gleaned from the reality of practice described in earlier chapters. An integrated form of response must satisfy five requirements:

1. a mechanism which mandates that restorative forms of response be accommodated in responses to wrongdoing;
2. a reframed sentencing rhetoric which is more closely aligned with the essential aims of justice;
3. a set of sentencing mechanisms better able to meet both punitive and restorative needs;
4. a network of community-based restorative justice providers to facilitate restorative encounters;
5. a clearer recognition of the part played by overt ceremonial forms of reintegration in addressing criminal wrongdoing.

1. Mandating the accommodation of restorative justice responses
There is a need to mandate that criminal justice processes accommodate restorative approaches in a way that is overt and explicit. The importance of this requirement was emphasized in both the New Zealand and Canadian experience, where legislative requirements to accommodate restorative responses resulted in the development of a strong restorative justice jurisprudence as a consequence. In both jurisdictions, localized integrative approaches followed only as a consequence of legislative and judicial requirements to 'reconcile restorative and punitive responses'. In the case of New Zealand, the approach was to *balance* both criminal and restorative approaches through mainstreaming the use of restorative encounters. In the case of Canada, the approach involved a variety of provincial institutional initiatives to satisfy the legislative and jurisprudential mandate to *consider* restorative means alongside punitive means in meeting sentencing obligations. A clear contrast is Australia, where no legislative mandate exists and where there has been little or no jurisprudential development.

2. Reframing the sentencing rhetoric/jurisprudence
There is a need to reframe sentencing prescriptions in ways that more closely align with the normative requirements of a full justice response to wrongdoing. This reframing can better highlight the capacity of restorative approaches to meet these requirements. Simply reforming legislative provisions to read in a more 'restorative' way is insufficient. The preferred approach is one that makes the legislative requirements prescriptive. In New Zealand's *Sentencing Act* of 2002, restatements have been reinforced with specific provisions which *require* courts

to take account of the outcomes of restorative conferences. Its general sentencing purposes in s.7 include the following (emphasis added):

> (a) to *hold the offender accountable* for harm done to the victim and the community by the offending; or
> (b) to *promote* in the offender a *sense of responsibility* for and an *acknowledgment of that harm*; or
> (c) to provide for *the interests of the victim* of the offence.

These requirements have been addressed by courts in ways that encourage restorative responses. In *R v Sami* (2006) NZDCR 128, referred to earlier, McElrea J specifically matched each of these factors to what had been achieved through 'a conference with a direct face-to-face meeting with the victim'. In his sentencing remarks he said of the offender:

> He has already been *held accountable in that face-to-face way for harm done*, and he has been held accountable in a way *to promote a sense of responsibility for harm* and some *personal acknowledgement of that harm*. The conference has also *provided for the interests of the victim* by making things easier for her and her family. (para. 26, emphasis added)

Such a prescriptive reframing of sentencing jurisprudence can move the use of restorative approaches from the periphery to the mainstream.

3. Establishing multifunctional sentencing mechanisms

There is a need to create sentencing mechanisms that allow punitive and restorative approaches to coexist within one form of response. Such devices are particularly necessary in cases of serious wrongdoing where restorative approaches would otherwise be dismissed as inadequate and unwarranted. A significant localized attempt to do so was the introduction of conditional sentences in the Canadian *Criminal Code*, discussed in Chapter 7. Conditional sentences were specifically designed where a 'term of imprisonment' was seen as warranted, but where it could be 'served in the community' subject to strict conditions.[2] This has allowed a punitive sentence to be satisfied in a form that also better accommodates restorative objectives. Conditional sentences can be limiting, particularly when they try to perform essentially conflicting functions. In the Canadian case of *Proulx*, discussed earlier, 'restorative purposes' were seen (paras. 109–112) as largely confined to

---

2 The notion of 'served in the community' is the key distinction between conditional sentences and 'suspended sentences', which are more commonplace in the Australian and New Zealand jurisdictions. For example, the ACT *Crimes (Sentencing) Act* s.12(2) provides that a court 'may make an order suspending all or part of the sentence of imprisonment' imposed. The effect is that a sentence is not then 'served' unless the offender reoffends or breaches some probation conditions which may result in his imprisonment.

addressing consequential aims, such as 'restitution', 'community service' and 'treatment', and were given little role in addressing some retributive aims. This will remain a difficulty with sentencing devices as long as 'restorative objectives cannot dominate ... [and indeed] cannot be given equal weight' (Healy 2000: ii.1). The UK's alternative of 'conditional cautioning' and 'community (probation) supervision' provisions in its *Criminal Justice Act* of 2003 (UK) have also been limited to facilitating rehabilitation of the offender and reparation for the offence and give no real scope for the restorative addressing of retributive aims (UK Home Office 2003; Sherman and Strang 2007). In order to more effectively balance restorative and punitive means, sentencing mechanisms must be multifunctional and responsive.

4. Developing community restorative practice networks

There is a need to develop a network of community-based restorative practices to provide necessary conferencing and support services to carry out subsequent outcome monitoring. Localized attempts at institutionalizing such networks have proven effective in New Zealand and in the province-wide program in Nova Scotia. The New Zealand network now carries out restorative interventions for both juvenile and adult offenders (NZ Ministry of Justice: Crime Prevention Unit 2008). The Nova Scotia network supports its juvenile program through regional nonprofit agencies coupled with the use of volunteers (Clairmont 2005a: 5). A somewhat similar community-based agency scheme provides a network of conferencing facilities in Victoria (Maxwell and Hayes 2006: 143). The existence of such a network of community-based restorative practices is crucial for ready accessibility for courts to consider restorative encounters.

5. Providing overt reintegrative milestones

Finally, there is a need for the importance of reintegration to be overtly recognized as a core component of criminal responses to wrongdoing, ideally through some sort of 'reintegrative ceremony' at the conclusion of the response. Such explicit milestones provide more than simply 'ceremonial value ... [that makes one] *feel* that something is being done ... whether the result is right or wrong' (Llewellyn 1940: 610, emphasis in original). What is also needed is a meaningful interaction that re-convinces people 'that legal institutions [can be] genuine purveyors of justice' in their responses to wrongdoing (Luban 1996: 160). Localized attempts to provide such interactions are particularly prominent in indigenous restorative practices. In New Zealand, the Te Whanau Awhina program has used its indigenous community connection to add ceremonial emphasis to reintegration by holding the encounter on the *marae* (traditional Maori meeting place having deep religious significance), with a panel of local *marae* members and with the offender accompanied by his or her *whanau* (extended family). The power of such an encounter to emphasize reintegration is illustrated in a report of one such conference in *R v Taparau & Ors* [1995] NZDCR 774:

> The voiced opinion from the people of Puatahi and Haranui *maraes* present is that such [punitive] approaches do not meet the needs of their people. They believe that the traditional ways of shaming, punishing and restoring their young people are a better way to deal with this situation.

Similarly in Canada, conventional justice practices have been adapted to add the power of indigenous ceremonial elements which emphasize reintegration. In the Gladue (Aboriginal Persons) Court, such atmosphere is created, underscoring reintegration through the promotion of Aboriginal values of ceremony and ritual. When the court diverts offenders to its community council program, each of its graduates is recognized with an 'honouring ceremony ... with all successful completion people coming together to celebrate at a community gathering together with prosecutors, judges and attorneys' (McCombs 2007). There is clearly room for this to occur as conventional justice practices in Australia have been adapted to add Koori and other indigenous elements in the form of sentencing circles which emphasize reintegration for Aboriginal offenders.

The ceremonial recognition need not only be indigenously-based. Becroft (2005) reports successful smaller-scale 'ceremonies' in New Zealand family group conferences where reintegration is marked in many diverse ways, such as 'an apology in song', an offender 'cooking a dinner for victims and their families' or by 'creating a CD of music which expresses apology'. Specialized domestic violence courts and drug courts give recognition to the importance of ceremony, with offenders applauded and congratulated by the bench on completion of program commitments.[3]

The five institutional design requirements outlined in this section are drawn from the earlier review of practice. Each specification contributes to widening the scope for restorative approaches to work within an integrated response. Envisaging such a model of integration is best accomplished from the perspective of answering the 'restorative question'.

The Minimalist 'Restorative Question' Model

Any model of integration should ideally display the hallmarks of 'democratic experimentalism' in the sense that justice institutions should take on a proactive role in 'monitoring the delivery of services', rather than simply confining their role to 'meting out justice' while remaining unconcerned with consequences or outcomes (Dorf and Sabel 1998: 938; Dorf 2003). The model is therefore proactive – it *requires* justice institutions to always ask the 'restorative question' in each case of wrongdoing so as to explicitly give voice to the need to address the harm done. This

3 Such symbolism is also important in traditional courtrooms. In answer to the question to the effect of 'What gives you a good feeling about your work as a judge?' one of Fellegi's (2013) judge respondents said, 'When the trial was done in a proper way. Even if we all know it is a kind of theatre.'

mirrors in many respects the way criminal courts have evolved to now routinely ask the 'rehabilitation question' in its responses where previously they did not. Asking the 'restorative question' in fact requires courts to make two specific inquires:

1. Firstly, to ask, 'Is there a restorative aspect to address in this wrongdoing?' That is, to consider whether persons affected by the wrongdoing (including the offender) have suffered harm as a consequence and whether this harm is capable of being restored in some way or by some degree. In most responses to criminal wrongdoing, the clear answer to the harm question is 'yes'. The model design provides a suggested set of principles for judges to gauge whether a particular incident of wrongdoing has produced personal or normative harm which is amenable to repair or reduction.
2. Secondly, to ask, 'Can restorative approaches address (all, or some of) the essential aims of justice required in response to this particular incident of wrongdoing?'

Again, the clear answer in most instances would be 'yes'. The model design provides a means to determine the responsive capacity of relevant restorative approaches to address different aspects of harm and provide different elements of repair or reduction.

As a fundamental, posing and answering these two questions is simplified if the response remains within existing institutional structures. As a comparison, McElrea (2007b: 108) has suggested using a network of 'Community Resolution Centres' where courts would relinquish this primary 'gate keeping' role with determinations of 'response tracks' being made 'by those [likely to] take part in the particular conference', that is to say, the persons directly affected by the wrongdoing (McElrea 2007b: 109).[4] Sherman and Strang propose a similar external triage device in their 'Restorative Justice Boards', which they envisage as 'tak[ing] RJ from the drawing board to its widespread construction' by removing the threshold gatekeeping role from the courts (2007: 8). The model suggested here retains the gatekeeping role within traditional justice institutions but with a mandated requirement to address the two aspects of the restorative question at the outset. A starting point for such a design is Sander's (1976) 'Dispute Resolution Centre' model, where determinative functions remain court-based. In Sander's model, civil disputes are allocated to different dispute resolution

4 McElrea (2005: 20) cites the Community Justice Houses in Colombia as an example of this model in practice. The Community Justice Houses began as a pilot in this Central American country in the mid-1990s, and by mid-2005 had expanded to more than 30 centres (Pearson 2004). Though their primary purpose has been to 'get basic justice services out into the community' by providing access to informal justice institutions for poor communities whose own 'informal conflict resolution alternatives ... tend to be violent', a lot of its processes were seen as 'being restorative justice without [necessarily being] called that' (Pearson 2004: unpaginated).

'streams' based upon predetermined criteria (such as 'the nature of the dispute', 'the relationship between disputants', 'the amount in dispute', and 'cost and timeliness considerations') (1976: 72–79). This is an approach that Preston (2007) has advocated in his design for procedural reform of the NSW Land and Environment Court. The benefit of retention of the function (coupled with an obligation) to make core procedurally determinative decisions within the existing institutional structure is that it requires minimalist change, potentially more likely to be adopted.[5] With this in mind, a suggested modification could simply impose:

1. a requirement to address the first aspect of the restorative question by routinely asking, 'Has harm been caused here?';
2. a set of criteria to apply to incidents of wrongdoing which can assist judges to make this determination;
3. a requirement to address the second aspect of the restorative question by considering the scope of restorative approaches available which could contribute to addressing various aspects of the essential justice aims;
4. a set of guidelines to be used by judges in selecting appropriate restorative programs.

Institutionalizing the Design Features

The process of institutionalizing such procedural changes has precedent. The Collingwood Neighbourhood Justice Centre (NJC) in suburban Melbourne provides a good example.[6] The NJC court performs decision-making and referral functions in tandem, within a single justice-based institutional structure. The court directs offenders at the outset to particular streams or tracks of response depending upon their circumstances, the nature of their offending behaviour and other relevant factors (Jordens 2008).[7] This approach provides one operational example that institutionalizing a requirement to ask "the restorative question" as a

5 Assertions that only the most minimalist change in sentencing practice is likely to be entertained by the judiciary is borne out by a search of the NSW Sentencing Bench Book (which is the judge's 'bible' on sentencing) which discloses no current reference whatsoever to 'restorative justice'; http://www.jirs.judcom.nsw.gov.au/menus/prin.php, accessed 19 May 2009. This is a potent reminder of Judge McElrea's comments that 'lawyers (including judges), prosecutors, government advisers and others [will be] slow to give up their old court-based, adversarial mindsets' (McElrea 2007b: 102).

6 The NJC draws its design and inspiration from the original multijurisdictional community courts, Red Hook Community Justice Center in Brooklyn, New York, and the North Liverpool Community Justice Centre in the UK.

7 Problem solving or 'problem-oriented' (Freiberg 2001a) courts already provide examples of successful modification to judicial practice in introducing therapeutic jurisprudence principles to criminal justice practice (Wexler, Winick et al. 2000). See the concerns Dorf (2006) raises about the 'accountability deficit' of such courts.

threshold step in criminal justice responses is potentially a workable practice. The requirements for mandating such a modification are as follows:

1. A consideration of whether harm has been caused

Requiring courts to consider whether harm has been caused clearly involves departure from traditional curial functions. Courts would still retain their neutral oversight function while adapting their practice to acknowledge the need to consider the restorative elements in a response to wrongdoing. Once a determination of the restorative question has been made (subject to the threshold assumption that criminal responsibility has been accepted by the offender or otherwise determined), it follows that a determination as to how to address restorative needs would logically follow.

2. Criteria to determine the extent of harm

It is certainly within the traditional curial function to make determinations as to the extent of harm caused (currently for the purposes of sentencing and to address considerations of proportionality and culpability, for instance). A set of criteria can be developed to further assist courts in making these determinations. Obvious criteria based on considerations such as the nature of the wrongdoing, the extent of harm suffered and by whom or the likelihood that such harm can be repaired or alleviated, provide an obvious starting point. These considerations are best framed as a set of 'restorative question criteria':

Table C.1 Criteria for determining restorative aspects

Restorative question criteria
A court *must*: 1. consider whether the wrongdoing involves personal violation of some kind; 2. consider the emotional and practical needs of victims vis-à-vis the offender and the wrongdoing; 3. consider the victim's views about the form of response; 4. consider potential benefits that may flow from engaging in a restorative form of response; 5. consider the possibility that any sanction imposed should have a community element; 6. consider the potential crime prevention benefits of a full, voluntary acceptance of responsibility.[1]

Note 1: A clear example of the superior offence prevention effects of strategies which focus on acceptance of responsibility is that of the Invitation to Responsibility program for family violence at the Mary Street Clinic in South Australia (Jenkins 1990).

3. A consideration of the scope to address the essential aims restoratively

The second determination is whether the appropriate response to the wrongdoing and the identified harm is (in whole or in part) through a restorative encounter or a judicial-managed approach. In broad terms, the court should either seek to deliver the restorative objectives itself with some institutional guidance or (and this is considered preferable) by referral to an external restorative provider to conduct some form of restorative encounter. There are a number of examples of how this could work in practice.[8] The method used in the NJC is for non-judicial 'assistance' to be specifically provided to the court in selecting suitable welfare and justice referrals which the court can then order.[9] NJC courtroom personnel include a 'justice centre caseworker' who has a specific courtroom presence and actively participates in proceedings to make such referral determinations (Jordens 2008; Lim and Bassett 2008). In the integrated model suggested here, judges would be assisted to make determinations as to the capacity of particular restorative approaches to address specific aspects of the wrongdoing. A 'restorative justice advisor' with the knowledge and skills about availability and suitability of various restorative approaches could fill a role similar to that of the NJC's justice centre caseworker. This restorative justice advisor would also act as an advocate for restorative approaches generally, with a role in highlighting the capacity of restorative approaches to address particular aspects of harm caused by the wrongdoing.

Adding the Restorative Perspective

Once the two parts of the restorative question are addressed as a threshold requirement, a restorative response can be provided in two ways. Either approach can satisfy 'the restorative question' requirement of ensuring that aspects of the essential retributive, restorative and consequential aims are met restoratively as much as possible. Broadly, these two approaches are the use of restorative-type sentences and the use of restorative encounters.

Using restorative-type sentences

Using restorative-type sentences means that the response remains a court-sanctioned approach, with imposed or agreed-upon conditions designed to meet

8 In New Zealand's adult restorative scheme, the selection is made by the court though suitability for restorative encounter is brought to the attention of judges by 'restorative justice co-ordinators' who have access to prosecution files and indicate a potential suitability for restorative intervention by 'tagging or stamping court papers "RJ"' (NZ Ministry of Justice 2005a: para. 3.2). Likewise, in some Canadian programs, such as the Ottawa Collaborative Justice Project, staff plays a significant role in the decision to refer (Mann 2007).

9 The referrals can be to community corrections, Aboriginal justice, alcohol and drug case officers, crime and violence prevention, legal aid, financial counselling, victim support, mental health, emergency relief, accommodation services and family violence support (Lim and Bassett 2008).

the essential aims. The difference is that explicit sentencing is delivered within a restorative framework. This is the approach in the development of Canadian restorative justice jurisprudence. Judges address the essential aims restoratively in these ways:

- Retribution – achieved through *denunciation* and *censure* rather than primarily through punishment, with retribution communicated by a *sanction* involving potential restrictions on liberty (such as house arrest, curfew, electronic monitoring, but ordinarily falling short of imprisonment), with the extent of such restrictions dependent on the severity of the harm done and not simply on the severity of the wrongdoing;
- Restoration – achieved through personal and normative harm being addressed by orders for *reparation* – symbolic reparation communicated by *apology*, and material reparation addressed through the payment of *compensation* or through the performance of appropriate *community services*;
- Consequential objectives – achieved through meeting:
  - the need for *deterrence* by the censure and restrictive measures;
  - the need for *rehabilitation* through requirements for attendance at treatment and/or education programs;
  - the need for *prevention*
    - by future restrictions on the liberty of the offender (reporting, curfew and residency conditions and the like);
    - by future target-hardening recommendations (for example, enhanced static security measures and improved community and police surveillance of trouble spots in the case of property-related offences or altered rules on the regulation of alcohol or illicit drugs in the case of violence-related offences) to act as practical disincentives for the commission of offences.

Using restorative encounters

Alternatively (and preferably), a separate restorative encounter provides the means to directly engage the offender with persons affected by the wrongdoing (subject to determinations of suitability and consent). Such an encounter has the potential to address each of the essential aims more directly as a consequence of the '*bringing together of all persons affected by wrongdoing*' that restorative justice implies. New Zealand restorative justice jurisprudence has developed in this way. The encounter is recognized as meeting the essential aims in these ways:

- Retribution – achieved through *denunciation* and *censure* (rather than through punishment) communicated in the process directly and through *remorse* similarly expressed by the offender directly to the persons affected;
- Restoration – achieved through the effects of personal and normative harm being explored in the conference; this need can be recognized symbolically

through *apology*, and met materially through *reparation* or through community engagement;[10]

- Consequential objectives – achieved through meeting:
  - the need for *deterrence* by *censure* and by agreed-upon restrictions on the offender and his or her behavior;[11]
  - the need for *rehabilitation* through agreement to participate in treatment and/or education programs;
  - the need for *prevention*[12]
    - by agreed-upon constraints on future behavior;
    - by the mobilization of community and police knowledge in order to craft targeted crime prevention measures;
    - by measures designed to provoke attitudinal change in the offender and to build upon any insights she or he has gained in the restorative process.[13]

Judicial recognition that restorative encounters can address many specifics of the essential aims is an important step in the move towards restorative justice practice. The value of a restorative process is not seen as confined only to addressing restorative aims but is also seen as capable of meeting some retributive and consequential requirements. When a restorative-type sentence is used and the management of the responses remains with the court the conditions remain imposed conditions, even though framed within a restorative context. When a restorative encounter is used the restorative potential is further realized, with the management of the response (at least for a time) returned to the persons affected, and many of the aims (particularly the difficult-to-achieve retributive aims of denunciation, remorse and censure) potentially met through negotiation at the encounter itself. Additionally, where encounters occur, consequential aspects may be more effectively met by agreed-on conditions which are accepted by, rather than imposed upon, the wrongdoer. Either approach nonetheless has the capacity

10 Angel's (2009) research has indicated participation in restorative conferencing can significantly reduce post-traumatic stress symptoms (PTSS), especially for female adult victims of serious crime. Gal's (2011) work suggests that restorative encounters may also better address the needs of child victims than legal approaches.

11 Shapland et al.'s (2008) evaluation of UK's randomized use of restorative conferencing in combination with 'conventional justice' has confirmed that significant reductions in reoffending rates for serious offenders can occur as a result of the encounter.

12 Restorative approaches can provide an effective vehicle for contextual crime prevention. Braithwaite (2002b: 111) has argued that 'there are many individuals with preventative capabilities who can be rendered responsible for mobilizing those capabilities through a restorative justice dialogue', such as an 'Uncle Harry' who can act as a strong, influential and effective restraint on potential reoccurrence of family violence.

13 Specifically, measures designed so as to begin the transformation of organizational, school or family cultures on matters like violence and alcohol abuse.

to allow restorative approaches to gain and maintain an institutional foothold. Requiring courts as a compulsory step to address the restoration question is key.

Using a minimalist model provides the best strategy for restorative approaches to become routinized and for a restorative justice jurisprudence to develop. The suggested reframing of the sentencing rhetoric to align with the essential aims of justice can then be explicitly met through addressing the second aspect of the restorative question. An integrated model encourages the development of multifunctional sentencing mechanisms so as to give courts wider options when the restorative-type sentencing option is adopted. The need for a community-based restorative practice network is specifically encouraged because these networks would be essential for both options of response to work effectively. The need to explicitly recognize integrative milestones can be met both directly through the restorative encounter, and indirectly through changed courtroom behaviour as exemplified in the Gladue Courts.

Conclusion

The model suggested here is deliberately a minimalist one, with certain categories of wrongdoing excluded from its reach. A traditional criminal justice response should remain the mandated form of response where responsibility for wrongdoing is denied and where culpability needs to be proven or dismissed by forensic means.

This book is about capitalizing on imminent developments in criminal justice reform. Criminal justice should be as much about restoration as it is about retribution or rehabilitation. It should be as much about repairing harm as it is about crime reduction or punishment. This is a valuable justice investment not beyond the ambit of the criminal justice law. The Canadian example shows how courts can move from an attention solely on individual responsibility for crime and restoration to one that takes proper consideration of the place and effect of systemic and historical factors. The New Zealand example shows how courts can confidently delegate to community conferences some aspects of retribution alongside restoration and repair. The innovative programs in Europe reveal the broad potential for communities to embrace this responsibility. There needs to be the judicial will to push these developments further.

Appendix

Methodology

An interview protocol approved for ethical purposes was used to conduct interviews to obtain the data reported in Chapter 9. Interviews of up to an hour were conducted face-to-face with 50 individuals closely involved in various restorative justice programs. The interview procedure was semi-structured, with the conduct of the interviews based on a written schedule focusing specifically on each of 12 generative mechanisms. Potential interviewees were either restorative practitioners (convenors, facilitators, program managers) or others (lawyers, judges, magistrates and so forth) involved directly in the programs or in the use of these programs as part of legal responses to criminal wrongdoing. No one approached for interview refused, though three interviews were not conducted due to the subject's unavailability at the time of the writer's visit. Interviews were held at the practice site mainly on a one-on-one basis, except for a small number of participants involved in the same program who preferred to be interviewed as a group. The interviews were conducted steadily from 2005 onwards, firstly in New Zealand, then in various Australian jurisdictions (the Australian Capital Territory, Victoria, South Australia and New South Wales) and in lastly in Canada.

Interviewees were asked to comment on 'a provisional list of elements seen as potentially essential to doing justice restoratively'. The definition of each mechanism developed in Chapter 4 was shown to interviewees on flash cards, read aloud or paraphrased to participants as each element was introduced. Comments were sought in response to two specific questions:

> Does [this mechanism] come into your program?
>
> Does your program have any particular views about the importance of [this mechanism] in achieving justice in your program?

Responses were recorded using a combination of contemporaneous note taking during the interview itself and subsequent note taking immediately following the interview. A typed version of the record of their interview was emailed to each interviewee soon after its completion, with the request that they check it for accuracy and make any corrections or additions they wished. Approximately one-third of respondents made some corrections or additions, mostly of a minor nature but in a few cases giving more detailed responses than before.

Interview data obtained was consolidated into responses concerning the 12 factors and analyzed using a variation of the constant comparative method, in which new comments obtained were consistently compared with all previous comments until no fresh perspectives were seen to emerge (Glaser and Strauss 1967; Parker 1999: 231–232). This detailed aggregation was then drawn on for this report. The interview and reporting methodology utilize similar methods as those adopted by Roche (2003) and Parker (1999) in reporting their empirical data. Direct quotations are indicated by italicizing the extract used. Words inserted within the quotations to retain sense and grammatical correctness are placed in square brackets. This reporting method is designed to weave together extracts from various responses seen as best capturing the consensus view about the importance of each of the mechanisms as justice generators in restorative practice.

List of References

Statutes

Charter of Human Rights and Responsibilities Act (Vic) 2006
Children, Young Persons and Their Families Act (NZ) 1989
Children, Youth and Families Act (Vic) 2005
Conditional Sentencing Reform Act C.9 2007
Constitution Act, being Schedule B to the Canada Act (UK) (C.11) 1982
Courts Legislation (Neighbourhood Justice Centre) Act (Vic) 2006
Crimes (Restorative Justice) Act (ACT) 2004
Criminal Code RSC C.46 1985
Criminal Justice Act (repealed) (NZ) 1985
Criminal Justice Act (UK) 2003
Criminal Procedure Act (NSW) 1986
Human Rights Act (ACT) 2004
Justice (Northern Ireland) Act (UK) 2002
Juvenile Justice Act (NT) 1997
Parole Act (NZ) 2002
Sentencing Act (Vic) 1991
Sentencing Act (NZ) 2002
Victims' Rights Act (NZ) 2002
Young Offenders Act (SA) 1993
Young Offenders Act RSC C.Y-1 (repealed) 1985
Young Offenders Act (NSW) 1997
Youth Criminal Justice Act SC, C.1 2002
Youth Justice Act (Tas) 1997
Youth Justice and Criminal Evidence Act (UK) 1999

Cases

Abahladi Basemjondolo Movement SA & Sibusiso Zikode v The Premier of the Province of Kwazulu-Natal [2010] BCLR 99 (CC)
Bugmy v The Queen [2013] HCA 37
D v Police [1999] Unreported High Court Auckland AP 161/99 (Nicholson J)
Dikoko v Mokhatla [2006] SA 235 (CC)
D'Orta-Ekenaike v Victoria Legal Aid [2005] 223 CLR 1
DPP v Dupas [2007] VSC 305

Environment Protection Authority v Waste Recycling and Processing Corporation [2006] NSWLEC 419
Feng v Police [2002] Unreported High Court Auckland A127/02 (Salmon J)
Garrett v Williams [2007] NSWLEC 96
Kalim v Police [2001] Unreported High Court Auckland A198/01 (Glazebrook J)
Kingi and McEwen v New Zealand Police [2007] CRI-2007-483-4 (High Court, Wanganui) (Simon France J)
Le Roux & Ors v Dey [2011] (3) SA 274 (CC)
Neal v The Queen [1982] 149 CLR 305
Occupiers of 51 Olivia Road & 197 Main Street v City of Johannesburg [2008] (3) SA 208 (C)
Police v Akurangi [1997] Unreported District Court Otahuhu CRN 60040709-2-7 (Mather J)
Police v Carter [2001] Unreported District Court Wanganui CRN 1083010524 (Becroft J)
Police v Currie [1996] NZDCR LEXIS 8
Police v Misikea [1996] Unreported District Court Auckland CRN 5204003944-45 (McElrea J)
Police v Stretch [2001] Unreported High Court Nelson AP9/01 (Durie J)
Port Elizabeth Municipality v Various Occupiers [2005] 1 SA 217 (CC)
R v Barci [2003] EWCA Crim 2816*R v Brizard* [2006] Unreported Ontario Court of Appeal O.J. No. 729
R v Bunn [2000] 1 SCR 183
R v Buttar [2008] NZCA 28
R v Cassidy [2003] Unreported High Court New Plymouth T2/03 (Paterson J)
R v Castles [2002] NZCA 109
R v Clotworthy [1998] Unreported District Court Auckland T.971545 (Thorburn J)
R v Clotworthy [1998] 15 CRNZ 651 (CA)
R v Collins [2003] EWCA Crim 1687
R v Collins [2011] ONCA 182
R v Fletcher [2000] Unreported District Court Auckland T.990070 (Gittos J)
R v Folaumoeloa [2004] Unreported District Court Auckland (Thorburn J)
R v Gladue [1999] 1 SCR 688
R v Ipeelee [2012] 1 SCR 433
R v Jeff [2010] BCSC 1800
R v Kakekagamick [2006] 214 OAC 127
R v L.F.W. [2000] 1 SCR 132
R v Logan [1999] CANLII 927
R v Martin [2011] ONCJ 423
R v Murphy [1996] Unreported District Court Auckland S151/96 (Hansen J)
R v Myke [2010] ONCJ 160
R v Nikolao & Ors [2005] Unreported Court of Appeal of New Zealand CA375/04; CA386/04; CA414/04
R v O'Brien [2004] EWCA Crim 2572

R v Police [2002] SASC 403
R v Proulx [2000] 1 SCR 61
R v Qutami [2001] NSWCCA 353
R v R.A.R. [2000] 1 SCR 163
R v R.N.S. [2000] 1 SCR 149
R v Sami [2006] NZDCR 128
R v Seet [2001] 2 DCLR (NSW) 192
R v Skani [2002] ABQB 1097
R v Symon [1995] Unreported High Court Auckland S64/95 (Tompkins J)
R v Taparau & Ors [1996] NZDCR 774
R v T.C. [2009] SKPC 80
R v Wells [2000] 1 SCR 207
R v Wilcox [2005] Unreported Court of Appeal of New Zealand CA14/05
Residents of Joe Slovo Community, Western Cape v Thubelisha Homes [2010] (3) SA 454 (CC)
S v M [2007] 2 SACR 539 (CC)
S v Saayman [2008] 1 SACR 393 (E)
The Citizen 1978 (Pty) Ltd and Ors v McBride [2011] (4) SA 191 (CC)

References

Aboriginal Corrections Policy Unit 1997. *The Four Circles of Hollow Water*. Ottawa: Solicitor General Canada.

Aboriginal Legal Services of Toronto 2007. *Community Council Program*. [Online]. Available at: http://aboriginallegal.ca [accessed: 13 October 2013].

Acorn, A. 2004. *Compulsory Compassion: A Critique of Restorative Justice*. Vancouver: University of British Columbia Press.

ACT Department of Justice and Community Safety 2006. *First Phase Review of Restorative Justice*. Canberra: JACS.

Ahmed, E. and V. Braithwaite 2006. Forgiveness, Reconciliation, and Shame: Three Key Variables in Reducing School Bullying. *Journal of Social Issues*, 62(2), 347–370.

Ahmed, E., N. Harris, J. Braithwaite and V. Braithwaite 2001. *Shame Management through Reintegration*. Cambridge: Cambridge University Press.

Alder, C. 2000. Young Women Offenders and the Challenge for Restorative Justice, in *Restorative Justice: Philosophy to Practice*, edited by H. Strang and J. Braithwaite. Aldershot: Ashgate, 105–119.

Allen, J. 1999. Balancing Justice and Social Unity: Political Theory and the Idea of a Truth and Reconciliation Commission. *University of Toronto Law Journal*, 49, 315–353.

Almond, B. 1991. Rights, in *A Companion to Ethics (Blackwell Companions to Philosophy)*, edited by P. Singer. Oxford: Blackwell, 259–269.

Anderson, E. 1999. What Is the Point of Equality? *Ethics*, 109, 287–337.

Angel, C. M. 2009. Effects of Restorative Justice Conferences on Post-traumatic Stress Symptoms among Robbery and Burglary Victims: A Randomised Controlled Trial. *The Ninth Annual Colloquium of The Campbell Collaboration*, Oslo, 18–20 May 2009.

Archibald, B. P. 2005. Coordinating Canada's Restorative and Inclusionary Models of Criminal Justice: The Legal Profession and the Exercise of Discretion under a Reflexive Rule of Law. *Canadian Criminal Law Review*, 9, 215–260.

Archibald, B. P. 2008. Let My People Go: Human Capital Investment and Community Capacity Building via Meta/Regulation in a Deliberative Democracy: A Modest Contribution for Criminal Law and Restorative Justice. *Cardozo Journal of International and Comparative Law*, 16(1), 1–86.

Archibald, B. P. and J. J. Llewellyn 2006. The Challenges of Institutionalizing Comprehensive Restorative Justice: Theory and Practice in Nova Scotia. *Dalhousie Law Journal*, 29(2), 297–343.

Aristotle 1984. *Nicomachean Ethics* (trans. E. Solomon), in *The Complete Works of Aristotle: The Revised Oxford Translation*, Vol. 2, edited by J. Barnes. Princeton: Princeton University Press.

Ashworth, A. 1983. *Sentencing and Penal Policy*. London: Weidenfeld & Nicolson.

Ashworth, A. 1993. Some Doubts about Restorative Justice. *Criminal Law Forum*, 4(2), 277–299.

Ashworth, A. 1998. Restorative Justice, in *Principled Sentencing*, edited by A. von Hirsch and A. Ashworth. Oxford: Hart Publishing, 300–311.

Ashworth, A. 2002. Responsibilities, Rights and Restorative Justice. *British Journal of Criminology*, 42, 578–595.

Augsburger, D. 1996. *Helping People Forgive*. Louisville: Westminster John Knox Press.

Bargen, J. 1996. Kids, Cops, Courts, Conferencing and Children's Rights: A Note on Perspectives. *Australian Journal of Human Rights*, 2(2), 209–238.

Bargen, J. 2001. Kids, Cops, Courts, Conferencing and Children's Rights: A Note on Perspectives and Update for 1996–98, in *Children on the Agenda: The Rights of Australia's Children*, edited by M. Jones and L. A. Basser Marks. Sydney: Prospect Press.

Bargen, J. 2003. Workshop: Training to Divert Young Offenders. *Juvenile Justice: From Lessons of the Past to a Road for the Future Conference*, Sydney, 1–2 December 2003.

Barker, E. 1959. *The Political Thought of Plato and Aristotle*. New York: Dover Publications.

Barnes, J. (ed). 1984. *The Complete Works of Aristotle*. Princeton: Princeton University Press.

Barton, C. 2000. Empowerment and Retribution in Criminal Justice, in *Restorative Justice: Philosophy to Practice*, edited by H. Strang and J. Braithwaite. Aldershot: Dartmouth, 55–76.

Barton, C. 2003. *Restorative Justice: The Empowerment Model*. Sydney: Hawkins Press.

Bassett, L. 2007. *Restorative Justice: Background and Discussion Paper*. Melbourne: Neighbourhood Justice Centre Project Team, Department of Justice Victoria.

Bassett, L. and K. Walker 2008. *Young Adult Restorative Justice Group Conferencing Program at the Neighbourhood Justice Centre*. Melbourne: Department of Justice Victoria.

Bazemore, G. 1996. Three Paradigms for Juvenile Justice, in *Restorative Justice: International Perspectives*, edited by B. Galaway and J. Hudson. Monsey, NY: Criminal Justice Press, 37–67.

Bazemore, G. and M. Schiff 2005. *Juvenile Justice Reform and Restorative Justice*. Cullompton: Willan Publishing.

Becker, L. C. 1986. *Reciprocity*. New York: Routledge & Kegan Paul.

Beckett, H., C. Campbell, D. O'Mahony, J. Jackson and J. Doak 2005. *Interim Evaluation of the Northern Ireland Youth Conferencing Scheme: Research and Statistical Bulletin* 1/2005. Belfast: Northern Ireland Statistics and Research Agency.

Becroft, A. 2003. Youth Justice: The New Zealand Experience; Past Lessons and Future Challenges. *Juvenile Justice: From Lessons of the Past to a Road for the Future Conference*, Sydney, 1–2 December 2003.

Becroft, A. 2005. Personal communication, 5 July 2005. Wellington, New Zealand.

Beebe, L., S. Williams, L. Chapman and D. Plecas 2003. The Fraser Valley Community Restorative Justice Programs Network: Private, Public, and Community Partners Working Together. *6th International Conference on Restorative Justice*, Vancouver, 1–4 June 2003.

Benn, S. 1980. The Nature of Justice, in *Justice: Alternatives Political Perspectives*, edited by J. Sterba. Belmont, CA: Wadsworth, 26–32.

Bentham, J. 1824. Anarchical Fallacies, in *The Works of Jeremy Bentham*, edited by J. Bowring. 1843. Bristol: Thoemmes Press.

Bix, B. 2006. *Jurisprudence: Theory and Context*. 4th edition. London: Sweet & Maxwell.

Blad, J. and J. Van Lieshout 2010. *Families Solving Their Problems: Family Group Conferencing on Family Problems in the Netherlands; European Best Practices of Restorative Justice in Criminal Procedure*. Conference publication. Budapest: Ministry of Justice and Law Enforcement.

Bolitho, J., J. Bruce and G. Mason (eds). 2012. Restorative Justice: Adults and Emerging Practice. *Institute of Criminology Series*, no. 30. Sydney: Institute of Criminology, University of Sydney Law School.

Bonta, J. and M. Gray 1996. *The Restorative Resolutions Project: Phase 2 Evaluation*. Ottawa: Solicitor General Canada.

Bonta, J., S. Wallace-Capretta and J. Rooney 1998. *Restorative Justice: An Evaluation of the Restorative Resolutions Project*. Ottawa: Solicitor General Canada.

Booth, T. 2005. Restoring Victims' Voices: Victim Impact Statements in the Sentencing Process. *Reform*, 86, 59–62.

Bottoms, A. 2003. Some Sociological Reflections on Restorative Justice, in *Restorative Justice and Criminal Justice*, edited by A. von Hirsch, J. V. Roberts and A. Bottoms. Oxford: Hart Publishing, 79–113.

Boutellier, H. 2002. Victimalization and Restorative Justice: Moral Backgrounds and Political Consequences, in *Restorative Justice and the Law*, edited by L. Walgrave. Cullompton: Willan Publishing, 19–30.

Bovens, M. 1998. *The Quest for Responsibility*. Cambridge: Cambridge University Press.

Bowen, H. and J. Boyack 2003. Adult Restorative Justice in New Zealand/ Aotearoa. *4th International Conference on Conferencing, Circles and other Restorative Practices*, Veldhoven, Netherlands, 28–30 August 2003.

Bowen, H., J. Boyack and J. Calder-Watson 2012. Recent Developments within Restorative Justice in Aotearoa/New Zealand, in *Restorative Justice: Adults and Emerging Practice*, edited by J. Bolitho, J. Bruce and G. Mason. Sydney: Institute of Criminology, University of Sydney Law School, 121–141.

Bowen, H. and J. Consedine 1998. Five Restorative Justice Court Judgments, in *Restorative Justice Contemporary Themes and Practices*, edited by H. Bowen and J. Consedine. Christchurch, NZ: Ploughshares Publications, 125–151.

Bowen, H. and T. Thompson 1999. Restorative Justice and the New Zealand Court of Appeal's Decision in the Clotworthy Case. *Journal of South Pacific Law*, 3(4), http://www.vanuatu.usp.ac.fj/journal_splaw/articles/Bowen1.htm.

Braithwaite, J. 1989. *Crime, Shame and Reintegration*. Cambridge: Cambridge University Press.

Braithwaite, J. 1996. Restorative Justice and a Better Future. *Dalhousie Review*, 76(1), 9–32.

Braithwaite, J. 1999a. Restorative Justice: Assessing Optimistic and Pessimistic Accounts, in *Crime and Justice: A Review of Research*, edited by M. Tonry. Chicago: University of Chicago Press, 25, 1–27.

Braithwaite, J. 2002a. Repentance Rituals and Restorative Justice. *Journal of Political Philosophy*, 8, 115–131.

Braithwaite, J. 2002b. *Restorative Justice and Responsive Regulation*. Oxford: Oxford University Press.

Braithwaite, J. 2002c. Restorative Justice and Therapeutic Jurisprudence. *Criminal Law Bulletin*, March–April, 244–262.

Braithwaite, J. 2002d. In Search of Restorative Jurisprudence, in *Restorative Justice and the Law*, edited by L. Walgrave. Cullompton: Willan Publishing, 150–167.

Braithwaite, J. 2002e. Setting Standards for Restorative Justice. *British Journal of Criminology*, 42, 563–577.

Braithwaite, J. 2005. Between Proportionality and Impunity: Confrontation =>Truth =>Prevention. *Criminology*, 43(2), 283–306.

Braithwaite, J. 2006. Accountability and Responsibility through Restorative Justice, in *Public Accountability: Designs, Dilemmas and Experiences*, edited by M. W. Dowdle. Cambridge: Cambridge University Press, 33–51.

Braithwaite, J. and V. Braithwaite 2001. Shame, Shame Management and Regulation, in *Shame Management through Reintegration*, edited by E. Ahmed, N. Harris, J. Braithwaite and V. Braithwaite. Cambridge: Cambridge University Press, 3–72.

Braithwaite, J., H. Charlesworth, P. Reddy and L. Dunn 2010. *Reconciliation and Architectures of Commitment: Sequencing Peace in Bougainville*. Canberra: ANU EPress.

Braithwaite, J. and P. Drahos 2000. *Global Business Regulation*. Cambridge: Cambridge University Press.

Braithwaite, J. and P. Pettit 1990. *Not Just Deserts: A Republican Theory of Criminal Justice*. Oxford: Oxford University Press.

Braithwaite, J. and D. Roche 2001. Responsibility and Restorative Justice, in *Restorative Community Justice*, edited by M. Schiff and G. Bazemore. Cincinnati: Anderson Publishing, 63–84.

Braithwaite, J. and H. Strang 2001. Introduction: Restorative Justice and Civil Society, in *Restorative Justice and Civil Society*, edited by H. Strang and J. Braithwaite. Cambridge: Cambridge University Press, 1–13.

Braithwaite, V. 1995. Games of Engagement: Postures within the Regulatory Community. *Law and Policy*, 17, 225–255.

Braithwaite, V., K. Murphy and M. Reinhart 2007. Taxation Threat, Motivational Postures, and Responsive Regulation. *Law and Policy*, 29(1), 137–158.

Brown, J. G. 1994. The Use of Mediation to Resolve Criminal Cases: A Procedural Critique. *Emory Law Journal*, 42, 1247–1308.

Buckle, S. 1991. Natural Law, in *A Companion to Ethics (Blackwell Companions to Philosophy)*, edited by P. Singer. Oxford: Blackwell, 161–174.

Burnside, J. and N. Baker (eds). 1994. *Relational Justice: Repairing the Breach*. Winchester: Waterside Press.

Campbell, C., R. Devlin, D. O'Mahony, J. Doak, J. Jackson, T. Corrigan and K. McEvoy 2005. *Evaluation of the Northern Ireland Youth Conference Service*. Belfast: Northern Ireland Office.

Campbell, T. 1996. *The Legal Theory of Ethical Positivism*. Aldershot: Dartmouth.

Campbell, T. 2001. *Justice*. 2nd edition. Basingstoke: Macmillan Press.

Campbell Research Associates 2006a. *Evaluation of the Aboriginal Legal Services of Toronto Gladue Caseworker Program, Year One: October 2004–September 2005*. Mississauga, ON: Campbell Research Associates.

Campbell Research Associates 2006b. *Evaluation of the Aboriginal Legal Services of Toronto Gladue Caseworker Program, Year Two: October 2005–September 2006*. Mississauga, ON: Campbell Research Associates.

Canadian Criminal Justice Association 2006. *C-9 Conditional Sentencing Bill: Submission to the Standing Committee on Justice, Human Rights, Public Safety and Emergency Preparedness*. Ottawa: Canadian Criminal Justice Association.

Canadian Sentencing Commission 1988. *Views of Sentencing: A Survey of Judges in Canada*. Ottawa: Research Reports of the Canadian Sentencing Commission, Department of Justice.

Cane, P. 2002. *Responsibility in Law and Morality*. Oxford: Hart Publishing.

Cant, R. and R. Downie 1998. *Evaluation of the Young Offenders Act (1994) and the Juvenile Justice Teams*. Perth: Social Systems and Evaluation.

Carruthers, D. 2005. Restorative Justice: A Judicial Perspective. *The SACRO (Safeguarding Communities - Reducing Offending) Annual Conference*, Edinburgh, 10 February 2005.

Carter, L. H. 1974. *The Limits of Order*. Lexington: Lexington Books.

Cashman, P. 1985. *A National Survey of Judges and Magistrates: Technical Report*. Sydney: Australian Law Reform Commission.

Cavadino, M. and J. Dignan 1997. Reparation, Retribution and Rights, in *Principled Sentencing*, edited by A. von Hirsch and A. Ashworth. Oxford: Hart Publishing, 348–358.

Chan, J., J. Bargen, G. Luke and G. Clancey 2004. Regulating Police Discretion: An Assessment of the Impact of the New South Wales Young Offenders Act 1997. *Criminal Law Journal*, 28, 72–92.

Chapman, T. 2012. The Problem of Community in a Justice System in Transition: The Case of Community Restorative Justice in Northern Ireland. *International Criminal Law Review*, 12, 1–15.

Charlesworth, H. 2002. Author! Author! A Response to David Kennedy. *Harvard Human Rights Journal*, 15, 127–131.

Christie, N. 1997. Conflicts as Property. *British Journal of Criminology*, 17(1), 1–15.

Clairmont, D. 2005a. The Nova Scotia Restorative Justice Initiative: Final Evaluation Report. Bedford, Nova Scotia: Atlantic Institute of Criminology, Dalhousie University.

Clairmont, D. 2005b. Penetrating the Walls: Implementing a System-Wide Restorative Justice Approach in the Justice System, in *New Directions in Restorative Justice: Issues, Practice, Evaluation*, edited by E. Elliott and R. M. Gordon. Cullompton: Willan Publishing, 245–265.

Clairmont, D. 2006. *Examining the Delivery of Extra-Judicial Sanctions Programs in a Complex Urban Community: An Assessment of the Nova Scotia Restorative Justice Initiative in Metropolitan Halifax*. Halifax, Nova Scotia: Atlantic Institute of Criminology.

Clairmont, D. 2007. Personal communication, 3 October 2007. Halifax.

Clairmont, D. and J. McMillan 2001. *Directions in Mi'kmaq Justice: An Evaluation of the Mi'kmaq Justice Institute and Its Aftermath*. Halifax: Tripartite Forum: Justice Subcommittee.

Coker, D. 2002. Transformative Justice: Anti-subordination Processes in the Case of Domestic Violence, in *Restorative Justice and Family Violence*, edited by H. Strang and J. Braithwaite. Cambridge: Cambridge University Press, 128–152.

Collaborative Justice Project 1999. *Collaborative Justice Project: Achieving Satisfying Justice through a Healing Restorative Approach*. Ottawa: Collaborative Justice Project.

Condliffe, P. 2006. *The Conferencing Handbook: Practising Restorative Justice*. Melbourne: Victorian Association for Restorative Justice.
Cowdery, N. 2006. Australian Avoidance of the Rule of Law. *NSW Law Society Journal*, September 2006, 63–65.
Crawford, A. 2000. Salient Themes towards a Victim Perspective and the Limitations of Restorative Justice, in *Integrating a Victim Perspective within Criminal Justice*, edited by A. Crawford and J. Goodey. Aldershot: Ashgate, 285–310.
Crawford, A. 2002. The State, Community and Restorative Justice: Heresy, Nostalgia and Butterfly Collecting, in *Restorative Justice and the Law*, edited by L. Walgrave. Cullompton: Willan Publishing, 101–129.
Crawford, A. and T. Newburn 2003. *Youth Offending and Restorative Justice: Implementing Reform in Youth Justice*. Cullompton: Willan Publishing.
Cretney, A. and G. Davis 1995. *Punishing Violence*. London: Routledge.
Cullen, F. T. and K. E. Gilbert 2009. Reaffirming Rehabilitation, in *Principled Sentencing: Readings on Theory and Policy*, edited by A. von Hirsch, A. Ashworth and J. V. Roberts. Portland: Hart Publishing, 28–32.
Cunneen, C. 2003. Thinking Critically about Restorative Justice, in *Restorative Justice: Critical Issues*, edited by E. McLaughlin, R. Fergusson, G. Hughes and L. Westmarland. London: Sage Publications, 182–194.
Daly, K. 1996. Diversionary Conferencing in Australia: A Reply to the Optimists and Skeptics. *American Society of Criminology Annual Meeting*, Chicago, November 1996.
Daly, K. 1999. Restorative Justice and Punishment: The Views of Young People. *American Society of Criminology Annual Meeting*, Toronto, 17–21 November 1999.
Daly, K. 2000. Revisiting the Relationship between Retributive and Restorative Justice, in *Restorative Justice: From Philosophy to Practice*, edited by H. Strang and J. Braithwaite. Aldershot: Ashgate Dartmouth, 33–54.
Daly, K. 2001. South Australian Juvenile Justice (SAJJ) Research on Conferencing. *Technical Report No. 2: Research Instruments in Year 2 (1999) and Background Notes*. Brisbane: School of Criminology and Criminal Justice, Griffith University.
Daly, K. 2002. Restorative Justice: The Real Story. *Punishment and Society*, 4(1), 55–79.
Daly, K. 2003. Mind the Gap: Restorative Justice in Theory and Practice, in *Restorative Justice and Criminal Justice*, edited by A. von Hirsch, J. V. Roberts and A. Bottoms. Oxford: Hart Publishing, 219–236.
Daly, K. 2006. The Limits of Restorative Justice, in *Handbook of Restorative Justice: A Global Perspective*, edited by D. Sullivan and L. Tifft. Oxford: Routledge, 134–146.
Daly, K. 2008. Girls, Peer Violence, and Restorative Justice. *Australian and New Zealand Journal of Criminology*, 41(1), 109–137.

Daly, K., S. Curtis-Fawley and B. Bouhours 2003. *Sexual Offence Cases Finalised in Court, by Conference, and by Formal Caution in South Australia for Young Offenders, 1995–2001*. Brisbane: School of Criminology and Criminal Justice.

Daly, K. and J. Stubbs 2006. Feminist Engagement with Restorative Justice. *Theoretical Criminology*, 10(1), 9–28.

Daly, K., M. Venables, L. McKenna and J. Christie-Johnston 1998. *South Australian Juvenile Justice (SAJJ) Research on Conferencing: Technical Report, No. 1; Project Overview and Research Instruments*. Brisbane: School of Criminology and Criminal Justice, Griffith University.

Davies, G. L. and K. L. Raymond 2000. Do Current Sentencing Practices Work? *Criminal Law Journal*, 24, 236–247.

Davies, M. 1999. Legal Separatism and the Concept of the Person, in *Judicial Power, Democracy and Legal Positivism*, edited by T. Campbell and J. Goldsworthy. Aldershot: Dartmouth, 115–137.

Davis, J. 2007b. Sentencing, and the Psychology of Justice. *Alternative Law Journal*, 32(3), 144–148.

Davis, J. 2009. Judicial Reasoning and the 'Just World Delusion': Using the Psychology of Justice to Evaluate Legal Judgments. *NJCA Conference Judicial Reasoning: Art or Science?* Canberra, 7–8 February 2009.

Department of Justice Canada 2002. *Youth Criminal Justice Act: Summary and Background*. Ottawa: Department of Justice Canada.

Department of Justice Canada 2005. *Youth Criminal Justice Act: 2005 Annual Statement*. Ottawa: Department of Justice Canada.

Derksen, W. 2009. Understanding Victims of Crime and Their Need to Deal with the Victim/Offender Trauma Bond: The 5 Elements of the Crime Victim Detour. *12th World Conference of the International Institute for Restorative Practices*, Bethlehem, PA, 21–23 October 2009.

Deutsch, M. 1969. *Distributive Justice: A Social-Psychological Perspective*. New Haven: Yale University Press.

Dignan, J. 2002. Restorative Justice and the Law: The Case for an Integrated, Systematic Approach, in *Restorative Justice and the Law*, edited by L. Walgrave. Cullompton: Willan Publishing, 168–190.

Dignan, J. 2003. Towards a Systematic Model of Restorative Justice: Reflections on the Concept, Its Context and the Need for Clear Constraints, in *Restorative Justice and Criminal Justice*, edited by A. von Hirsch, J. V. Roberts and A. Bottoms. Oxford: Hart Publishing, 135–156.

Dignan, J. and K. Lowey 2000. *Restorative Justice Options for Northern Ireland: A Comparative View. Northern Ireland Criminal Justice Review Group*. Belfast: Northern Ireland Office.

Doak, J. 2011. Honing the Stone: Refining Restorative Justice as a Vehicle for Emotional Redress. *Contemporary Justice Review*, 14(4), 439–456.

Dorf, M. C. 2003. Legal Indeterminacy and Institutional Design. *New York University Law Review*, 78(3), 875–981.

Dorf, M. C. 2006. Problem-solving Courts and the Judicial Accountability Deficit, in *Public Accountability: Designs, Dilemmas and Experiences*, edited by M. Dowdle. Cambridge: Cambridge University Press, 301–328.

Dorf, M. C. and C. Sabel 1998. A Constitution of Democratic Experimentalism. *Columbia Law Review*, 98, 267–473.

Drumgold, S. 2004. *Restorative Justice Programs for Indigenous Offenders in the USA, Canada and New Zealand.* Canberra: Churchill Fellowship 2003, Winston Churchill Memorial Trust of Australia.

Duff, R. A. 1986. *Trials and Punishments*. Cambridge: Cambridge University Press.

Duff, R. A. 1990. *Intention, Agency and Criminal Liability*. Oxford: Blackwell.

Duff, R. A. 1992. *Alternatives to Punishment: Or Alternative Punishments?* in *Retributivism and Its Critics*, edited by W. Cragg. Stuttgart: Franz Steiner, 46–68.

Duff, R. A. 2002. Restorative Punishment and Punitive Restoration, in *Restorative Justice and the Law*, edited by L. Walgrave. Cullompton: Willan Publishing, 83–100.

Duff, R. A. 2003. Restoration and Retribution, in *Restorative Justice and Criminal Justice*, edited by A. von Hirsch, J. V. Roberts and A. Bottoms. Oxford: Hart Publishing, 43–59.

Durkheim, E. 1933. *The Division of Labour in Society*. New York: New York University Press.

Durkheim, E. 1912. *The Elementary Forms of the Religious Life* (trans. J. Swain: 1915). New York: The Free Press.

Dworkin, R. 1978. *Taking Rights Seriously*. Cambridge, MA: Harvard University Press.

Dworkin, R. 1984. Rights as Trumps, in *Theories of Rights*, edited by J. Waldron. Oxford: Oxford University Press, 153–167.

Dworkin, R. 2000. Must Our Judges Be Philosophers? Can They Be Philosophers? *Council for the Humanities Scholar of the Year Lecture*. New York.

Dworkin, R. 2006. *Is Democracy Possible Here? Principles for a New Political Debate*. Princeton: Princeton University Press.

Dyzenhaus, D. 2003. Judicial Independence, Transitional Justice and the Rule of Law. *Otago Law Review*, 10(3), 345–366.

Edney, R. and M. Bagaric 2007. *Australian Sentencing: Principles and Practice*. Melbourne: Cambridge University Press.

Elster, J. 1989. *Nuts and Bolts for the Social Sciences*. Cambridge: Cambridge University Press.

Elster, J. 2007. *Explaining Social Behavior: More Nuts and Bolts for the Social Sciences*. New York: Cambridge University Press.

Erez, E. 1999. Who's Afraid of the Big Bad Victim? Victim Impact Statements as Empowerment and Enhancement of Justice. *Criminal Law Review*, 545–546.

Farrar, J. 1997. Reasoning by Analogy in the Law. *Bond Law Review*, 9, 149–175.

Farrar, J. 2009. Reasoning by Analogy in the Law. *NJCA Conference Judicial Reasoning: Art or Science?* Canberra, 7–8 February 2009.

Feeley, M. M. 1979. *The Process Is the Punishment*. New York: Russell Sage Foundation.

Feenan, D. (ed). 2002. *Informal Criminal Justice*. Aldershot: Ashgate.

Feinberg, J. 1970a. The Expressive Theory of Punishment, in *Doing and Deserving: Essays in the Theory of Responsibility*, edited by J. Feinberg. Princeton and Oxford: Princeton University Press, 95–118.

Feinberg, J. 1970b. The Nature and Value of Rights. *Journal of Value Inquiry*, 4(4), 243–257.

Feinberg, J. 1973. *Social Philosophy*. Englewood, NJ: Prentice-Hall.

Feinberg, J. 1984. *The Moral Limits of the Criminal Law: Harm to Others*. New York: Oxford University Press.

Feld, B. C. 1999. Rehabilitation, Retribution and Restorative Justice: Alternative Conceptions of Juvenile Justice, in *Restorative Juvenile Justice: Repairing the Harm of Youth Crime*, edited by G. Bazemore and L. Walgrave. Monsey, NY: Criminal Justice Press, 19–43.

Fellegi, B. 2013. Retribution and/or Restoration? The Purpose of Our Justice System through the Lens of Judges and Prosecutors, in *Civilising Criminal Justice: An International Agenda for Penal Reform*, edited by M. Wright, J. Blad and D. J. Cornwell. Hook, Hampshire: Waterside Press.

Finnis, J. 1980. *Natural Law and Natural Rights*. Oxford: Clarendon Press.

Fiss, O. 1984. Against Settlement. *Yale Law Journal*, 93, 1073–1090.

Fletcher, G. 1978. *Rethinking Criminal Law*. Boston: Little, Brown & Co.

Foucault, M. 1977. *Discipline and Punish: The Birth of the Prison*. London: Allen Lane.

Foucault, M. 2003. *Society Must Be Defended: Lectures at the College de France, 1975–1976*. New York: Picador.

Frankel, M. E. 1978. *Partisan Justice: Too Much Fight? Too Little Truth?* New York: Hill & Wang.

Fredriksen, E. and V. Andersen 2008. The National Mediation Services: Northern Contexts and Challenges, in *Restoring Peace and Justice: Exploring Methodological and Theoretical Challenges; CPS Working Papers*, No. 11, edited by Centre for Peace Studies. Tromso, Norway: University of Tromso, 23–32.

Freiberg, A. 2001. Affective versus Effective Justice: Instrumentalism and Emotionalism in Criminal Justice. *Punishment and Society*, 3(2), 265–278.

Fuller, L. L. 1964. *The Morality of Law*. New Haven: Yale University Press.

Gaita, R. 1991. *Good and Evil: An Absolute Comparison*. London: Macmillan.

Gal, T. 2011. *Child Victims and Restorative Justice: A Needs-Rights Model*. Oxford: Oxford University Press.

Garvey, S. 1999. Punishment as Atonement. *UCLA Law Review*, 46, 1801–1858.

Gilligan, C. 1982. *In a Different Voice*. Revised edition, 1993. Cambridge, MA: Harvard University Press.

Glaser, B. and A. Strauss 1967. *The Discovery of Grounded Theory: Strategies for Qualitative Research*. Chicago: Aldine.

Glendon, M. A. 1992. Rights in Twentieth-Century Constitutions. *University of Chicago Law Review*, 59, 519–538.

Goffman, E. 1971. *Relations in Public*. New York: Basic Books.

Golding, M. P. 2005. Responsibility, in *The Blackwell Guide to the Philosophy of Law and Legal Theory*, edited by M. P. Golding and W. A. Edmundson. Malden, MA: Blackwell Publishing, 221–235.

Goldman, A. H. 1982. Towards a New Theory of Punishment. *Law and Philosophy*, 1, 57–76.

Goldsmith, A., M. Halsey and D. Bamford 2005. *Adult Restorative Justice Conferencing Pilot: An Evaluation*. Adelaide: South Australian Courts Administrative Authority and Flinders University of South Australia.

Gramsci, A. 1971. *Selections from the Prison Notebooks*. London: Lawrence & Wishart.

Green, R. G. 1998. *Justice in Aboriginal Communities: Sentencing Alternatives*. Saskatoon, Saskatchewan: Purich Publishing.

Griffiths, C. T. and R. Hamilton 1996. Sanctioning and Healing: Restorative Justice in Canadian Aboriginal Communities, in *Restorative Justice: International Perspectives*, edited by B. Galaway and B. Hudson. Monsey, NY: Criminal Justice Press, 175–191.

Grotius, H. 1925. *De Jure Belli ac Pacis*. Oxford: Clarendon Press.

Habermas, J. 1996. *Between Facts and Norms*. Cambridge: Polity Press.

HALT 2008. *Halt: An Alternative and Successful Approach to Juvenile Crime in the Netherlands*. [Online]. Available at: http://www.efus.eu/wpcontent/uploads/fileadmin/efus/pdf/GeneralInformationHalt.pdf [accessed: 13 October 2013].

Hampton, J. 1998. Punishment, Feminism, and Political Identity: A Case Study in the Expressive Meaning of the Law. *Canadian Journal of Law and Jurisprudence*, 11(1), 23–45.

Harris, N. 2001. Shame and Shaming: Regulating Drink-driving, in *Shame Management through Reintegration*, edited by E. Ahmed, N. Harris, J. Braithwaite and J. Braithwaite. Cambridge: Cambridge University Press, 73–210.

Hart, D. and G. Pirc 2012. Forum Sentencing: Using Research and Experience to Improve Practice, in *Restorative Justice: Adults and Emerging Practice*, edited by J. Bolitho, J. Bruce and G. Mason. Sydney: Institute of Criminology Press, University of Sydney Law School, 57–79.

Hart, H. L. A. 1961. *The Concept of Law*. 2nd edition. Oxford: Oxford University Press.

Hart, H. L. A. 1968. *Punishment and Responsibility*. Oxford: Clarendon Press.

Hatzistergos, J. 2008. *Victims of Crime to Assist in Sentencing* [press release]. [Online]. Available at: http://www.lawlink.nsw.gov.au/lawlink/Corporate/ll_corporate.nsf/pages/LL_Media_Centre_attorney_general_2008.

Hayden, A. 2001. *Restorative Conferencing Manual of Aotearoa New Zealand*. Wellington: Department for Courts.

Hayes, H. 2005. Assessing Reoffending in Restorative Justice Conferences. *Australian and New Zealand Journal of Criminology*, 38(1), 77–101.

Hayes, H. and K. Daly 2004. Conferencing and Re-Offending in Queensland. *Australian and New Zealand Journal of Criminology*, 37(2), 167–191.
Hayes, H., T. Prenzler and R. Wortley 1998. *Making Amends: Final Evaluation of the Queensland Community Conferencing Pilot*. Brisbane: Centre for Crime Policy and Public Safety, Griffith University.
Healy, P. 2000. The Punitive Nature of the Conditional Sentence, in *The Changing Face of Conditional Sentencing*. Ottawa: Department of Canada.
Hedström, P. and R. Swedberg 1996. Social Mechanisms. *Acta Sociologica*, 39(3), 281–308.
Hedström, P. and R. Swedberg (eds). 1998. *Social Mechanisms: An Analytical Approach to Social Theory*. Cambridge: Cambridge University Press.
Hobbes, T. 1996. *The Leviathan*, in *Leviathan (Cambridge Texts in the History of Political Thought)*, edited by R. Tuck. Cambridge: Cambridge University Press.
Holmes, O. W. 1918. Natural Law. *Harvard Law Review*, 32, 40–44.
Hudson, B. 1998a. Restorative Justice: The Challenge of Sexual and Racial Violence. *Journal of Law and Society*, 25(2), 237–256.
Hudson, B. 1998b. Doing Justice to Difference, in *Fundamentals of Sentencing Theory*, edited by A. Ashworth and M. Wasik. Oxford: Oxford University Press, 223–250.
Hudson, B. 2000. Punishing the Poor: Dilemmas of Justice and Difference, in *From Social Justice to Criminal Justice*, edited by W. C. Heffernan and J. Kleinig. New York: Oxford University Press, 189–216.
Hudson, B. 2002. Restorative Justice and Gendered Violence. *British Journal of Criminology*, 42, 616–634.
Hudson, B. 2003. *Justice in the Risk Society*. London: Sage Publications.
Husak, D. 2008. *Overcriminalization: The Limits of the Criminal Law*. New York: Oxford University Press.
Hutchinson, A. C. and P. Monahan (eds). 1987. *Rule of Law: Ideal or Ideology?* Toronto: Carswell.
Hydle, I. 2008. From Local Trial Projects to State-Owned Services: Empirical Research on Restorative Justice in Norway, in *Restoring Peace and Justice: Exploring Methodological and Theoretical Challenges; CPS Working Papers*, No. 11, edited by Centre for Peace Studies. Tromso, Norway: University of Tromso, 106–121.
Hydle, I. and S. Kemény 2010. From Local Trial Projects to State-Owned Services: Empirical Research on Restorative Justice in Norway, in *Restorative Justice Realities: Empirical Research in a European Context*, edited by I. Vanfraechem, I. Aertsen and J. Willemsens. The Hague: Eleven International Publishing, 207–217.
Independent Commission on Policing 1999. *A New Beginning: Policing in Northern Ireland; Report of the Independent Commission on Policing for Northern Ireland*. Belfast: HMSO.

Independent Commission on Youth Crime and Antisocial Behaviour 2010. *Time for a Fresh Start: The Report of the Independent Commission on Youth Crime and Antisocial Behaviour*. London: Police Foundation.

Jenkins, A. 1990. *Invitations to Responsibility*. Adelaide: Dulwich Centre Publications.

Jesuit Social Services 2005. *Group Conferencing*. Melbourne: JSS.

Joanknecht, L. 2004. Family Group Conference and Domestic Violence. *Cooperating Netherlands Foundations for Central and Eastern Europe (CNF) Quarterly Journal*, February 2004, 4–6.

Johnson, D. T. 2002. *The Japanese Way of Justice: Prosecuting Crime in Japan*. New York: Oxford University Press.

Johnstone, G. and D. W. Van Ness (eds). 2011. *Handbook of Restorative Justice*. Cullompton: Willan Publishing.

Jordens, J. 2008. Eighteen Problem-Solving Months at the Neighbourhood Justice Centre. *21st Annual Australian and New Zealand Society of Criminology Conference*, Canberra, 25–28 November 2008.

Joseph, J. (ed). 2002. *Hegemony: A Realist Analysis*. New York: Routledge.

Joutsen, M. 1987. Listening to the Victim: The Victim's Role in European Criminal Justice Systems. *Wayne Law Review*, 34, 95–124.

Kant, I. 1981. *Groundwork of the Metaphysics of Morals*. Indianapolis: Hackett Publishing Co.

Keməny, S. 2005. Victim-Offender Mediation with Juvenile Offenders in Norway, in *Victim-Offender Mediation with Youth Offenders in Europe: An Overview and Comparison of 15 Countries*, edited by A. Mestitz and S. Ghetti. Dordrecht: Springer, 101–114.

Kennard, K. L. 1989. The Victim's Veto: A Way to Increase Victim Impact on Criminal Case Dispositions. *California Law Review*, 77(2), 417–453.

Kennedy, D. 1993. Autumn Weekends: An Essay on Law and Everyday Life, in *Law in Everyday Life*, edited by A. Sarat and T. R. Kearns. Ann Arbor: University of Michigan Press, 191–236.

Kennedy, D. 2000. When Renewal Repeats: Thinking Against the Box. *New York University Journal of International Law and Politics*, 32, 335–500.

Kennedy, D. 2002. The International Human Rights Movement: Part of the Problem? *Harvard Human Rights Journal*, 15, 101–125.

Kennedy, D. 2008. Modern War and Modern Law. *Toyota-ANU Public Lecture Series*, Canberra, 2 June 2008.

Kennedy, D. 2009. *Deterrence and Crime Prevention: Reconsidering the Prospect of Sanction* Abingdon, Oxon: Routledge.

King, M., A. Freiberg, B. Batagol and R. Hyams (eds). 2009. *Non-Adversarial Justice*. Sydney: Federation Press.

Kiss, E. 2005. Righting Wrongs: Two Visions of Transitional Justice. *CAPPE Seminar*, University of Melbourne, 12 October 2005.

Kleiman, M. 2009. *When Brute Force Fails: How to Have Less Crime and Less Punishment* Princeton and Oxford: Princeton University Press.
Kleinig, J. 1973. *Punishment and Desert*. The Hague: Martinus Nijhoff.
Kleinig, J. 2010. Paternalismus und Menschenwürde (Paternalism and Human Dignity), (trans. Antje Du Bois-Pedain), in *Paternalismus: Die Kriminalisierung von selbstschädigendem Verhalten*, edited by A. von Hirsch, U. Neumann & K. Seelmann. Baden-Baden: Nomos Verlagsgesellschaft, 145–171.
Knazan, B. 2003. Sentencing Aboriginal Offenders in a Large City: The Toronto Gladue (Aboriginal Persons) Court. *National Judicial Institute Aboriginal Law Seminar*, Calgary, 23–25 January 2003.
Knazan, B. 2005. The Toronto Gladue (Aboriginal Persons) Court: An Update. *National Judicial Institute Aboriginal Law Seminar*, St John's, Newfoundland, April 2005.
Lacey, N. 1988. *State Punishment: Political Principles and Community Values*. London: Routledge.
Lacey, N. 2008. *The Prisoners' Dilemma: Political Economy and Punishment in Contemporary Democracies (The Hamlyn Lectures)*. Cambridge: Cambridge University Press.
Lajeunesse, T. 1993. *Community Holistic Circle Healing: Hollow Water First Nation Canada; Aboriginal Peoples Connection*. Ottawa: Solicitor General Canada.
Lamont, J. and C. Favor 2007. Distributive Justice. *The Stanford Encyclopedia of Philosophy*. [Online]. Available at: http://plato.stanford.edu/archives/spr2007/entries/justice-distributive.
Laster, K. 2001. *Law as Culture*. Sydney: Federation Press.
Landau, T. 2004. How to Put the Community in Community-Based Justice: Some Views of Participants in Criminal Court Diversion. *Howard Journal of Criminal Justice*, 43(2), 131–148.
Law Commission of Canada 2003. *Transforming Relationships through Participatory Justice*. Ottawa: Law Commission of Canada.
Legislative Assembly for the Australian Capital Territory 2004. *Crimes (Restorative Justice) Bill 2004 Explanatory Statement*. Canberra: ACT Government.
Leiter, B. 2001. Legal Realism and Legal Positivism Reconsidered. *Ethics*, 111(2), 278–301.
Lerner, M. J. 1980. *The Belief in a Just World: A Fundamental Delusion*. New York: Plenum Press.
Lerner, M. J. 2002. Pursuing the Justice Motive, in *The Justice Motive in Everyday Life*, edited by M. Ross and D. T. Miller. Cambridge: Cambridge University Press, 10–40.
Lewis, R., R. E. Dobash, R. P. Dobash and K. Cavanagh 2001. Law's Progressive Potential: The Value of Engagement with the Law for Domestic Violence. *Social and Legal Studies*, 10(1), 105–130.
Lim, H. and L. Bassett 2008. *The Neighbourhood Justice Centre and Restorative Justice*. Melbourne: Victorian Association of Restorative Justice.

Littleton, C. 1987. Reconstructing Sexual Equality. *California Law Review*, 75, 1279–1337.

Llewellyn, J. J. 2002. Dealing with the Legacy of Native Residential School Abuse in Canada: Litigation, ADR, and Restorative Justice. *University of Toronto Law Journal*, 53, 253–300.

Llewellyn, J. J. 2006. Restorative Justice in Transitions and Beyond: The Justice Potential of Truth Telling Mechanism for Post-Peace Accord Societies, in *Telling the Truths: Truth Telling and Peace Building in Post-Conflict Societies*, edited by T. A. Borer. Notre Dame: University of Notre Dame Press, 83–114.

Llewellyn, J. J. 2006. Truth and Reconciliation Commissions: Restorative Justice in Response to Genocide and Mass Violence, in *Handbook of Restorative Justice*, edited by G. Johnstone and D. W. Van Ness. Cullompton: Willan Publishing, 351–371.

Llewellyn, J. J. and R. Howse 1998. *Restorative Justice: A Conceptual Framework*. [Online]. Available at: http://www.lcc.gc.ca/en/themes/sr/rj/howse/howse_main.asp.

Llewellyn, J. J. and R. Howse 1999. Institutions for Restorative Justice: The South African Truth and Reconciliation Commission. *University of Toronto Law Journal*, 49, 355–388.

Llewellyn, K. 1940. On Reading and Using the Newer Jurisprudence. *Columbia Law Review*, 40, 581–614.

Locke, J. 1970. *Locke: Two Treatises on Government*. Cambridge: Cambridge University Press.

Luban, D. J. 1996. The Publicity Principle, in *The Theory of Institutional Design*, edited by R. E. Goodin. Cambridge: Cambridge University Press, 154–194.

Luke, G. and B. Lind 2002. Reducing Juvenile Crime: Conferencing versus Court. *Crime and Justice Bulleti*n, 69. Sydney: NSW Bureau of Crime Statistics and Research.

Luna, E. 2003. Punishment Theory, Holism, and the Procedural Conception of Restorative Justice. *Utah Law Review*, 205–302.

MacIntyre, A. 1985. *After Virtue*. 2nd edition. London: Duckworth.

Mack, K. and S. Roach Anleu 2008. The National Survey of Australian Judges: An Overview of Findings. *Journal of Judicial Administration*, 18, 5–22.

MacKinnon, C. A. 1989. *Towards a Feminist Theory of the State*. Cambridge, MA: Harvard University Press.

Markel, D. 1999. The Justice of Amnesty? Towards a Theory of Retributivism in Recovering States. *University of Toronto Law Journal*, 49, 389–445.

Markiewicz, A., B. Lagay, H. Murray and L. Campbell 1997. *Juvenile Justice Group Conferencing in Victoria: An Evaluation of a Pilot Program; Phase 1*. Melbourne: School of Social Work, University of Melbourne.

Markiewicz, A., B. Lagay, H. Murray and L. Campbell 1997a. *Juvenile Justice Group Conferencing in Victoria: An Evaluation of a Pilot Program; Phase 2*. Melbourne: School of Social Work, University of Melbourne.

Marshall, T. 1996. The Evolution of Restorative Justice in Britain. *European Journal of Criminal Policy and Research*, 4(4), 21–43.

Marshall, T. 1999. *Restorative Justice: An Overview*. London: Home Office Research, Development and Statistics Directorate.

Marshall, T. and S. Merry 1990. *Crime and Accountability: Victim and Offender Mediation in Practice*. London: HMSO.

Maruna, S. 2001. *Making Good: How Ex-Convicts Reform and Rebuild Their Lives*. Washington, DC: American Psychological Association.

Maruna, S. and R. Immarigeon (eds). 2004. *After Crime and Punishment: Pathways to Offender Reintegration*. Cullompton: Willan Publishing.

Maslow, A. 1970. *Motivation and Personality*. 3rd edition. New York: Harper & Rowe.

Mautner, T. 1996. *The Penguin Dictionary of Philosophy*. London: Penguin Books.

Maxwell, G. and H. Hayes 2006. Restorative Justice Developments in the Pacific Region: A Comprehensive Study. *Contemporary Justice Review*, 9(2), 127–154.

Maxwell, G. and A. Morris 1993. *Family, Victims and Culture: Youth Justice in New Zealand*. Wellington: Social Policy Agency and Institute of Criminology, Victoria University.

Maxwell, G., A. Morris and T. Anderson 1999. *Community Panel Adult Pre-Trial Diversion: Supplementary Evaluation*. Wellington: Crime Prevention Unit, Department of the Prime Minister and Cabinet and Institute of Criminology, Victoria University.

McCold, P. and T. Wachtel 2003. In Pursuit of Paradigm: A Theory of Restorative Justice. *13th World Congress of Criminology*, Rio de Janeiro, 10–15 August 2003.

McCorry, T. 2010. Alternatives to the Traditional Criminal Justice System: An Assessment of Victim-Offender Mediation and Neighborhood Accountability Boards in the United States. *The New York Sociologist*, 4, 75–86.

McElrea, F. W. M. 1994. The New Zealand Youth Court: A Model for Development in Other Courts? *Journal of Judicial Administration*, 4, 33–54.

McElrea, F. W. M. 1998. Taking Responsibility in Being Accountable, in *Restorative Justice: Contemporary Themes and Practices*, edited by H. Bowen and J. Consedine. Christchurch: Ploughshares Publications, 56–63.

McElrea, F. W. M. 2005. The New Zealand Experience of Restorative Justice Legislation. *11th Annual Restorative Justice Conference*, California, 23–24 September 2005.

McElrea, F. W. M. 2007a. Restorative Justice as a Procedural Revolution: Some Lessons from the Adversary System. *Fourth International Winchester Restorative Justice Conference*, Winchester, UK. 10 October 2007.

McElrea, F. W. M. 2007b. Restorative Justice for Adult Offenders: Practice in New Zealand Today, in *Restorative Justice and Practices in New Zealand: Towards a Restorative Society*, edited by G. Maxwell and J. H. Liu. Wellington: Institute of Policy Studies, Victoria University of Wellington, 95–110.

McElrea, F. W. M. 2011. Twenty Years of Restorative Justice in New Zealand: Reflections of a Judicial Participant. *Journal of Commonwealth Criminal Law*, 1, 44–54.

McEvoy, K. and A. Eriksson 2008. Who Owns Justice? Community, State, and the Northern Ireland Transition, in *Justice, Community and Civil Society: A Contested Terrain Across Europe*, edited by J. Shapland. Cullompton: Willan Publishing.

McGloin, J. M. 2006. A Historical Consideration of the Police and Prosecution/Courts in Northern Ireland. *International Criminal Justice Review*, 16, 77–98.

Merton, R. K. 1968. *Social Theory and Social Structure*. New York: Free Press.

Meyer, M. J. 1987. Kant's Concept of Dignity and Modern Political Thought. *History of European Ideas*, 8(3), 319–332.

Miers, D. 2001. *International Review of Restorative Justice*. London: Home Office Research, Development and Statistics Directorate.

Miller, D. 1987. Justice, in *The Blackwell Encyclopaedia of Political Thought*, edited by D. Miller. Oxford: Blackwell.

Milner, K. 2012. Restorative Justice and Adult Offending: 12 Years of Post-Sentence Practice, in *Restorative Justice: Adults and Emerging Practice*, edited by J. Bolitho, J. Bruce and G. Mason. Sydney: Institute of Criminology Press, University of Sydney Law School, 80–99.

Minichiello, V., R. Aroni, E. Timewell and R. Alexander 1990. *In-Depth Interviewing: Researching People*. Melbourne: Longman Cheshire.

Ministry of Justice 2010a. *Breaking the Cycle: Effective Punishment, Rehabilitation and Sentencing of Offenders*. London: Stationery Office Limited.

Ministry of Justice 2010b. Green Paper Evidence Report. *Breaking the Cycle: Effective Punishment, Rehabilitation and Sentencing of Offenders*. London: Stationery Office Limited.

Minow, M. 1990. *Making All the Difference: Inclusion, Exclusion and American Law*. Ithaca, NY: Cornell University Press.

Minow, M. 1998. *Between Vengeance and Forgiveness: Facing History after Genocide and Mass Violence*. Boston: Beacon Press.

Mokgoro, Y. 1998. Ubuntu and the Law in South Africa. *Buffalo Human Rights Law Review*, 4, 15–24.

Mokgoro, Y. 2009. The Role of Legislation and Courts in Promoting Socio-Economic Rights: The South African Experience. *RegNet Seminar ANU*, Canberra, 24 July 2009.

Montgomery, A. 1997. *Alternative Measures in Nova Scotia: A Comprehensive Review*. Halifax: Nova Scotia Department of Justice.

Moore, D. B. 1993. Shame, Forgiveness, and Juvenile Justice. *Criminal Justice Ethics*, 12(1), 3–25.

Moore, S. F. 1978. Law and Social Change: The Semi-Autonomous Social Field as an Appropriate Subject of Study, in *Law as Process: An Anthropological Approach*, edited by S. F. Moore. London: Routledge & Kegan Paul, 54–81.

Morris, A. and G. Maxwell 2003. Restorative Justice in New Zealand, in *Restorative Justice and Criminal Justice*, edited by A. von Hirsch, J. V. Roberts and A. Bottoms. Oxford: Hart Publishing, 257–271.

Morris, H. 1968. Persons and Punishment. *Monist*, 52, 475–501.

Morrison, B. 2007. *Restoring Safe School Communities: A Whole School Response to Bullying, Violence and Alienation*. Sydney: Federation Press.

Murphy, M. C. 2005. Natural Law Theory, in *The Blackwell Guide to the Philosophy of Law and Legal Theory*, edited by M. P. Golding and W. A. Edmundson. Malden, MA: Blackwell Publishing, 15–28.

Narayan, U. 1993. Appropriate Responses and Preventive Benefits: Justifying Censure and Hard Treatment in Legal Punishment. *Oxford Journal of Legal Studies*, 13(2), 166–182.

New South Wales Law Reform Commission 1996. *Sentencing (Discussion Paper No. 33)*. Sydney: NSW LRC.

Norrie, A. 2005. The Limits of Justice: Finding Fault in Criminal Law, in *Law and the Beautiful Soul*, edited by A. Norrie. London: Grasshouse Press, 75–92.

North, D. C. 1990. *Institutions, Institutional Change and Economic Performance*. New York: Cambridge University Press.

Northern Ireland Office 2007. *Protocol for Community-Based Restorative Justice Schemes*. Belfast: Northern Ireland Office.

Nova Scotia Department of Justice 1998. *Restorative Justice: A Program for Nova Scotia*. Halifax: Department of Justice.

Nova Scotia Department of Justice 2005a. *Restorative Justice Program Protocol*. Halifax: Department of Justice.

Nova Scotia Department of Justice 2005b. *Nova Scotia Restorative Justice Program: Program Activity Report 2003/04*. Halifax: Department of Justice.

Nova Scotia Department of Justice 2005c. *Nova Scotia Restorative Justice: Best Practice Standards*. Halifax: Department of Justice.

Nozick, R. 1974. *Anarchy, State, and Utopia*. New York: Basic Books.

NSW Attorney General's Department 2005. *Community Conferencing for Young Adults Operating Procedure*. Sydney: NSW Attorney General's Department.

Nuffield, J. 1997. *Final Report: Evaluation of the Adult Victim-Offender Mediation Program, Saskatoon Community Mediation Services*. Saskatoon, Saskatchewan: Saskatchewan Justice.

NZ Ministry of Justice 2004. *Restorative Justice in New Zealand: Best Practice*. Wellington: Ministry of Justice.

NZ Ministry of Justice 2005a. *New Zealand Court-Referred Restorative Justice Pilot Evaluation*. [Online]. Available at: http://www.justice.govt.nz/pubs/reports/2005/nz-court-referred-restorative-justice-pilot-evaluation/index.html [accessed: 29 May 2005].

NZ Ministry of Justice 2005b. *Stocktake Restorative Justice Programmes*. Wellington: NZ Ministry of Justice.

NZ Ministry of Justice 2010. *Restorative Justice in New Zealand.* Wellington: NZ Ministry of Justice.

NZ Ministry of Justice: Crime Prevention Unit 2008. *Reviewing Arrangements for the Delivery of Restorative Justice Services*. [Online]. Available at: http://www.justice.govt.nz/cpu/restorative-justice/review.html.

O'Neill, O. 1991. Kantian Ethics, in *A Companion to Ethics*, edited by P. Singer. Oxford: Blackwell Reference, 175–185.

Paine, T. 1995. *Collected Writings* (ed.). Eric Foner. New York: Library of America.

Parker, C. 1999. *Just Lawyers*. Oxford: Oxford University Press.

Parker, C. 2004. Restorative Justice in Business Regulation? The Australian Competition and Consumer Commission's Use of Enforceable Undertakings. *Modern Law Review*, 67(2), 209–246.

Paulin, J. and V. Kingi 2005. *The Wanganui Community-Managed Justice Programme: An Evaluation.* Wellington: NZ Ministry of Justice.

Paulin, J., V. Kingi and T. Huirama 2005. *The Rotorua Second Chance Community-Managed Justice Programme: An Evaluation.* Wellington: NZ Ministry of Justice.

Pavlich, G. 2001. The Force of Community, in R*estorative Justice and Civil Society*, edited by H. Strang and J. Braithwaite. Cambridge: Cambridge University Press, 56–68.

Pavlich, G. 2005. *Governing Paradoxes of Restorative Justice*. London: Glasshouse Press.

Payne, B., V. Conway, C. Bell, A. Falk, H. Flynn, C. McNeil and F. Rice 2010. *Restorative Practices in Northern Ireland: A Mapping Exercise*. Belfast: School of Law, Queen's University.

Pearson, A. 2004. Can Colombian Community Justice Houses Help the New Criminal Justice System Achieve Restorative Results? *The New Frontiers in Restorative Justice: Advancing Theory and Practice Conference*, Massey University at Albany, New Zealand, 2–5 December 2004.

Pelikan, C. 2000. *Victim-Offender-Mediation in Domestic Violence Cases: A Research Report*. Vienna: United Nations Crime Congress Ancillary Meeting.

People, J. and L. Trimboli 2007. *An Evaluation of the NSW Community Conferencing for Young Adults Pilot Program*. Sydney: NSW Bureau of Crime Statistics and Research.

Perelman, C. 1980. *Justice, Law and Argument*. Boston: D. Reidal.

Pettit, P. 1997. *Republicanism*. Oxford: Clarendon Press.

Plato 1975. *The Republic* (trans. D. Lee). Harmondsworth: Penguin Books.

Posner, R. 1990. *The Problems of Jurisprudence*. Cambridge, MA: Harvard University Press.

Poulson, B. 2003. A Third Voice: A Review of Empirical Research on the Psychological Outcomes of Restorative Justice. *Utah Law Review*, 167–203.

Preston, B. J. 2007. The Land and Environment Court of New South Wales: Moving Towards a Multi-Door Courthouse. *LEADR NSW Chapter Annual Dinner*, Sydney, 15 November 2007.

Pritchard, J. 2002. Parent-Child Dynamics in Community Conferences: Some Questions for Reintegrative Shaming, Practice and Restorative Justice. *Australian and New Zealand Journal of Criminology*, 35(3), 330–346.

Pritchard, J. 2004. *Juvenile Conferencing and Restorative Justice in Tasmania.* Hobart: Faculty of Law, University of Tasmania.

Proulx, C. 2003. *Reclaiming Aboriginal Justice, Identity, and Community.* Saskatoon, Saskatchewan: Purich Publishing.

Public Inquiry into the Administration of Justice and Aboriginal People 1991. *Report of the Aboriginal Justice Inquiry of Manitoba: The Justice System and Aboriginal People, Vol. 1*. Winnipeg: Inquiry.

Putnam, R. A. 1995. Why Not a Feminist Theory of Justice? in *Women, Culture and Development: A Study of Human Capabilities*, edited by M. C. Nussbaum and J. Glover. Oxford: Clarendon Press, 298–331.

Rawls, J. 1955. Two Concepts of Rules. *The Philosophical Review*, 64(1), 3–32.

Rawls, J. 1971. *A Theory of Justice*. Oxford: Oxford University Press.

Rawls, J. 1985. Justice as Fairness: Political, not Metaphysical. *Philosophy and Public Affairs*, 14(3), 223–251.

Rawls, J. 2001. *Justice as Fairness: A Restatement*. Cambridge, MA: Belknap Press.

Raz, J. 1975. *Practical Reasons and Norms*. London: Hutchinson.

Reddy, P. 2012. *Peace Operations and Restorative Justice: Groundwork for Post-Conflict Regeneration*. Farnham: Ashgate.

Reiman, J. 1990. *Justice and Modern Moral Philosophy*. New Haven: Yale University Press.

Rescher, N. 1966. *Distributive Justice*. Indianapolis: Bobbs-Merrill.

Restorative Justice Council 2011. *A New Way of Doing Justice: The Response of the Restorative Justice Council to the Sentencing Green Paper; Breaking the Cycle*. [Online]. Available at: http://www.restorativejustice.org.uk/resource/a_new_way_of_doing_justice__restorative_justice_council_response_to_breaking_the_cycle_green_paper_gncn5/#.UiVLJHc9_2w [accessed: 12 October 2013].

Retzinger, S. M. and T. J. Scheff 1996. Strategy for Community Conferences: Emotions and Social Bonds, in *Restorative Justice: International Perspectives*, edited by B. Galaway and J. Hudson. Monsey, NY: Criminal Justice Press, 315–335.

Richardson, G. and B. Galaway 1995. *Evaluation of the Restorative Resolutions Project of the John Howard Society of Manitoba*. Ottawa: Solicitor General Canada.

Roach, K. 2000. Conditional Sentences, Restorative Justice, Net-Widening and Aboriginal Offenders, in *The Changing Face of Conditional Sentencing*, No. 3. Ottawa: Department of Justice Canada.

Roach, K. and J. Rudin 2000. Gladue: The Judicial and Political Reception of a Promising Decision. *Canadian Journal of Criminology*, 42(3), 355–388.

Roberts, J. V., A. Doob and V. Marinos 1999. *Judicial Attitudes to Conditional Terms of Imprisonment: Results of a National Survey*. Ottawa: Department of Justice Canada.

Roberts, J. V. and T. Gabor 2003. The Impact of Conditional Sentencing: Decarceration and Widening of the Net. *Canadian Criminal Law Review*, 8, 33–50.

Roberts, J. V., M. Hough and J. M. Hough (eds). 2002. *Changing Attitudes to Punishment: Public Opinion, Crime and Justice*. Cullompton: Willan Publishing.

Roberts, J. V. and C. LaPrairie 2000. *Conditional Sentencing in Canada: An Overview of Research Findings*. Ottawa: Department of Justice Canada.

Roberts, J. V. and R. Melchers 2003. The Incarceration of Aboriginal Offenders: Trends from 1978–2001. *Canadian Journal of Crime and Criminal Justice*, 45, 211–226.

Roberts, J. V. and K. Roach 2003. Restorative Justice in Canada: From Sentencing Circles to Sentencing Principles, in *Restorative Justice and Criminal Justice*, edited by A. von Hirsch, J. V. Roberts and A. Bottoms. Oxford: Hart Publishing, 237–256.

Roberts, P. 2003. Restoration and Retribution in International Criminal Justice: An Exploratory Analysis, in *Restorative Justice and Criminal Justice*, edited by A. von Hirsch, J. V. Roberts and A. Bottoms. Oxford: Hart Publishing, 115–134.

Roberts, T. 1995. *Evaluation of the Victim-Offender Mediation Project Langley, BC.* Ottawa: Solicitor General Canada.

Roche, D. 2003. *Accountability in Restorative Justice*. Oxford: Oxford University Press.

Rosenberg, G. N. 1991. *The Hollow Hope: Can Courts Bring about Social Change?* Chicago: University of Chicago Press.

Ross, D. 2009. *Ross on Crime*. 4th edition. Sydney: Thomson Lawbook Co.

Rousseau, J.-J. 1990. *The Collected Writings of Rousseau* (ed.). C. Kelley and R. Masters. Hanover: University Press of New England.

Rowe, C. 1991. Ethics in Ancient Greece, in *A Companion to Ethics*, edited by P. Singer. Oxford: Blackwell Reference, 121–132.

Royal Commission on Aboriginal Peoples 1996. *Bridging the Cultural Divide: A Report on Aboriginal People and Criminal Justice in Canada*. Ottawa: Supply and Services Canada.

Rudin, J. 2008. Aboriginal Over-Representation and *R. v. Gladue*: Where We Were, Where We Are and Where We Might Be Going, in *The Charter and Criminal Justice: Twenty-Five Years Later*, edited by J. Cameron and J. Stribopoulos. Markham, ON: LexisNexis Canada, 687–713.

Rugge, T. A., J. Bonta and S. Wallace-Capretta 2005. *Evaluation of the Collaborative Justice Project: A Restorative Justice Program for Serious Crime*. Ottawa: Public Safety and Emergency Preparedness Canada.

Rugge, T. A. and R. B. Cormier 2003. Restorative Justice in Cases of Serious Crimes: An Evaluation. *6th International Conference on Restorative Justice*, Vancouver, 1–4 June 2003.

Ryan, A. (ed). 1993. *Justice*. Oxford: Oxford University Press.

Sadurski, W. 1985. *Giving Desert Its Due: Social Justice and Legal Theory*. Dordrecht: Reidel.

Sandel, M. J. 1982. *Liberalism and the Limits of Justice*. Cambridge: Cambridge University Press.

Sandel, M. J. (ed). 1984. *Liberalism and Its Critics*. Oxford: Basil Blackwell.

Sander, F. E. A. 1976. Varieties of Dispute Processing, in *The Pound Conference: Perspectives on Justice in the Future*, edited by A. L. R. Wheeler. St. Paul, MN: West Pub. Co, 65–87.

Schmidtz, D. 2006. *Elements of Justice*. Cambridge: Cambridge University Press.

Schweigert, F. 1997. *Learning the Common Good: Principles of Community-Based Moral Education in Restorative Justice*. Unpublished paper; copy with author.

Shapland, J., A. Atkinson, H. Atkinson, B. Chapman, E. Colledge, J. Dignan, M. Howes, J. Johnstone, G. Robinson and A. Sorsby 2006. *Restorative Justice in Practice: The Second Report of the Evaluation of Three Schemes*. Sheffield: Centre for Criminological Research, University of Sheffield.

Shapland, J., A. Atkinson, H. Atkinson, B. Chapman, J. Dignan, M. Howes, J. Johnstone, G. Robinson and A. Sorsby 2007. Restorative Justice: The Views of Victims and Offenders. *Ministry of Justice Research Series 3/07*. London: Ministry of Justice.

Shapland, J., A. Atkinson, H. Atkinson, J. Dignan, L. Edwards, J. Hibbert, M. Howes, J. Johnstone, G. Robinson and A. Sorsby 2008. Does Restorative Justice Affect Reconviction? The Fourth Report from the Evaluation of Three Schemes. *Ministry of Justice Research Series 10/08*. London: Ministry of Justice.

Shapland, J., A. Atkinson, E. Colledge, J. Dignan, M. Howes, J. Johnstone, R. Pennant, G. Robinson and A. Sorsby 2004. Implementing Restorative Justice Schemes (Crime Reduction Programme): A Report on the First Year. *Home Office Online Report 32/04*. London: Home Office Research, Development and Statistics Directorate.

Shapland, J., G. Robinson and A. Sorsby 2011. *Restorative Justice in Practice: Evaluating what Works for Victims and Offenders*. London: Routledge.

Shaw, J. W. 1997. *Second Reading Speech, Young Offenders Act*. Sydney: NSW Legislative Council.

Shearing, C. and L. Johnson 2005. Justice in the Risk Society. *The Australian and New Zealand Journal of Criminology*, 38(1), 25–38.

Sherman, L., D. Gottfredson, D. L. MacKenzie, J. Eck, P. Reuter and S. Bushway 1997. *What Works, What Doesn't, What's Promising*. Washington, DC: Department of Justice.

Sherman, L. W. and H. Strang 1997a. *The Right Kind of Shame for Crime Prevention: RISE Working Papers*, No. 1. Canberra: Law Program, Research School of Social Sciences, Australian National University.

Sherman, L. W. and H. Strang 2007. *Restorative Justice: The Evidence*. London: Smith Institute.

Sherman, L. W., H. Strang and D. J. Woods 2000. *Recidivism Patterns in the Canberra Reintegrative Shaming Experiments (RISE): Final Report*. Canberra: Centre for Restorative Justice, Research School of Social Sciences, Australian National University.

Shklar, J. 1990. *The Faces of Injustice*. New Haven: Yale University Press.

Shy, Y. 2006. *Restorative Justice Jurisprudence in New Zealand (1998–2005)*. Paper submitted for JD, School of Law, Northeastern University, Boston.

Singer, J. 1984. The Player and the Cards: Nihilism and Legal Theory. *Yale Law Journal*, 94, 1–70.

Skelton, A. 2010. Face to Face: Sachs on Restorative Justice. *South African Public Law*, 25(1), 94–107.

Skelton, A. 2013. The South African Constitutional Court's Restorative Justice Jurisprudence. *Restorative Justice*, 1(1), 122–145.

Smith, L. T. and F. Cram 1998. *An Evaluation of the Community Panel Diversion Pilot Programme: A Report to the Crime Prevention Unit*. Auckland: Auckland Uniservices Ltd.

Sourdin, T. (ed). 2004. *Alternative Dispute Resolution and the Courts*. Sydney: Federation Press.

Spader, D. J. 1988. Criminal Justice and Distributive Justice: Has the Wall of Separation Been Reduced to Rubble? *Justice Quarterly*, 5(4), 589–614.

Spencer, F. and G. McIvor 2000. Conferencing as a Response to Youth Crime. *Selected Papers from the 1999 British Criminology Conference*. Liverpool.

Statistics Canada 2000. *Youth Court Statistics*. Ottawa: Canadian Centre for Justice Statistics.

Statistics Canada 2006. *Cases in Adult Criminal Court by Type of Sentence*. [Online]. Available at: http://www40.statcan.ca/l01/cst01/legal22a-eng.htm [accessed: 2008].

Stewart, H. 2001. Harms, Wrongs and Set-Backs in Feinberg's Moral Limits of the Criminal Law. *Buffalo Criminal Law Review*, 5(1), 47–67.

Stone, J. 1980. Equal Protection and the Search for Justice. *Arizona Law Review*, 22, 1–17.

Strang, H. 2002. *Repair or Revenge: Victims and Restorative Justice*. Oxford: Oxford University Press.

Strang, H. 2009. Restorative Justice: The Campbell Collaboration Review and Victims of Violence. *RegNet Seminar ANU*, Canberra, 18 August 2009.

Strang, H. 2012. Conclusion: Emerging Practice and Future Directions, in *Restorative Justice: Adults and Emerging Practice*, edited by J. Bolitho, J. Bruce and G. Mason. Sydney: Institute of Criminology Press, University of Sydney Law School, 231–239.

Strang, H. and J. Braithwaite (eds). 2002. *Restorative Justice and Family Violence*. Cambridge: Cambridge University Press.

Stuart, B. 1997a. *Building Community Justice Partnerships: Community Peacemaking Circles*. Ottawa: Aboriginal Justice Directorate Department of Justice of Canada.

Stubbs, J. 2004. *Restorative Justice, Domestic Violence and Family Violence (Issues Paper No. 9)*. Canberra: Australian Domestic and Family Violence Clearinghouse.

Stubbs, J. 2012. Justice for Gendered Violence: What Does Restorative Justice Offer? in *Restorative Justice: Adults and Emerging Practice*, edited by J. Bolitho, J. Bruce and G. Mason. Sydney: Institute of Criminology, University of Sydney Law School, 194–213.

Sullivan, D. and L. Tifft 1998. The Negotiated and Economic Dimensions of Restorative Justice. *Humanity and Society*, 22(1), 38–48.

Sunstein, C. 1990. *After the Rights Revolution: Reconceiving the Regulatory State*. Cambridge, MA: Harvard University Press.

Sunstein, C. 1992. Commentary on Analogical Reasoning. *Harvard Law Review*, 106, 741–790.

Sypnowich, C. 1994. Social Justice and Legal Form. *Ratio Juris*, 7, 72–79.

Tavuchis, N. 1991. *Mea Culpa: A Sociology of Apology and Reconciliation*. Stanford: Stanford University Press.

Taylor, A. J. W. 2003. Justice as a Basic Human Need. *New Ideas in Psychology*, 21, 209–219.

Taylor, A. J. W. 2007. Restorative Justice Serving the Need for Justice, in *Restorative Justice and Practices in New Zealand: Towards a Restorative Society*, edited by G. Maxwell and J. H. Liu. Wellington: Institute of Policy Studies, 265–274.

Thorburn, S. 2005. Observing the Application of Restorative Justice in Courts of New Zealand. *Latest Developments in International Criminal Justice Reform*, Shenzhen, China, 19–20 August 2005.

Tonry, M. 1994. Proportionality, Parsimony and Interchangeability of Punishments, in *Penal Theory and Practice*, edited by R. A. Duff, S. Marshall, R. E. Dobash and R. P. Dobash. Manchester: Manchester University Press, 59–83.

Tonry, M. 1996. *Sentencing Matters*. New York: Oxford University Press.

Tonry, M. 2004. *Punishment and Politics: Evidence and Emulation in the Making of English Crime Control Policy*. Cullompton: Willan Publishing.

Triggs, S. 2005. *New Zealand Court-Referred Restorative Justice Pilot: Two-Year Follow-up of Reoffending*. Wellington: Ministry of Justice.

Trimboli, L. 2000. *An Evaluation of the NSW Youth Justice Conferencing Scheme*. Sydney: NSW Bureau of Crime Statistics and Research.

Truth and Reconciliation Commission 1998. *Report of the South African Truth and Reconciliation Commission*. Cape Town: Truth and Reconciliation Commission.

Tuebner, G. 1998. After Privatisation? The Many Autonomies of Private Law, in *Legal Theory at the End of the Millennium*, edited by M. Freeman. Oxford: Oxford University Press, 393–424.

Turpel-Lafond, M. E. 1999. Sentencing within a Restorative Justice Paradigm. *Canadian Institute for the Administration of Justice Conference 'Changing Punishment at the Turn of the Century'*, Saskatoon, Saskatchewan, 26–29 September 1999.

Tushnet, M. 1984. An Essay on Rights. *Texas Law Review*, 96, 1363–1403.

UK Home Office 2003. *Conditional Cautioning, Section 22-27 Criminal Justice Act 2003: Code of Practice and Associated Annexes*. London.

Umbreit, M. and A. Roberts 1996. *Mediation of Criminal Conflict in England: An Assessment of Services in Coventry and Leeds*. Minneapolis: University of Minnesota: Center for Restorative Justice and Peacemaking.

Unger, R. 1975. *Knowledge and Politics*. New York: Free Press.

United Nations Office on Drugs and Crime 2006a. *Basic Principles for the Use of Restorative Justice Programmes in Criminal Matters*. New York: United Nations.

Valley Restorative Justice 2007. *Annual Report 2006–2007*. Kentville, Nova Scotia: Valley Restorative Justice.

Van Doosselaere, D. and I. Vanfraechem 2010. Research, Practice and Policy Partnerships: Empirical Research on Restorative Justice in Belgium, in *Restorative Justice Realities: Empirical Research in a European Context*, edited by I. Vanfraechem, I. Aertsen and J. Willemsens. The Hague: Eleven International Publishing, 57–94.

Van Ness, D. W. 1993. New Wine and Old Wineskins: Four Challenges of Restorative Justice. *Criminal Law Forum*, 4, 251–276.

Van Ness, D. W. 1996. Restorative Justice and International Human Rights, in *Restorative Justice: International Perspectives*, edited by B. Galaway and J. Hudson. Monsey, NY: Criminal Justice Press, 17–35.

Van Ness, D. W. 1999. Legal Issues of Restorative Justice, in *Restorative Juvenile Justice*, edited by G. Bazemore and L. Walgrave. Monsey, NY: Criminal Justice Press, 263–284.

Van Ness, D. W. 2003. Proposed Basic Principles on the Use of Restorative Justice: Recognising the Aims and Limits of Restorative Justice, in *Restorative Justice and Criminal Justice*, edited by A. von Hirsch, J. V. Roberts and A. Bottoms. Oxford: Hart Publishing, 157–176.

Van Ness, D. W. and K. H. Strong 1997. *Restoring Justice*. Cincinnati: Anderson Publishing Co.

Van Ness, D. W. and K. H. Strong. 2010. *Restoring Justice*. 4th edition. New Providence, NJ: Matthew Bender & Company.

Vanfraechem, I. 2001. Implementing Family Group Conferences in a Legalistic Justice System. *Third International Conference on Conferencing, Circles and Other Restorative Practices: 'Dreaming of a New Reality'*. Minneapolis, August 2002.

Vanfraechem, I. 2003. Family Group Conferences in Belgium, in *Youth Violence: New Patterns and Local Responses: Experiences in East and West*, edited by F. Dünkel and K. Drenkhahn. Mönchengladbach: Forum Verlag Godesberg.

Vanfraechem, I. 2005. Evaluating Conferencing for Serious Juvenile Offenders, in *Restorative Justice: Emerging Issues in Practice and Evaluation*, edited by E. Elliott and R. Gordon. Cullompton: Willan Publishing, 278–295.

Vanfraechem, I. 2006. *Herstelgericht groepsoverleg: Op zoek naar een constructief antwoord op ernstige jeugddelinquentie; Proefschrift tot het behalen van de graad van doctor in de criminologische wetenschappen*. PhD dissertation. Leuven: Catholic University of Leuven.

Vanfraechem, I., I. Aertsen and J. Willemsens (eds). 2010. *Restorative Justice Realities: Empirical Research in a European Context*. The Hague: Eleven International Publishing.

Vanseveren, B. 2010. HERGO in Belgium: Flanders Developments in Flanders and HERGO in Sexual Assault Cases. *Expert Seminar on Conferencing*, Leuven, Belgium.

Victorian Department of Human Services 2007. *Youth Fact Sheet: Youth Justice Group Conferencing*. Melbourne: Victorian Department of Human Services.

Vlastos, G. 1970. Justice and Equality, in *Human Rights*, edited by A. I. Melden. Belmont, CA: Wadsworth Publications, 41–76.

Von Hirsch, A. 1976. *Doing Justice: The Choice of Punishments*. New York: Hill & Wang.

Von Hirsch, A. 1985. *Past or Future Crimes: Deservedness and Dangerousness in the Sentencing of Criminals*. New Brunswick: Rutgers University Press.

Von Hirsch, A. 1993. *Censure and Sanctions*. New York: Oxford University Press.

Von Hirsch, A., A. Ashworth and J. V. Roberts (eds). 2009. *Principled Sentencing: Readings on Theory and Policy*. Portland: Hart Publishing.

Von Hirsch, A., A. Ashworth and C. Shearing 2003. Specifying Aims and Limits for Restorative Justice: A 'Making Amends' Model? in *Restorative Justice and Criminal Justice*, edited by A. von Hirsch, J. V. Roberts and A. Bottoms. Oxford: Hart Publishing, 21–41.

Von Hirsch, A. and N. Jareborg 1991. Gauging Criminal Harm: A Living Standard Analysis. *Oxford Journal of Legal Studies*, 11, 1–38.

Waldron, J. 1987. Nonsense upon Stilts? A Reply, in *Nonsense upon Stilts: Bentham, Burke and Marx on the Rights of Man*, edited by J. Waldron. London: Methuen, 151–209.

Waldron, J. 1992. *Liberal Rights*. Cambridge: Cambridge University Press.

Waldron, J. 2000. Judicial Ethics and the Rule of Law. *Judicial Ethics Conference*, Rotorua, New Zealand, September 2000.

Waldron, J. 2008. Dignity and Rank. *Political Philosophy Workshop*, Brown University, Providence, , 14 February 2008 [Online]. Available at: http://www.brown.edu/Research/ppw/files/dignity%20and%20rank5%20 WALDRON%20Brown.pdf.

Walgrave, L. 2000a. How Pure can a Maximalist Approach to Restorative Justice Remain? Or Can a Purist Model of Restorative Justice Become Maximalist? *Contemporary Justice Review*, 3(4), 415– 432.

Walgrave, L. 2000b. Restorative Justice and the Republican Theory of Criminal Justice: An Exercise in Normative Theorising on Restorative Justice, in *Restorative Justice: Philosophy to Practice*, edited by H. Strang and J. Braithwaite. Aldershot: Ashgate, 165–183.

Walgrave, L. 2002. Restorative Justice and the Law: Socio-Ethical and Juridical Foundations for a Systemic Approach, in *Restorative Justice and the Law*, edited by L. Walgrave. Cullompton: Willan Publishing, 191–218.

Walgrave, L. and H. Geudens 1996. The Restorative Proportionality of Community Service for Juveniles. *European Journal of Crime, Criminal Law and Criminal Justice*, 4, 361–380.

Walzer, M. 1994. *Thick and Thin: Moral Argument at Home and Abroad.* Notre Dame: University of Notre Dame Press.

Wardak, A. 2004. Building a Post-War Justice System in Afghanistan. *Crime, Law and Social Change*, 41, 319–341.

Warner, K. 1994. Family Group Conferences and the Rights of the Offender, in *Family Conferencing and Juvenile Justice: The Way Forward or Misplaced Optimism?* edited by C. Adler and J. Wundersitz. Canberra: Australian Institute of Criminology, 141–152.

Weber, M. 1947. *The Theory of Social and Economic Organizations*. New York: Oxford University Press.

Webster, B. 2000. Restorative Justice Developments in New Zealand: Community-Managed Restorative Justice Programmes, from Inception to Evaluation. *Australian Crime Prevention Council, 19th Biennial Conference*, October 1999, Melbourne, Crime Prevention Unit, Ministry of Justice. Revised and updated 25 July 2000.

Weil, S. 1951. *Waiting on God.* London: Routledge & Kegan Paul.

Weinreb, L. L. 2005. *Legal Reason: The Use of Analogy in Legal Argument.* Cambridge: Cambridge University Press.

Wengert, M. 2008. Personal communication, 3 January 2008. Queanbeyan, NSW.

West, R. (ed). 2001. *Rights (The International Library of Essays in Law and Legal Theory)*. Aldershot: Dartmouth.

West, R. 2003. *Re-Imagining Justice*. Aldershot: Ashgate.

Wexler, D. B., B. J. Winick and D. P. Stolle (eds). 2000. *Practicing Therapeutic Jurisprudence: Law as a Helping Profession*. Durham, NC: Carolina Academic Press.

Whitman, J. Q. 2003. *Harsh Justice: Criminal Punishment and the Widening Divide between America and Europe*. Oxford: Oxford University Press.

Wilczynski, A., A. Wallace, B. Nicholson and D. Rintoul 2004. *Evaluation of the Northern Territory Agreement*. Canberra: Urbis Keys Young.

Woodyatt, L. and M. Wenzel 2013. Self-Forgiveness and the Restoration of Offenders after an Interpersonal Transgression. *Journal of Social and Clinical Psychology*, 32(2), 225–259.

Wynne, J. 1996. Leeds Mediation and Reparation Service: Ten Years' Experience of Victim-Offender Mediation, in *Restorative Justice: International Perspectives*, edited by B. Galaway and J. Hudson. Monsey, NJ: Criminal Justice Press, 445–462.

Yeung, K. 2001. *The Public Enforcement of Australian Competition Law*. Canberra: Australian Competition and Consumer Commission.

Young Adult Restorative Justice Group Conferencing Program 2008. *Operating Guidelines*. Melbourne: Neighbourhood Justice Centre.

Young, I. M. 1990. *Justice and the Politics of Difference*. Princeton: Princeton University Press.

Young, I. M. 2000. *Inclusion and Democracy*. New York: Oxford University Press.

Young, I. M. 2006. Responsibility and Global Justice: A Social Connection Model, in *Justice and Global Politics*, edited by E. F. Paul, F. D. Miller and J. Paul. Cambridge: Cambridge University Press, 102–130.

Youth Justice Agency 2007–2008. *Annual Report and Accounts: Report on the Work of the Youth Justice Agency of Northern Ireland, 2007–2008*. London: Stationery Office Limited.

Youth Justice Agency 2009–2010. *Annual Report and Accounts: Report on the Work of the Youth Justice Agency of Northern Ireland, 2009–2010*. London: Stationery Office Limited.

Zedner, L. 1994. Reparation and Retribution: Are They Reconcilable? *Modern Law Review*, 57, 228–250.

Zehr, H. 2004. Commentary: Restorative Justice; Beyond Victim-Offender Mediation. *Conflict Resolution Quarterly*, 22(1–2), 305–315.

Zimring, F. E. and G. J. Hawkins 1973. *Deterrence: The Legal Threat in Crime Control*. Chicago: University of Chicago Press.

Zinsstag, E., M. Teunkens and B. Pali 2011. *Conferencing: A Way Forward for Restorative Justice in Europe*. Leuven: European Forum for Restorative Justice.

Zipursky, B. C. 2005. Philosophy of Tort Law, in *The Blackwell Guide to the Philosophy of Law and Legal Theory*, edited by M. P. Golding and W. A. Edmundson. Malden, MA: Blackwell Publishing, 122–137.

Index